Classic Grounded Theory

SAGE was founded in 1965 by Sara Miller McCune to support the dissemination of usable knowledge by publishing innovative and high-quality research and teaching content. Today, we publish over 900 journals, including those of more than 400 learned societies, more than 800 new books per year, and a growing range of library products including archives, data, case studies, reports, and video. SAGE remains majority-owned by our founder, and after Sara's lifetime will become owned by a charitable trust that secures our continued independence.

Los Angeles | London | New Delhi | Singapore | Washington DC | Melbourne

Classic Grounded Theory

Applications With Qualitative and Quantitative Data

Judith A. Holton

Mount Allison University, Canada

Isabelle Walsh

SKEMA Business School, France

Los Angeles | London | New Delhi
Singapore | Washington DC | Melbourne

FOR INFORMATION:

SAGE Publications, Inc.
2455 Teller Road
Thousand Oaks, California 91320
E-mail: order@sagepub.com

SAGE Publications Ltd.
1 Oliver's Yard
55 City Road
London, EC1Y 1SP
United Kingdom

SAGE Publications India Pvt. Ltd.
B 1/I 1 Mohan Cooperative Industrial Area
Mathura Road, New Delhi 110 044
India

SAGE Publications Asia-Pacific Pte. Ltd.
3 Church Street
#10–04 Samsung Hub
Singapore 049483

Acquisitions Editor: Helen Salmon
Editorial Assistant: Anna Villarruel
Production Editor: Veronica Stapleton Hooper
Copy Editor: Colleen Brennan
Typesetter: Hurix Systems Pvt. Ltd.
Proofreader: Wendy Jo Dymond
Indexer: Sheila Bodell
Cover Designer: Alexa Turner
Marketing Manager: Susannah Goldes

Printed in the United States of America

Library of Congress Cataloging-in-Publication Data

Names: Holton, Judith A., author. | Walsh, Isabelle, author.

Title: Classic grounded theory : applications with qualitative and quantitative data / Judith A. Holton, Mount Allison University, Canada, Isabelle Walsh, SKEMA Business School, France.

Description: Los Angeles : SAGE, [2017] | Includes bibliographical references and index.

Identifiers: LCCN 2015041977 | ISBN 9781483372549 (pbk. : alk. paper)

Subjects: LCSH: Grounded theory.

Classification: LCC H61.24 .H65 2017 | DDC 001.42--dc23 LC record available at http://lccn.loc.gov/2015041977

16 17 18 19 20 10 9 8 7 6 5 4 3 2 1

Brief Contents

Detailed Contents

Preface

Since the publication of *The Discovery of Grounded Theory* (Glaser & Strauss, 1967), grounded theory (GT) has grown in popularity to become one of the most frequently cited research methodologies. GT researchers come from a wide range of professional fields, such as social work, nursing, medicine, allied health, education, management, and business. They are practitioners and scholars seeking to explain patterns of behavior from within their disciplines. Grounded theories offer a "sensitizing recognition" (Glaser, 1998, p. 62) through high-impact variables that succinctly yet eloquently explain experienced reality. The wide interest in GT has resulted in many journal articles and texts intended to guide researchers in using the methodology. This interest in studying the nature and practice of GT—what Glaser has so aptly termed "the rhetorical wrestle" (Glaser, 1998, Chap. 3)—extends to established scholars as well as the novice researcher (Walsh, Holton, Bailyn, Fernandez, Levina, & Glaser, 2015a).

The "draw and grab" (Glaser, 1998, p. 62) of GT is highly motivating, but learning and doing GT is a delayed action learning process (Glaser, 1978, p. 6; 2001, p. 1; 2003, p. 78). The importance of learning through doing cannot be overestimated. As Glaser has often commented in his troubleshooting seminars, a grounded theory (a theory that is grounded in data) is asymptotic; it is very close to what is happening but never fully captures reality. Its propositional nature allows for its modification with additional data and with further skill development on the part of the theorist. What one misses in the first grounded theory study can be realized and modified in subsequent studies.

Novice classic grounded theorists often find that they are breaking new territory at their institutions. They are striving to master a methodology that not only is new to them but also is often unfamiliar to supervisors and colleagues or misinterpreted as a qualitative research approach situated within an interpretivist paradigm. While it has become common practice for many qualitative researchers to apply some GT techniques in their data analysis (e.g., **constant comparison, theoretical sampling**)—drawing on the "tenets of GT" so to speak—it is important to differentiate such practices from studies that employ full classic GT methodology.

Our goal in this text is twofold. First, we take the reader back to the roots of GT to illustrate how those roots are important to a full appreciation of GT as much more than a qualitative method. Our purpose is in no way intended to suggest that the immensely productive collaboration between Glaser and Strauss was not an important milestone in the development of GT. However, we feel strongly that failing to recognize the significance of GT's early roots has led some scholars to accord to GT a paradigmatic position that not only has restricted its use to qualitative data but, in doing so, has remodeled and reduced its theory-generating power.

Second, we offer practical guidance in undertaking a research study staying true to the classic GT practice paradigm and using the full classic GT methodology package. The topics covered in this text are grounded in the experiences of many novice researchers who have participated in GT troubleshooting seminars or who have contacted us with questions and problems. The challenges faced are universal in that they are routinely encountered as part of the GT learning curve. Offering some practical advice and examples for troubleshooting these challenges will help readers develop their own GT expertise.

● OUR PHILOSOPHICAL PERSPECTIVE

In this text, we emphasize the philosophical flexibility of classic GT as a "full package" approach that can be applied to any study and any type of data where the goal is to discover and generate a conceptually integrated theory. While GT is philosophically unbiased, we believe that no methodological book can be fully epistemologically and ontologically neutral. Hence, it is essential to state from the outset that both authors of this text are critical realists, and this has probably influenced the examples that we have chosen to illustrate various aspects of the GT process.

A discussion about critical realism is beyond the purpose of this book. However, it might be useful to stress that, for a critical realist, reality is multifaceted and may be perceived differently by different individuals and in different contexts. Critical realists consider, however, that an *intransitive domain* exists independent of our perceptions. In the ontological domain, critical realism holds a realist view and, in the epistemological domain, it accepts the "relativism of knowledge as socially and historically conditioned" (Mingers, 2004, p. 91). Through retroduction, critical realism aims to discover the underlying structures that generate specific patterns of events or non-events, and welcomes quantitative and/or qualitative data, methods, and techniques. The critical realist retroductive approach to knowledge creation, well elaborated by Zachariadis, Scott, and Barrett (2013), is fully congruent with the necessary emergent quality of grounded theories.

It is also essential to clarify what causality means for a critical realist, as theories are often conceived as centered on causality, that is, the relationship between a cause and an event (Gregor, 2006). The notion of causality as a *generative mechanism* is a core and defining feature of critical realism (Bhaskar, 2002). Generative mechanisms are best understood as *tendencies,* as their activation is highly context dependent (Bhaskar, 2002). In contrast with the Humean vision of causality (A causes B) commonly accepted in traditional positivist quantitative circles, a generative mechanism can be reformulated as "A generates B in context C" (Cartwright, 2003; Smith, 2010). For a critical realist, causality is, thus, a process of how causal powers are actualized in some particular context; a process in which the generative mechanisms of that context shape (modulate, dampen, etc.) the particular outcomes. For instance, wood in a camp fire (A) will have a tendency to generate heat (B) if somebody has put together the right elements for the fire to burn adequately and has put a light to it and if it does not rain on the fire (C). Thus, even though some regularity in events may be empirically derived, critical realism does not look for universal laws and recognizes the significant role of context, social structures, and individual agencies in causal explanations.

SOME DEFINITIONS ●

We refer the reader to Walsh (2014c) for a full discussion on mixed design GT and the various works that may be found in the literature to fit such a description. Some of these works use, within the same research project, an exploratory GT stance with qualitative data and a confirmatory hypothetical-deductive stance with quantitative data. In this book we are concerned with adopting an exploratory GT stance with any data, both qualitative and/or quantitative, and from any philosophical/epistemological perspective that may be adopted by a researcher. When we mention "mixed GT" or "GT using mixed data," it implies that all data are analyzed as one set and that the constant comparative analyses of qualitative and quantitative data are not separated but *embedded.*

At the outset, it is also essential to propose some definitions for constitutive elements that may be found in the design of any research project. As highlighted by Mingers (2001), certain words may be interpreted in many different ways by different researchers; this sometimes leads to misunderstandings. To avoid this, it is important to define some terms. We do not claim these definitions to be correct across domains, but they will be used consistently throughout this book.

Data are the necessary basis on which we build theories (Evermann & Tate, 2011, p. 634), and in most cases, we need good data to produce good theory (Lyytinen, 2009). Creswell (2014) refers to qualitative data as consisting of text and images and quantitative data as numbers. The term *quantitative data* is mostly used to describe a type of information that may be counted or expressed numerically and is amenable to statistical analysis whereas qualitative data provides explanation for and information about something in the form of words and involves in-depth description (Monette, Sullivan, & Delong, 2011). However, a researcher may choose to *quantitize* qualitative data (Sandelowski, Voils, & Knafl, 2009) or to *qualify* (Creswell, 2007), or *qualitize* (Sandelowski, 2000), quantitative data. A researcher may also use **secondary data** in various ways, with different techniques, regardless of the methods used to collect these data.

Methods are the data-collection methods used in the research project, such as interviews, observation, filming, or surveys. Contrary to commonly accepted beliefs, we do not consider that specific methods will produce specific data: Methods traditionally understood as quantitative may produce qualitative data (e.g., one may include open-ended questions in a survey that will yield qualitative data), and methods traditionally understood as qualitative may produce data that may subsequently be quantitized (Sandelowski et al., 2009), for example, the number of times a term is found in an interview.

Techniques are the instruments used in the research project to help analyze and make sense of the collected data, such as text analysis, cluster analysis, or structural equation modeling. Here again, we depart from traditional beliefs considering qualitative and quantitative instruments as completely distinct. Some techniques traditionally believed to belong to the qualitative realm may be perceived to be extremely close to the quantitative realm. For instance, Glaser's (1978) substantive and **theoretical coding** may be realized through text analysis but also through elaboration analysis, factor/cluster analyses, and *soft* structural equation modeling—traditionally considered as quantitative techniques and often used in quantitative studies.

Methodology is the specific combination of research methods and techniques used in a research project. Each research project may be considered as having a specific methodology, as we understand researchers as important stakeholders in their own research, who may adapt the methods and techniques they adopt.

Framework *is* the general set of guidelines proposed by some authors that a researcher may choose to follow in a given project, such as action research (Baskerville & Pries-Heje, 1999), case-study research (Eisenhardt, 1989), quantitative grounded theory (Glaser, 2008), or Straussian grounded theory (Strauss, 1987).

Paradigm has been understood and used in social sciences at different levels of generality (Morgan, 2007). The four versions of paradigms found in the literature and highlighted by Morgan (2007) are worldviews, epistemological stance, shared beliefs in a research field, and model examples. These are not mutually exclusive but "nested within each other" (p. 54). In all four versions, paradigms are "shared belief systems that influence the kinds of knowledge researchers seek and how they interpret the evidence they collect" (p. 50).

Another issue that has to be addressed up front is the meaning of the term *grounded theory* itself, because it leads to misunderstanding as already highlighted by Bryant and Charmaz (2007). When asked the question, "What is grounded theory?" Barney Glaser has responded that GT is a set of "interrelated grounded concepts based on an emergent theoretical code."[1] Walsh, Holton, Bailyn, Fernandez, Levina, and Glaser (2015b) elaborate on this definition:

> GT is the systematic generation of theory from data that has itself been systematically obtained (Glaser, 1978, p. 2). GT's exploratory approach may be adopted irrespective of the researcher's philosophical positioning. It may include qualitative and quantitative data, or both.

The term *grounded theory* describes at the same time both the research process (the way the research is conducted) and the end result (a new theory that is empirically grounded in data); it also serves as a guide for the research design. In this book, and while also contextualizing our discourse, we use the abbreviation *GT* when we mean the research process and the full term *grounded theory* when we mean the end result of a GT study.

• HOW WE HAVE ORGANIZED THIS BOOK

Chapters 1 to 4 provide an overview of classic GT by situating GT on the research landscape (Chapter 1), discussing theory discovery as the end purpose of GT (Chapter 2), elaborating the foundational pillars of classic GT (Chapter 3), and clarifying common sources of confusion in GT (Chapter 4).

Chapters 5 to 7 offer practical guidance in the application of a classic GT framework using both qualitative and quantitative data. Chapter 5 explores the process of data collection, Chapter 6 guides the reader through classic GT's data analysis procedures, and Chapter 7 elaborates the various procedures applied in classic GT for shaping the emergent theory.

Chapters 8 to 10 offer the reader advice on writing as an important part of the classic GT process (Chapter 8) as well as on writing for an audience, that is, for publication (Chapter 9). Chapter 10 addresses the issue of evaluating grounded theories.

Each chapter features a short quiz (**Test Your Knowledge**) to help you quickly check your knowledge and understanding of the material covered. We identify additional works (**Further Reading**) at the end of each chapter that may also assist in enhancing your knowledge of classic GT. Also included are five appendices, to which we regularly refer as illustrations of some issues examined in several chapters.

Appendix A provides comparative examples of data collection and analysis using a preformulated, descriptive qualitative approach with classic GT's emergent, conceptual approach.

Appendix B provides an overview and selected excerpts from Holton's (2006) thesis, illustrating the application of classic GT to qualitative data.

Appendix C provides selected methodological excerpts from Walsh (2014a) illustrating the use of a classic GT approach with mixed data, methods, and techniques.

Appendix D is extracted and adapted from Walsh (2014c). It provides some examples of theoretical coding using mixed qualitative and quantitative data. It also illustrates how the literature may be used as secondary data, once the core category of a grounded theory has emerged.

Appendix E is extracted from Walsh, Renaud, and Kalika (2013) and shows an example of diagrams that helped the emergence of a theory and guided its writing up.

Finally, while we have no intention in this book to replicate or summarize Barney Glaser's many publications on classic grounded theory, we make frequent reference to his work. Studying the original work of Barney Glaser is a must for anyone seeking to do classic grounded theory (CGT).

ACKNOWLEDGMENTS ●

This book has been "in the works" for more than 10 years. In 2004, Barney Glaser suggested that I write a "troubleshooting book" based on the many questions and blocks to doing classic GT that the novice researcher encounters. I have since had the privilege of attending many of Barney's troubleshooting seminars as well as offering several seminars myself internationally. Many of these seminars were collaborations with Fellows of the Grounded Theory Institute, including Tom Andrews, Toke Barfod, Ólavur Christiansen, Foster Fei, Astrid Gynnild, Tina Johnston, Andy Lowe, Vivian Martin, Antoinette McCallin, Alvita Nathaniel, Anna Sandgren, Helen Scott, Odis Simmons, Michael Thomas, and Hans Thulesius. The seminars and my 8 years as editor in chief of *The Grounded Theory Review* have provided me with a greater appreciation for the power of doing classic GT as well as offering valuable insights into the challenges met by those new to the GT experience. In conversations with Barney over the ensuing years, I have had my perspective at times validated and at other times challenged! All has been wonderful learning for which I owe Barney a great debt of gratitude.

A chance e-mail exchange in October 2012 (in response to an Academy of Management electronic mailing list posting titled "Whoever said that grounded theory (GT) was a qualitative methodology?") has led to another fruitful collaboration with my coauthor, Isabelle Walsh. In a very short period of intense exchange, our collaboration has included co-organizing both a symposium (2013) and a professional development workshop (2014) on GT through the Academy of Management, as well as the publication of a special issue on grounded theory in a top-tier journal, *Organizational Research Methods*.

Isabelle and I have had very different GT learning journeys but share a common philosophical perspective as critical realists and as management scholars. In this collaboration as well, I have at times had my perspective on GT both validated and challenged. Our collaboration has further stretched my learning and helped to firm up the unique concept for this book—*a guide to the fundamentals of classic GT highlighting applications with both qualitative and quantitative data.*

—Judith Holton, September 2015

I was not directly trained by Barney Glaser as such. I only attended one of his seminars, which I organized in Paris during the spring of 2014. Beyond the very limited aspects of GT that I learned from some methodological seminars I attended during my doctoral years, my knowledge of GT is empirically grounded (I learned about GT as I was doing it). However, I have to highlight that I was guided by Barney's numerous publications in my methodological endeavors. Through the years and as I was conducting my various research projects, every time I wondered what I should do methodologically, which methods or techniques I could use, I just referred to the seminal book about GT (Glaser & Strauss, 1967) and then to Barney's subsequent writings. These freed my creativity, allowed me to produce some theories considered of some worth, and sent me on the way to becoming a recognized scholar in my own research field.

I started collaborating with Judith and Barney only 3 years ago, after putting, out of desperation and loneliness, a post on the Academy of Management electronic mailing list: "Whoever said that grounded theory (GT) was a qualitative methodology?" This post was like a bottle thrown from my own little intellectual island into the ocean of knowledge that was out there. It was sent out of desperation as I had been working on a GT methodological article for the previous 5 years and was, at the time, fighting to have my vision of GT recognized by a top-tier journal of my research field. Going against the mainstream in one's research field is difficult enough. Doing it alone is a thankless task that I was spared, at least for the past couple of years, thanks to Judith's help. She was one of the many people who picked up and answered the message I had posted. Our subsequent meeting and the start of our friendship and work together happened at a time when I needed support to be able to express my findings. I could not have done it without her. I needed reassurance that what I understood as the scope and reach of classic GT were indeed what I saw them to be. And then, I wanted to share what I had found through the methodological article I had been working on for many years and which I finally published in 2014.

This post on the Academy of Management listserv marked a turning point in my intellectual journey to the land of theories. It brought within my reach fabulously rich intellects and opened the way to some deep friendships. The past few years have been interwoven with sharp intellectual challenges, and I certainly would not have achieved what I have done during these years without Judith and Barney's encouragement and reassurance.

Judith is so close to Barney's work and Barney's thinking that, as we were cowriting this book, I would call her "Barnette" during our intellectual fights! She has the unique asset of a thorough knowledge not only of Barney's work but also of Barney himself as an exceptional man and of his thoughts and their evolution over the years.

The present book aims to give a clear and savory taste of classic GT and its fundamentals. Ultimately, it should motivate readers to start reading, or to read again with fresh eyes, Barney Glaser's seminal publications.

—Isabelle Walsh, September 2015

Finally, we would be remiss if we did not acknowledge the guidance, encouragement, and support that we have received from the editorial team of Sage Publications, in particular, Helen Salmon, Anna Villarruel, Veronica Stapleton Hooper, and Colleen Brennan. We are also grateful for the feedback of the following SAGE reviewers: Wayne A. Babchuk, University of Nebraska–Lincoln; Vivian B. Martin, Central Connecticut State University; Sebastien Point, EM Strasbourg Business School; and Karthigeyan Subramaniam, University of North Texas.

ENDNOTE

1. E-mail exchange with second author, February 12, 2015.

PowerPoint slides to accompany the text are available to instructors at study.sagepub.com/holton.

About the Authors

Judith A. Holton completed her Masters in Leadership at Royal Roads University, Victoria (Canada) and her PhD in Management Studies at the University of Northampton (UK). During her PhD research, she was closely mentored by Barney Glaser. She has written a number of methodological papers and coedited books about classic grounded theory and was the founding editor of *The Grounded Theory Review* as a peer-reviewed journal dedicated to classic grounded theory research. She is currently Associate Professor of Management in the Ron Joyce Centre for Business Studies at Mount Allison University, Sackville (Canada), where she teaches strategy, leadership, and organizational change.

Isabelle Walsh defended her PhD and HDR (Habilitation à Diriger des Recherches: Habilitation to Supervise Research) in Paris–Dauphine University (France). Beside methodological and research design issues, her research themes include information systems usage, cultural issues, and change management. Her research has been published in several international top tier outlets (the *European Journal of Information Systems,* the *Journal of Strategic Information Systems, Organizational Research Methods, Systèmes d'Information & Management,* etc.). Beyond her research achievements, she has extensive corporate and consultancy experience and is currently a full professor at SKEMA Business School in France and Head of the Project Management, Information Systems and Supply Chain department; her teaching is aligned with her research themes.

1

Situating Grounded Theory on the Research Landscape

After studying this chapter, you will:

- *understand the origins of grounded theory*
- *understand grounded theory as a general research paradigm*

THE EARLY DEVELOPMENT OF GROUNDED THEORY ●

Barney Glaser has often commented that grounded theory (GT) was discovered, not invented (Glaser, 1992, p. 7; 1998, p. 21). He explains that after completing their famous awareness of dying study (Glaser & Strauss, 1965a), he and Anselm Strauss were frequently asked to explain how they had developed their theory. Glaser suggested to Strauss that they write up their methodology; the result was the publication of *The Discovery of Grounded Theory* (Glaser & Strauss, 1967).[1] Although the book is generally acknowledged as the seminal work on GT, Glaser (1992, 1998) reveals that he had begun developing the methodological ideas that would form the foundation of GT during his doctoral work at Columbia University. What were these ideas, and what precipitated their emergence?

Barney Glaser's Early Influences and Ideas

Glaser completed his doctoral degree at Columbia University in 1961, later publishing his dissertation (Glaser, 1964b). It is worth noting the societal context of the time as one of tension and turmoil with taken-for-granted ideas and accepted norms being challenged everywhere, including the scientific community where the preeminence of the positivist, hypothetical-deductive paradigm in scientific research was being persistently questioned, particularly in terms of its effectiveness for the development of theory. This debate reflects the debate between the logic of discovery and the logic of verification.[2] Gibson and Hartman (2014) suggest that *Discovery* clearly developed from this debate with Glaser and Strauss's particular innovation being the specification of procedures for the discovery of theory from data (p. 75).

Hans Zetterberg, Glaser's doctoral supervisor, has described the climate at Columbia at this time as a long-standing debate between those favoring the advancement of sociology through theory, led by Robert Merton, and those favoring its advancement through methodology, led by Paul Lazarsfeld (Zetterberg, 1954, as cited in Holton, 2011). Theory was logically elaborated with empirical data used simply to verify conjectured hypotheses. In this environment, Glaser was exposed to departmental tensions and methodological innovations through the work of Lazarsfeld, Merton, and contemporaries (Glaser, 2008). He describes being steeped in Lazarsfeld's elaboration analysis and the use of secondary data for discovering latent patterns and unanticipated relationships among variables. Key elements of GT would later emerge from quantitative methodology and "qualitative mathematics," both taught by Lazarsfeld (Glaser, 1998, pp. 22–27).

Paul Lazarsfeld's focus on methodology over methods and data and over ideology—his "quantomania" (Glaser, 2008, p. 4)—would inspire Glaser's focus on theory discovery over verification. His methodological focus would aid in systematizing Glaser's inherent propensity to identify and integrate ideas, to recognize and conceptualize patterns and structures in data. Lazarsfeld's interest in identifying unobserved variables through latent structure analysis taught Glaser to avoid preconceiving a research focus and to instead look for the unexpected, the unanticipated in the data.

Glaser has specifically acknowledged Lazarsfeld's influence as "seeding" him with important methodological contributions to the development of GT: index formation, interchangeability of indicators, constant comparative analysis, and core variable analysis (Glaser, 2005b).[3] The first two methods come directly from Lazarsfeld's work

(Lazarsfeld & Thielsens, 1958, pp. 402–407) while Glaser used Lazarsfeld's method of comparative analysis as a starting point for his own discovery and development of constant comparative analysis, a foundational pillar of GT methodology. Glaser has commented that Lazarsfeld "missed this one. . . . The power of this procedure to generate theory is phenomenal. What a theoretical yield of discovery. What a miss. The constant comparative technique became the influential analytic procedure of GT to generate and discover theory" (Glaser, 2005b, in Holton, 2011, p. 208). Gibson and Hartman (2014) suggest that "rather than specifying a **concept** and then seeking out indicators to illustrate it, in the manner of Lazarsfeld, Glaser (1978) reversed the relationship and argued that indicators indicate concepts" (p. 75). This switch from comparative analysis for testing and verifying theory to theory discovery, they suggest, was a major departure in research methodology at the time and marked a significant methodological innovation in Glaser's work.

Robert Merton's approach to theory construction was also a considerable influence on Glaser's methodological development (Glaser, 1998, pp. 29–31). From Merton, Glaser learned to read for ideas, underlining and noting **concepts** as they emerged from careful reading of text (Glaser, 1998, pp. 29–30). This close reading approach complemented his earlier training in *explication de texte* (meaning literally, in French, "explanation of a text"), which he had acquired during a year of study at the Sorbonne in Paris. Merton's influence on Glaser's methodological development is perhaps most apparent through Merton's emphasis on conceptual integration (i.e., theoretical coding in classic GT) as essential to theory development (Merton, 1968, p. 143).

It was not Merton or Lazarsfeld, however, who supervised Glaser's doctoral studies at Columbia but rather the quiet-spoken Hans Zetterberg (1954, 1961, 1962, 1965). Glaser was particularly taken with Zetterberg's focus on the practical value of social theory and the importance of empirical research as the basis for theory development. Glaser's concern for the practical value of sociology would surface in the later articulation of criteria for evaluating a good grounded theory—that is, a theory that fits, works, has relevance, and is readily modifiable on the basis of new data (Glaser, 1978). Zetterberg admonished the definitional and descriptive nature of contemporary sociology and called for more effort at moving past simply setting forth findings and simple propositional statements in favor of integrating propositions into systems, or theories (Zetterberg, 1954). He railed against conjectured theory and called instead for "research-grounded theories" (Zetterberg, 1954, p. 20); albeit, like Lazarsfeld, his primary concern was with theory verification.

While Glaser has frequently acknowledged the influence of Lazarsfeld, Merton, and Zetterberg on his conceptual ideation of GT, it was Glaser's autonomous creativity (Holton, 2011) that enabled him to stand outside the shadow of these great men of science to develop his own ideas about science and social behavior, ideas that would progress and develop throughout his scholarly career and foster his determined advancement of GT. This autonomous creativity enabled him to transcend the dominant positivist tradition, effectively rejecting that paradigm's premise of preconceived theoretical bases in favor of developing theory from empirical data. Glaser's ability to conceptually transcend the dominant positivist view with respect to theory development would later enable him to approach Anselm Strauss's qualitative realm, with its rich possibilities for data, open to discovery without imposing the structures of positivism's logic of justification; this was an intellectual stance that not only facilitated the emergence of GT but also laid the foundation for GT as a general methodology for research open to any epistemological perspective and using any type of data (Glaser, 2003, 2005a; Holton, 2008) and as an integrative research "paradigm for discovery" (Glaser, 2005a, p. 145).

Glaser and Strauss: From Collaboration to Difference

Having completed his PhD studies in 1961, Glaser moved back to the San Francisco Bay area, where he met and began to work with Anselm Strauss (1916–1996). Strauss had moved from Chicago to the University of California at San Francisco (UCSF) in 1960. His expertise was in qualitative methods with a symbolic interactionist perspective. The shift in the philosophy of science in the 1960s (Gibson & Hartman, 2014) had considerable momentum at the Chicago school during Strauss's time there, with efforts focused on displacing the privileged status of quantitative methodologies (e.g., variable analysis). A leading proponent of the Chicago school, Herbert Blumer asserted that these methodologies produced "disconnected findings" absent of the context that characterizes a sociological variable as "an intricate and inner-moving complex" (1956, pp. 684, 688). As such, both Glaser and Strauss were sensitive to this emerging tension in methodological approaches to theory development.

Glaser would join Strauss at UCSF to commence work on what would become their famous study of dying in American hospitals (Glaser & Strauss, 1965a).[4] The study relied largely on interviews and observational data captured through **field notes**. Their collaboration afforded distinct yet complementary roles for the new research partners. While Strauss led the fieldwork, Glaser's focus was methodological as he applied his attention to conceptual coding of the data. What emerged fairly quickly in the process was his recognition that the study was that of another index (i.e., a core category)—an awareness index—methodologically similar to Lazarsfeld's apprehension index (Lazarsfeld & Thielens, 1958) and his own recognition index (Glaser, 1961, 1964a, 1964b).

By affording Glaser a first opportunity to work extensively with qualitative data, the *Awareness* study offered an opportunity to further refine methodological ideas that he had begun to develop through his doctoral work. An early paper (Glaser, 1965) sets down his procedures for taking explicit coding strategies from quantitative methodology and combining these with methods for generative theory development in contrast to more conventional approaches to qualitative analysis through analytic induction. Thus, *Awareness* became another arena for Glaser's elaboration and refinement of earlier methodological ideas as seeded during his days at Columbia—reading carefully the data, conceptually labeling ideas, comparing them for interchangeable indicators, theoretically saturating and integrating them to explain a pattern of social behavior. "The process was the same: the data was a little softer, but no less rigorously dealt with" (Glaser, 1998, p. 27).

Awareness generated significant interest at the time, not simply for its theoretical contribution to understanding the process of dying in hospitals but also for its methodological innovation. This interest prompted Glaser to suggest publishing their methodology (Glaser, 1998, pp. 21–22). Strauss had not been trained in methodology but encouraged Glaser to proceed. Glaser claims that he authored the first draft of *Discovery* while Strauss was on sabbatical in Europe, later sharing it with Strauss, who then added comments and wrote an additional three chapters (pp. 21–22). Suddaby (2006) suggests that "the genius of Glaser and Strauss's original methodology is that it outlines a procedure by which formerly tacit approaches are made explicit" (p. 640). However, this first seminal book was more an introduction than a procedural guide. Hence, Glaser went on to write a second book, *Theoretical Sensitivity* (1978), detailing more specifically what has become the classic methodology for doing GT.

As is well documented, Glaser and Strauss were to later disagree about the precise nature of GT and would discontinue their professional collaboration. Consistent with their respective backgrounds, Strauss would continue his research and writing from within the qualitative realm while Glaser denied holding any particular perspective, instead espousing his relentless dictum: "All is data." Glaser, however, is generally recognized as having retained both the spirit and the substance of their original work (Locke, 2001, p. 64).

● ARE GLASERIAN AND STRAUSSIAN GT RECONCILABLE?

Glaser and Strauss (1967) start from a common position of GT as a general method of comparative analysis for the generation of theory from empirical data (p. 1) in opposition to other approaches where data were collected and analyzed to verify speculative theory. Indeed, Glaser (1991) reflected on their common quest and achievement in a tribute to Anselm Strauss in which he credits their respective contributions—Strauss's ability for sociological conceptualization and his own for theoretical integration and formulation via the central role of core categories—as fundamental to the emergence of GT.

Juliet Corbin, the other individual widely recognized for her collaboration with Anselm Strauss, acknowledges the contribution that Barney Glaser made to Strauss's methodological advancement in her tribute to Strauss in the same 1991 festschrift. She comments that, early in his career, Strauss struggled to analyze collected data and that his frustration was in how to penetrate the surface of data, what procedures to use to identify and label concepts, and how to relate concepts in theoretical formulations. She suggests that it is doubtful that Strauss would ever have been able to clarify procedures if he had not worked with Barney Glaser.

It is generally accepted that *Discovery* is more an outline of the approach than it is a procedural guide. We can, however, look to subsequent texts to explore more specifically each author's approach to teaching GT, offering insight into their eventual methodological divergence. Glaser's 1978 publication of *Theoretical Sensitivity* was based in large measure on his experiences of teaching GT to graduate students at UCSF. Nine years later, Strauss published *Qualitative Analysis for Social Scientists* (1987), which draws heavily on his experiences of teaching qualitative methodology to graduate students, including his approach to GT. In these two texts, we glimpse a marked contrast in how each author "teaches" GT that may offer us a view to their respective perspectives.

Glaser's (1978) text extends the discussion commenced in *Discovery* by setting forth a systematic approach to analysis and also by explicating the general and specific nature of GT, integrating and elaborating on methodological advances discovered and developed through his years of teaching. Beginning with a chapter on the importance of theoretical pacing, Glaser leads the reader through the full package of GT techniques—sampling, coding, **memoing**, integrating, and writing up. Indeed, his explication of GT methods is so well articulated that 9 years later, Strauss quotes extensively from the 1978 text in the introduction to one of his own texts (Strauss, 1987). As Strauss comments in his Preface, "indeed the second half of that chapter is essentially his [Glaser's] except for some amplification" (1987, p. xiv). However, we believe that what Strauss proceeds to offer in his text illustrates a fundamental difference in how each author perceives GT and what each considers essential to doing GT.

Glaser (1978) explains the various GT procedures largely absent of specific detailed examples. He writes conceptually, giving the reader a sense of the methods and how they might be employed without pre-scribing precisely how they need to be employed. He does so without detailed procedural specification, leaving the researcher more scope for creativity and flexibility. Partington (2000) suggests that "Glaser was less keen to see grounded theorists following an orthodoxy of approach, preferring to direct his attention to ways of enhancing researchers' latent creativity" (p. 94). Options are offered, as in theoretical coding families, but none is prescribed as required. Apart from suggesting questions for **substantive coding** of data, the actual mechanics of coding, for example, are left largely to the researcher's discretion. Examples are footnoted for the reader's convenience, but they do not interfere with general explanations offered in the text.

By contrast, Strauss (1987) emphasized a need for structure to aid analysis—in particular, his coding paradigm and axial coding with emphasis on conditions, interactions, strategies, tactics, and consequences (pp. 27–28, 32–33). He described GT as

> a style of doing qualitative analysis that includes a number of distinct features, such as theoretical sampling, and certain methodological guidelines, such as the making of constant comparisons and the use of a coding paradigm, to ensure conceptual development and density. (p. 5)

His emphasis in theory generation is on change as a constant in social life, social interaction and social processes at the center of attention (p. 6). The approach is much more descriptive. While Strauss (1987) embraced the general ideas and the power in doing GT, unlike Glaser he was clearly less comfortable trusting in the creative ideation that emerges from trusting in the systematic and sustained analysis of data. His insistence on structure in advance and throughout the process preempts encouraging the researcher to remain open and to trust in **emergence**. Corbin (1991) affirms Strauss's more structured approach with its emphasis on action, interaction, conditions, constraints, and consequences.

As a guide to doing qualitative research, Strauss (1987) offers some excellent advice and many rich descriptive examples. However, he tends to overthink the process, potentially undermining researcher autonomy by restraining the creativity and flexibility inherent in GT's theory-generating power. Perhaps Strauss's many years as a supervisor of students had produced in him a need for cautionary control of the novice researcher. Apart from the Introduction chapter, which, as noted earlier, draws largely on Glaser's (1978) text, subsequent chapters contain extensive detailed descriptive excerpts from Strauss's own research and that of various students. It would seem that each man valued something different as crucial to developing the ability to do GT. For Glaser, it was presenting the methodological ideas and trusting in the researcher's ability to understand and work with those ideas, developing skill over time. For Strauss, what was most important was ensuring sufficient descriptive examples, perhaps feeling that with good examples "how qualitative analysis is actually done is made vivid" and that "one can literally see it being taught" (Strauss, 1987, p. xii).

The Straussian approach suggests that the experience, knowledge, and interest of the researcher should come into play in the initial focusing of the study (see Strauss, 1987, pp. 10–11). While acknowledging that the researcher will be motivated to explore a general area of interest, the Glaserian approach challenges the researcher to set aside preconceived professional ideas and remain open to what emerges as the **main concern** in the area under study. While some may simply reject Glaser's call for openness as impossible, opting instead for the Straussian approach with its specified analytic tools and coding frameworks, the latter can be a slippery slope, particularly for those trained in qualitative methods. As is illustrated in many published papers (that wrongly and with a very limitative perspective) identify GT as a qualitative method, authors mistakenly apply standard precepts of established research procedures traditionally applied within academia (e.g., initial literature reviews, theoretical frameworks, specified research questions, interview protocols, taping and transcribing) as standard aspects of the GT package.

This emphasis on preconceiving the research process, a need to know in advance and to map out in detail the research journey, became so evident in the work of Strauss and Corbin (1990) that it would mark a clear methodological divergence from their earlier collaboration. Glaser's (1992) response sets forth in great detail the inconsistencies with the basic tenets of GT in Strauss and Corbin's (1990) text, declaring their work to be a completely different methodology. Gibson and Hartman (2014) affirm Glaser's concerns, suggesting that

in the need to make things simple, [Strauss and Corbin] presented the name of the things that made up grounded theory
but changed the notion of what grounded theory was. They
did so without carefully justifying their changes with reference
to the original texts. (p. 97)

Referring to Strauss and Corbin (1998), Hernandez (2010) asserts
that

the method described in that book, published after Strauss's
death in 1996, deviated completely from original grounded
theory methodology (Glaser & Strauss, 1967) because of its
descriptive, deductive, and verificational focus—as opposed
to a grounded theory's explanatory, inductive, and discovery
focus. (p. 152)

Hernandez continues: "Corbin (2007) has called their method
Straussian Grounded Theory and has asserted that it is not a research
methodology but rather a qualitative data analysis approach" (p. 152).
Glaser would conceptualize this lexical takeover in his 2009 book,
Jargonizing: Using the Grounded Theory Vocabulary, in which he suggests
that, perhaps ironically, vocabulary is GT's greatest gift to the research
world.

Given the strong positions that appear to exist within the research
community regarding this famous split, it is worth noting that *Basics
of Grounded Theory Analysis: Emergence vs. Forcing* (1992)[5] was written
only after Glaser had made several attempts to convince Strauss to
withdraw the earlier book that Strauss had coauthored with Juliet
Corbin (Strauss & Corbin, 1990). Rather than withdraw, Strauss
encouraged Glaser to publish his objections. While much has been
made of the famous schism, with supporters on both sides defending
clearly divergent positions, it is worth noting that Glaser's criticism
was confined to asserting an absence of good scholarship on the part
of Strauss and Corbin in not differentiating their methods for qualitative analysis from the original GT methodology and for not acknowledging the roots of GT in quantitative methodology and qualitative
mathematics.[6]

In the opening paragraphs of Strauss and Corbin's (1998) second
edition, they relate a story about two famous French artists, Cezanne
and Monet, in which Cezanne is purported to have said of Monet, "He
is only an eye—but *what* an eye!" They suggest that although Monet's
way was different from Cezanne's way, it was indeed just as insightful

and valuable. This story perhaps epitomizes the "great divide" between the Glaserian (i.e., classic GT) and Straussian approaches. Here, Corbin (writing after Strauss's death in 1996) subtly acknowledges that what they (Strauss and Corbin) had produced was indeed a different methodology—just as insightful and valuable but different. Here we agree with Gibson and Hartman (2014) that Strauss and Corbin's approach had fundamentally changed the notion of GT as it had been intended.

● THE NATURE AND POWER OF CLASSIC GT

GT is the systematic generation of theory from data that has itself been systematically obtained (Glaser, 1978, p. 2). A grounded theory, the result of a GT study is not the reporting of facts but the generation of probability statements about the relationships between concepts, a set of conceptual hypotheses/propositions developed from empirical data (Glaser, 1998, pp. 3, 22). GT offers a transcending view of a main concern in a substantive area and the social behavior that explains how that concern is processed, managed, or resolved.

To understand the nature of the classic GT methodology, one must understand the distinction between conceptualization and description. Classic GT is not about accurate, descriptive reporting of findings in a study, nor is it an act of interpreting meaning as ascribed by the participants in a study; rather, it is an act of conceptual abstraction. For a classic grounded theorist, what matters are the concepts, the relationships among those concepts, and their power to offer the reader a conceptual explanation of significant behavior within the social setting under study, free of the particularistic details of specific empirical incidents (indicators). "Without abstraction from time, place and people, there can be no multivariate, integrated theory based on conceptual, hypothetical relationships—descriptions cannot be related to each other as hypotheses as there is no conceptual handle" (Glaser, 2002, p. 26[7]).

While descriptive findings in qualitative research are most certainly valuable, they do not provide conceptual abstraction. A GT must explain, not merely describe, what is happening in a social setting. This ability to abstract the conceptual idea from empirical indicators (incidents in the data under analysis), without the burden of descriptive detail, is what distinguishes classic GT methodology from qualitative data analysis. This abstraction to a conceptual level theoretically explains rather than describes behavior that occurs conceptually and generally in many diverse groups with a common concern (Glaser, 2003).

With this goal of conceptual abstraction, classic GT methodology uses data of all types and media and accommodates a range of epistemological and ontological perspectives without having to espouse any one perspective; that is, the methodology is epistemologically and ontologically flexible. Whether data are viewed as interpreted or objective is immaterial in classic GT methodology, as it is not the descriptive detail or the way in which the data are "constructed" that concerns the grounded theorist; rather, it is the discovery of abstract concepts that lie within the data. Conceptual abstraction frees the researcher from the emphasis on detailed description and elucidation of multiple perspectives. The skill of the grounded theorist is to abstract concepts by leaving the detail of the data behind, lifting the concepts above the data and integrating them into a theory that explains the latent social pattern underlying the behavior in a substantive area (Locke, 2001). Researchers' philosophical stance will certainly come into play in whatever substantive area of interest they may choose as their initial focus and what they consider to be appropriate data sources. This aside, however, the full package of GT can be applied to any data, and indeed, this full package needs to be applied to merit its distinction as a grounded theory.

EMERGENCE OF THE CLASSIC GT PARADIGM ●

Despite the widespread embrace of GT by qualitative researchers, a growing number of theorists are adopting Glaser's view that GT is a general research methodology occupying its own distinct paradigm on the research landscape (Holton, 2008). The use of any and all types of data in classic GT, together with its ontological and epistemological flexibility, clearly distinguishes GT from the precepts of other research paradigms. Many qualitative studies labeled as grounded theories simply fall short of the criteria of a **classic grounded theory**. Such studies have been "remodeled" to meet the criteria of a qualitative framework (Glaser, 2003; Glaser & Holton, 2004). In the process, researchers sacrifice the power of emergence that is fundamental to classic GT.

As a general research methodology, GT uses any and all types of data. For grounded theorists, using both qualitative and quantitative data opens a vast realm of additional empirical possibilities for generating theory. Embracing GT with mixed qualitative and quantitative data (Walsh, 2014a, 2014b, 2014c) will also encourage further scholarship among established GT researchers eager to advance their analytic skills by learning to work with quantitative indices as sources of data.

Perhaps it is inevitable that GT's tremendous power and its inherent flexibility invite methodological evolution and plurality. That being said, when evolution and its consequent plurality create "drift" whereby the key tenets of GT are not sustained as they were intended, can we still accept claims to grounded theory? While much excellent research is done under the banner of some qualitative frameworks, only studies that have employed the full GT methodological package should be accepted as grounded theory. It is our position in this text that recognizing this distinction is important to advancing methodological scholarship. This distinction, of course, raises a key question that we address in this text: *What are the essential elements of methodology that must be evident for a study to claim that it is a grounded theory in the classic sense?*

IN SUMMARY

GT is about the discovery of theory from data systematically collected and analyzed without structured forcing through predetermined theoretical frameworks. Contrary to popular belief, GT is not a qualitative research method. It is a general research methodology that uses any and all types of data, both quantitative and qualitative. As such, GT is not confined to any one philosophical perspective. It is ontologically and epistemologically flexible, accommodating any philosophical perspective as espoused by the researcher. Classic GT is a "full package" methodology that progresses a study from initial data collection and analysis through to the presentation of an integrated theoretical explanation of a latent pattern of social behavior. Classic GT originated with the early work of Barney Glaser using quantitative data and was further developed and articulated through Glaser's famous collaboration with Anselm Strauss. More recently, a growing community of classic GT scholars has espoused GT as a distinct research paradigm with its own distinct perspective and practices.

TEST YOUR KNOWLEDGE

In the following questions, one or several answers may be correct.

1. GT is about
   a. Theory verification
   b. Theory building
   c. Deductive reasoning

    d. Inductive reasoning

    e. None of the above

2. GT originated

    a. From Glaser and Strauss's 1967 book

    b. From Glaser and Strauss's collaboration

    c. From Glaser's doctoral work

    d. From Strauss's doctoral work

    e. None of the above

3. GT can be applied

    a. Only with qualitative data

    b. Only with quantitative data

    c. With any type of data

    d. Only with data collected from interviews

    e. None of the above

4. In classic GT it is important to

    a. Describe in detail a substantive area

    b. Report on facts in a detailed manner

    c. Maintain an interpretive stance

    d. Conceptualize from empirical indicators

    e. None of the above

FURTHER READING

Glaser, B. G. (1998). The roots of grounded theory. In *Doing grounded theory: Issues and discussions* (pp. 21–33). Mill Valley, CA: Sociology Press.

Holton, J. A. (2011). The autonomous creativity of Barney G. Glaser: Early influences in the emergence of classic grounded theory methodology. In A. Gynnild & V. Martin (Eds.), *Grounded theory: The philosophy, method and work of Barney Glaser* (pp. 201–223). Boca Raton, FL: BrownWalker Press.

Walsh, I. (2014). Using quantitative data in mixed-design grounded theory studies: An enhanced path to formal grounded theory in information systems. *European Journal of Information Systems*. Advance online publication. doi:10/1057/ejis.2014.23

ENDNOTES

1. Hereafter referred to as *Discovery*.

2. Gibson and Hartman (2014) offer valuable insight into this context. See in particular pp. 5–13.

3. See also Glaser and Strauss (1967, Chap. 8).

4. Hereafter referred to as *Awareness*.

5. Hereafter referred to as *Basics*.

6. Despite Glaser and Strauss's obvious methodological divergence, Glaser has continued to acknowledge and respect Anselm Strauss as a close personal friend.

7. The Creative Commons-Attribution-NonCommercial-ShareAlike License 4.0 International applies to all works published by the International Journal of Qualitative Methods. Copyright for articles published in the International Journal of Qualitative Methods remains with the first author.

2

Discovering New Theory as the End Purpose of Classic Grounded Theory[1]

After studying this chapter, you will:

- *be aware of the different meanings attached to the word* theory *as they relate to different philosophical assumptions*
- *understand GT as a process aimed at theory discovery and congruent with any philosophical perspective*

M any social sciences are still lacking in the area of theorizing, and we need a plurality of theories in order to make sense of the complex and dynamic world that surrounds us (Junglas et al., 2011). "Developing theory is what we are meant to do as academic researchers and it sets us apart from practitioners and consultants" (Gregor, 2006, p. 613). Hence, the ultimate aim of GT being theory building, there is little doubt of its importance and fit in any academic career. However, it is first essential to stop and reflect on the meaning of the word *theory*.

● WHAT IS A THEORY?

As we saw in the introduction, we recently asked Barney Glaser, "What is a grounded theory?" His answer was "interrelated grounded concepts based on an emergent theoretical code" (personal communication, February 12, 2015). However, many different views of what a theory is have been given in the literature from *etic* (i.e., nomothetic) or *emic* (i.e., idiographic) perspectives; we need to examine these views in detail in order to truly understand the various ways in which GT is being applied all over the world and in many different disciplines. These perspectives are often linked to the researcher's background, training, and philosophical assumptions. For instance, Bacharach (1989) views a theory "as a system of constructs and variables in which the constructs are related to each other by propositions and the variables are related to each other by hypotheses"' (p. 498), whereas Weick (1995) views theories as "approximations" of a complex reality that one has to make sense of. However, these definitions are not philosophically neutral. We accept the all-encompassing definition provided by Gregor (2006), which is as philosophically neutral as possible and which views "theories as abstract entities that aim to describe, explain, and enhance understanding of the world and, in some cases, to provide predictions of what will happen in the future and to give a basis for intervention and action" (Gregor, 2006, p. 616).

Gregor investigates the structure and form of theories. She argues that the four primary goals of theory are analysis and description, explanation, prediction, and prescription (Gregor, 2006). She shows that combinations of these goals lead to five types of theories that are interrelated, answer different types of questioning, and which should be combined: analytic (type I: What is?), explanatory (type II: What is? How? Why? When? Where?), predictive (type III: What is? What will be?), explanatory and predictive (type IV: What is? How? Why? When? Where? What will be?), and theory for design and action (type V: How to do?). Usually, one must analyze before one can explain, predict, or act. And, preferably, one must attempt to explain and predict, if at all possible, before one actually acts. This is summarized in Table 2.1.

When doing classic GT, type I is not sufficient, and at least type II must be achieved. As we emphasize in this book, classic GT may be applied with any data, qualitative and/or quantitative, and is compatible with any philosophical assumptions. Different data may be collected

Table 2.1   Different Types of Theory (Adapted from Gregor, 2006)

	Theory type	Answers the following questions . . .	Description
I	Analytical	What is it? What is happening?	The theory analyzes and describes phenomena but no causal relationship is highlighted.
II	Explanatory	What is it? What is happening? How? Why? When? Where?	The theory explains but does not predict. It does not highlight propositions.
III	Predictive	What is it? What is happening? What will be? What will happen?	The theory predicts and highlights testable propositions but does not develop justified causal explanations.
IV	Explanatory and predictive	What is it? What is happening? How? Why? When? Where? What will be? What will happen?	The theory predicts and also highlights testable causal explanations.
V	Prescriptive	What should be done? How should it be done?	The theory explicitly prescribes (methods, techniques, principles).

through various methods (e.g., interviews, focus groups, photograph-ing, filming, surveys, etc.) and analyzed with the help of different tech-niques (e.g., text analysis, cluster analysis, etc.) through the constant comparative method. The resulting theory may differ from one researcher to the next, depending on researchers' philosophical assumptions, the data they choose as appropriate, and their previous training.

Over the past 20 years, an important debate has ensued about the rationale for combining methods and techniques previously consid-ered as incompatible due to philosophical assumptions and world-views presumed to be linked to these (Bryman, 1998; Hall, 2012). This dispute has led to *philosophical caricatures* (Bryman, 1998) at each end of a continuum (see Figure 2.1).

Figure 2.1   Caricatures at Each End of the Philosophical Continuum (Adapted from Walsh, Holton, Bailyn, Fernandez, Levina, & Glaser, 2015a)

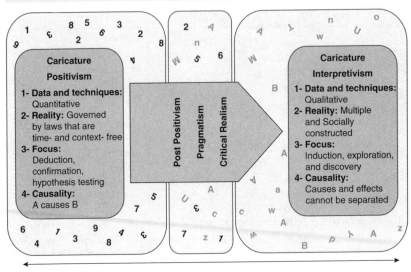

Philosophical Continuum

At one end, quantitative purists espouse a positivist philosophy and adopt the "natural science model" (Bryman, 1998) with independent and dependent variables and quantitative data (Lee & Hubona, 2009): The observer is separate from the object of study; science is objective and aims to uncover laws that are time- and context-free; and the focus is on deduction, confirmation, hypothesis testing, and quantitative analysis (Johnson & Onwuegbuzie, 2004). Causality is understood from a Humean perspective ("A causes B").

At the other end of the continuum, qualitative purists espouse an interpretive philosophy associated with ethnography, hermeneutics, and some forms of case research, interpreting settings and contexts to take the "natives' point of view" (Lee & Hubona, 2009, p. 238): Realities are multiple and socially constructed so that knower and known cannot be separated; research is subjective and value-bound; causes and effects cannot be differentiated; and the focus is on induction, exploration, discovery, and qualitative analysis (Johnson & Onwuegbuzie, 2004).

However, many researchers have now reached an agreement on some major issues (Johnson & Onwuegbuzie, 2004) regarding theorizing, whether they use qualitative or/and quantitative data and techniques and even if their philosophical assumptions may vary

Figure 2.2   Consensual Perspective

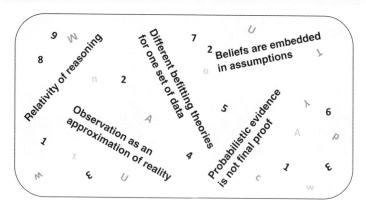

(see Figure 2.2): Reasoning is relative and varies among people; observation is an approximation of reality; a single set of empirical data can yield different befitting theories; hypotheses are linked to assumptions; probabilistic evidence is not final proof; and researchers' beliefs are embedded in the assumptions of their respective communities.

One reason these caricatures developed is that philosophical assumptions have been mapped mainly as an opposition between nomothetic perspectives and more idiographic perspectives. This element, and the coupling of quantitative data and techniques with a nomothetic approach versus qualitative data and techniques with an idiographic approach, completely ignores another dimension that opposes confirmatory, theory-driven research and exploratory data-driven research.

The Possibility of Using Any Type of Data With Any Philosophical Stance to Do GT

In *Awareness* (Glaser & Strauss, 1965a), and through the use of qualitative data, Glaser and Strauss highlight an *awareness index* that explains the social interactions surrounding a dying person. This index makes sense at the same time in Glaser's post-positivist worldview and in Strauss's symbolic interactionist perspective. Walsh (2010, 2014a) uses mixed qualitative and quantitative data/techniques in a critical realist stance to propose a *digital culture index* that explains information technology usage; that is, why people use (or do not use) information technologies, for what purpose, and how they do so through the emergence of their digital needs.

● THE DRIVE FROM SUBSTANTIVE TO FORMAL GT

When theorizing, researchers produce theories at different levels of generalization; these are sometimes linked to the theory's level of abstraction. For instance, a metatheory is at a high level of abstraction and provides "a way of thinking about other theories" (Gregor, 2006, p. 616); a grand theory is abstract, scarce in observational details, and "'unbounded in space and/or time' (p. 616), whereas some empirical generalizations are rich in observational details but often "bounded in space and time" (Bacharach, 1989, p. 500). There are, however, different conceptions of generalizability, which "refers to the validity of a theory in a setting different from the one where it was empirically tested and confirmed" (Lee & Baskerville, 2003, p. 221). Lee and Baskerville (2003) identify different types of generalizability and generalizing beyond statistical, sampling-based generalizability: generalizing from empirical statement to empirical statement (i.e., from data to description), from empirical statement to theoretical statement (i.e., from description to theory), from theoretical statement to empirical statement (i.e., from theory to description), and from theoretical statement to theoretical statement (i.e., from concepts to theory). This is summarized in Table 2.2.

In the case of a grounded theory, the generalization is done from data to theory through conceptualization, even though one often starts from data to description in order to see through and understand the data, that is, what they are *telling* us (i.e., indicating) in order to conceptualize. It must, however, be highlighted that one cannot claim to have done classic GT if one remains at the descriptive level, short of producing a conceptual theory.

Table 2.2   Different Types of Generalization (Adapted from Lee and Baskerville, 2003)

Generalization	Toward empirical elements	Toward theoretical elements
	Description of data	From description to theory
From empirical statements	The researcher measures, observes, describes	The researcher conceptualizes from her/his data
	From theory to description	From concepts to theory
From theoretical statements	The researcher applies to a given context a theory developed and confirmed in another context	The researcher highlights propositions linking concepts

Grounded theories may be developed at both the substantive and formal levels. A **substantive grounded theory** reaches beyond observed incidents and analyzed data but applies to the substantive area of inquiry (Urquhart, Lehmann, & Myers, 2010). A **formal grounded theory** is abstract in terms of time, place, and people until it is applied (Glaser, 2007); it has been defined by Glaser (2007) as "a theory of SGT [substantive GT] core category's general implications, using, as widely as possible other data and studies in the same substantive area and in other substantive areas" (p. 99). A formal GT has no predetermined level of abstraction, as this will be determined by the theoretical sampling and the data used. It allows generalizing on a core category from different substantive areas "with more multivariate conceptual complexity" (Glaser, 2007, p. 1). Hence, and in order to reach formal GT, a substantive GT first has to be developed. Formal GT makes substantive findings "meaningful on a larger scale" (Kearney, 2007, p. 131) and extends the applicability of a substantive grounded theory across contexts, settings, or both.

The formalization of a substantive grounded theory involves starting with an existing substantive theory; its aim, however, is to "enhance the theory, widen its scope or in other ways improve it—but not to verify or falsify it" (Urquhart et al., 2010, p. 4). The formalization of a substantive grounded theory will therefore always involve the full GT process. To sum up, theorizing is a continuum (Runkel & Runkel, 1984; Weick, 1995): A substantive grounded theory can be understood as what Weick (1995) terms an "interim struggle," an early stage of formal theoretical development leading toward further development and stronger

From Substantive to Formal Theory

In their famous collaboration, Glaser and Strauss first developed a general substantive theory related to dying patients (*Awareness*, 1965). They then extended their core category (i.e., patients' changing status from living to dying) to build a formal theory of status passage (Glaser & Strauss, 1971) related to many different settings (e.g., career changes, mobility within organizations, etc.).

Walsh, Kefi, and Baskerville (2010) proposed a substantive theory related to the process of acculturation to information technologies and a digital culture index developed from qualitative data collected in some given contexts (corporate and societal) but bounded by qualitative data. This index was then amended and the theory formalized into a general substantive theory by extension to other substantive contexts through supplementary quantitative data slices (Walsh, 2014a; Walsh & Gettler-Summa, 2010).

formal theory at a "higher gradation of abstractness and generality" (p. 385). Glaser (2011) stresses that the procedures required to generate formal GT are the same as those to generate substantive GT. The multiple differences between the two are in the theoretical sampling:

> In SGT [substantive GT], one samples within a substantive chosen site or population. In doing FGT [formal GT], one samples widely in other substantive sites and populations both within and outside the substantive area in order to make the theory more general, as one constantly compares, adding new properties and categories to the core category being generalized. (Glaser, 2011, p. 257)

Doing GT does not imply an idiographic (i.e., local) or nomothetic (i.e., universal) perspective. Both are possible, depending solely on the researcher's philosophical stance. Idiographic, substantive theories lead to different types of nomothetic, formalized theories, using any kind of data (qualitative and/or quantitative) while always remaining in an exploratory, data-driven stance (Figure 2.3). As highlighted by Glaser (2007), a formal theory may be a so called middle-range theory or "grand theory" in Merton's (1967) sense.

Glaser and Strauss (1967) differentiated between substantive and formal GT through their differing degrees of abstraction and generality; however, they cautioned that they lacked hindsight and experience in this area. Glaser (1978) suggested that between a theory (e.g., the change of status of patients in one hospital) in a specific area (e.g., dying patients) and a formal theory (e.g., status passage) in its full generality (e.g., career changes, mobility within organizations), "there is a type of theory in between which we call general substantive theory" (p. 52), for example, the awareness of dying related to patients in any hospital. To fully understand the process of formalization of a substantive theory, and in a critical realist stance, we would propose to replace the term *generality* as used by Glaser and Strauss (1967) by *substantive formalization* and "abstraction" by *conceptual formalization*. The substantive formalization of a substantive theory may be obtained through sampling different substantive groups, contexts, and/or social units within the same setting/substantive area; it increases the scope of a grounded theory. The conceptual formalization, which can mostly be achieved once the substantive formalization has been ensured, may be obtained through sampling in different settings/ substantive areas; it increases the reach of a grounded theory. This is summarized in Figure 2.4. The two examples provided in the previous boxed text are illustrated in Figure 2.5.

Figure 2.3   The *Land* of Theories (Adapted from Walsh et al., 2015a)

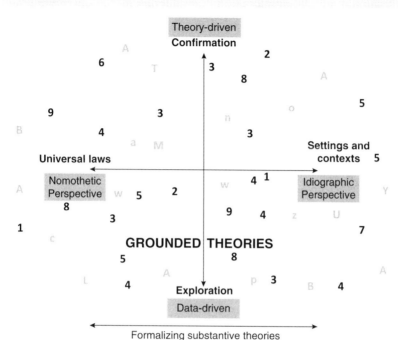

Figure 2.4   From Substantive to Formal Grounded Theory (Translated and adapted from Walsh, 2015)

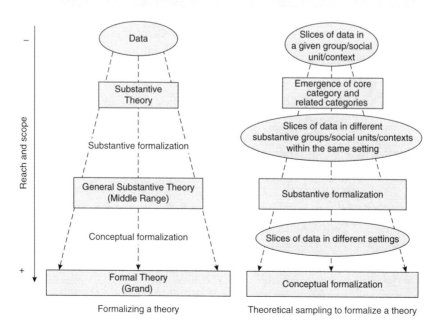

Figure 2.5 Examples of Substantive and Conceptual Formalization

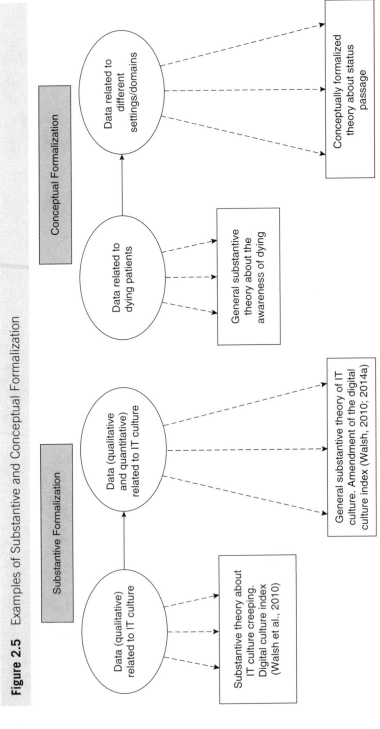

THEORIZING IN RUPTURE WITH EXISTING LITERATURE   ●

Beyond the various classifications aimed at describing theories proposed by different authors, we propose a further consideration that is acutely needed to understand fully the contribution of classic GT to the scientific research process. When researchers theorize, they can do so through what we term *incremental theorizing* (theorizing while using existing concepts/constructs) or *rupture theorizing* (theorizing while using new concepts/constructs; Walsh, 2014c). Incremental theorizing, although essential to help a research field mature and grow, represents additional information and gradual developments on existing concepts/constructs. Rupture theorizing uses *nascent* concepts/constructs, which were previously unrevealed and unstudied in the literature, or which were previously applied in, and adapted to, completely different domains.

Rupture theorizing may involve defining and specifying these new concepts/constructs and/or investigating relationships between these and other previously established and studied concepts/constructs. For instance, in a hypothetical-deductive stance, the literature is usually first investigated for clues to lay down hypotheses in a linear research approach (Creswell, 2014; Zachariadis, Scott, & Barrett, 2013). Hypothetical-deductive research has led to data poverty (as data collected are used for theory testing and not for theory building; Evermann & Tate, 2011; Lyytinen, 2009) and, consequently, to incremental theorizing. In the case of rupture theorizing, if a concept/construct has never been previously studied in a field, the literature will be of little help to describe or explain it or to develop propositions or hypotheses involving this new construct. As all **preconceptions** are to be set aside when doing GT (Glaser, 1978), adopting a classic GT exploratory stance naturally leads to the emergence of new concepts/constructs and to theorizing in rupture with existing literature. Thus, as the main concern emerges while doing GT, it may lead the researcher to investigate either new phenomena, never before investigated in the literature, or, alternatively, the GT process will lead to studying phenomena already investigated in past literature but from different and alternative perspectives.

IN SUMMARY

Classic GT may accommodate any philosophical perspective. The ultimate purpose of classic GT is to go beyond description and to discover new theories grounded in empirical data; either a new theoretical perspective on a well-established and theoretically developed phenomenon or a theory *in rupture* with existing literature. A grounded theory may be substantive and framed in an idiographic perspective, or it may be formal (i.e., with greater reach and scope) and framed in a more nomothetic perspective. Depending on a researcher's philosophical stance, the potential resulting grounded theories may vary widely.

TEST YOUR KNOWLEDGE

In the following questions one or several answers may be correct.

1. A theory
   a. Is the same thing whatever your philosophical stance
   b. May be only descriptive in classic GT terms
   c. Always involves causal elements whatever your philosophical stance
   d. None of the above

2. A substantive grounded theory
   a. Reaches beyond analyzed data and observed incidents
   b. Applies to the substantive area of inquiry
   c. Generalizes from empirical data to theoretical statement
   d. None of the above

3. A formal grounded theory
   a. Has no predetermined level of abstraction
   b. Allows generalizing on a core category from different substantive areas
   c. Develops further a substantive GT
   d. Is at a greater level of abstraction and/or generality than a substantive GT
   e. None of the above

FURTHER READING

Gibson, B., & Hartman, J. (2014). *Rediscovering grounded theory* (Chapter 2). London: Sage.

Glaser, B. G. (1978). *Theoretical sensitivity* (Chapter 1). Mill Valley, CA: Sociology Press.

Glaser, B. G. (2007). *Doing formal grounded theory.* Mill Valley, CA: Sociology Press.

Glaser, B. G., & Strauss, A. L. (1967). *The discovery of grounded theory: Strategies for qualitative research* (Chapters 1 & 2). New York: Aldine de Gruyter.

Gregor, S. (2006). The nature of theory in information systems. *MIS Quarterly, 30*(3), 611–642.

ENDNOTE

1. Some materials in this chapter were previously published in Walsh (2014c).

3

Foundational Pillars of Classic Grounded Theory

After studying this chapter, you will:

- *understand the foundational pillars of grounded theory*
- *appreciate the necessary frame of mind for doing grounded theory*

I t is common to read in published accounts of grounded theory that doing GT is not easy, that it is a "difficult subject" (Suddaby, 2006, p. 633), "worryingly messy" (Partington, 2002, p. 155), "problematic" (Backman & Kyngas, 1999, p. 148), and a source of "methodological confusion" (Goulding, 1999, p. 866). Reading such accounts would be enough to discourage any novice from adopting GT as a methodological choice! If one looks beyond such assessments, it is generally the case that the authors have conflated GT with some of the precepts of traditional qualitative research. Such precepts are often misaligned with GT's precepts, and therein frequently rest the struggles. Partington (2002) suggests this conflation has resulted in a loss of attention to key principles of GT.

Suddaby's (2006) editorial in the *Academy of Management Journal* is a leading example of this qualitative assumption applied to GT. He confuses GT's emergent paradigm with a lack of systematic procedure when he suggests that "totally unstructured research produces totally unstructured manuscripts that are unlikely to make it past the desk editor at any credible journal of social science" (p. 633). Suddaby also confuses the way GT research is actually conducted and the way it is written to fit within the constraints of established academic publishing standards (de Vaujany, Walsh, & Mitev, 2011). Similar to Partington (2002), Suddaby advocates for a clear research question and theoretical framework up front. Furthermore, he misinterprets Glaser and Strauss (1967, p. 79) as calling for grounded theory to be generated from extant theory. Here, he confuses their reference to generating formal theory as applying more broadly to substantive theory generation. What Glaser and Strauss are actually proposing is that a formal grounded theory is best generated when it follows from a substantive grounded theory using its core category as the basis for more formal theory development. They are *not* suggesting that to develop a grounded theory, one must start from existing theory.

What Glaser and Strauss (1967) actually said about the use of extant theory:

> A substantive theory generated from the data must first be formulated in order to see which of diverse formal theories are, perhaps, applicable for furthering substantive formulations … allowing substantive concepts and hypotheses to emerge first, on their own, enables the analyst to ascertain which, if any, existing formal theory may help him to generate his substantive theories. (p. 34)

We agree with Suddaby's advice that GT is not an excuse to ignore the literature. GT is not about ignoring the literature but rather about staying open by holding the literature in abeyance until the core category of the theory has emerged. Doing so avoids the potential of forcing of the study's theoretical direction; instead, it enhances the potential to discover a true main concern in the area under study and a novel way to explain it through a core category. As a prominent scholar, Suddaby is influential, but his conception of GT as a qualitative method only adds to the confusion for those wishing to pursue the classic GT approach.

The purpose of this chapter is to help clarify some of this confusion and hopefully relieve the angst of "doing it wrong" by being very clear about the foundational pillars of classic GT and how these shape the necessary mindset for doing GT. We offer three components of GT as foundational and essential to its application: emergence, constant comparative analysis, and theoretical sampling. By emergence, we refer to the result of GT's open and exploratory stance in relation to the research field. Constant comparative analysis refers to the process through which all data are analyzed as they are collected and together with all previously collected data. Theoretical sampling is the process through which empirical data are selected and collected as guided by the emerging theory.

● EMERGENCE

The GT approach is a general methodology for the discovery of theory. The researcher enters the field and explores a substantive area by allowing the chief concerns of those actively engaged therein to guide the emergence of a core issue or problem. The conceptualization of that issue (or problem) becomes the basis for the articulation of a grounded theory that explains how the issue is processed, managed, or resolved. As such, a defining characteristic of GT is its rejection of preconceived theorizing. Contrary to the traditional quantitative approach, which implies the articulation of hypotheses in advance, or the traditional qualitative approach, which implies a theoretical framework to be applied, GT does not require as a starting point the identification of a gap in the literature from which precise research questions are framed to guide the study. A GT study begins with the researcher being open to discovering latent patterns that can be theorized to explain social behavior.

Those who have been trained in other research methodologies often find it a challenge to set aside learned habits, but doing so is fundamental to undertaking a grounded theory study where the focus of the study and its theorization cannot be decided at the outset of the study by preconceived notions resident within the researcher's worldview, an initial professional problem, or an extant theory and framework. Such preconception is simply forced conjecture—what Glaser and Strauss (1965b) refer to as "logical speculation" (p. 11). Preconceiving a study based on extant theory blocks the emergent potential with "categories that do not seem to emerge in the data but, rather, are imposed on it as existing theory which ought to be applicable. Their relevance is implicitly assumed" (Glaser, 1966, p. 332).

Our philosophical stance does preconceive our research approach to some degree as it can limit what we consider to be appropriate data and how we approach the analysis of those data. As an example, constructivism privileges interview and focus group data and would commonly reject the use of observational or documentary data as not appropriate for conveying the perspectives of the participants. GT's openness to all data creates a form of triangulation in data sources, thereby reducing the potential for a *perspective bias* (whether that of the researcher or the participants) being introduced through restricted use of data types.

In a GT study, if a researcher chooses to use quantitative data and/or techniques traditionally considered by some as confirmatory, it is not the technique in itself that is important but how it is used and applied with an exploratory purpose. As early as 1980, Tukey highlighted that "exploratory (quantitative) data analysis is an attitude and a flexibility" (p. 24). For instance, factor analysis that helps to group emerging variables, and/or cluster analysis that helps to classify objects/people/concepts based on their similarities and differences, could fruitfully be used in an exploratory fashion. Structural equation modeling (SEM) in the soft exploratory version of the partial least squares (PLS) approach can also help theorizing. Researchers may use many other techniques, if they always take care not to impose hypotheses on the data. When one uses quantitative data, it may be useful to remember that the numbers themselves are not what matters in social sciences: It is the meaning behind the numbers that is important. Hence, quantitative techniques may be used; they should, however, never be used in a mechanical fashion without fully understanding the meaning behind the techniques (Glaser, 2008). It might be useful for the reader to refer to Appendix C as an illustration of some quantitative techniques used in an exploratory GT stance.

While doing GT, concepts come from the data; they are not preconceived or imposed on data. This is particularly important when data, methods, and techniques are mixed. The quantitative and qualitative components are not used for verification or testing but for further elaboration of the theory. There should be no *forcing*, where it is assumed that particular constructs will occur in the data. Thus, and whatever the data that are being used, exploration and emergence of the theory from the data have to remain central.

Our preconceptions about the social worlds we wish to study can creep in unawares as this statement in one methodology guide illustrates: "In management research, you will often find that the more senior the manager the more useful the interview data" (Partington, 2002, p. 144). Concepts in vogue (e.g., context) are often assumed and forced upon a study, but in GT they are simply potential variables that may or may not emerge as relevant through constant comparative analysis. How such variables may influence a latent pattern within your data must emerge as relevant to the substantive area that is investigated and not be assumed and forced into the analysis (Glaser, 1992, 2013). Studies in disciplines that are highly theorized (e.g., management, economics, psychology) are particularly susceptible to preconception; this is what Alvesson and Sandberg (2014) refer to as "'boxed-in research'... encouraging specialization, incremental adding-to-the-literature contributions and a blinkered mindset" (p. 967). Undertaking a grounded theory study in such disciplines necessitates that researchers appreciate from the outset the undermining effect of preconceiving the research focus through the lens of their professional research interests, extensive preliminary literature reviews, precise research questions, defined sample populations, structured interview protocols, and other factors. Emergence as a foundational pillar necessitates that researchers remain open to discovering a main concern motivating the interest or action within the area under study and offers a conceptual theory to explain the behavior.

Glaser (2013) has identified several types of preconception that frequently derail GT intentions. Among those commonly adopted are the following:

- Conducting an extensive preliminary literature review to identify a gap in the research around which to focus a proposed study

- Assuming the relevance of a "pet theoretical code" (Glaser, 2005a) such as social network, **basic social process**, conditional matrix, and so on, as a lens through which the data are analyzed

- Specifying research questions around which all data collection is focused

- Assuming the relevance of face sheet data (e.g., gender, age, income, etc.) to the analysis and theory development

Misconceptions such as all grounded theories are basic social processes (Langley, 1999) or actions (Creswell, 2013) lead to forcing a theory to fit the misconception. While Glaser (1978) highlighted basic social processes as an important theoretical **code**, he did so to empha-size the patterned nature of grounded theory in contrast to unit analysis, which invariably leads to descriptive findings rather than conceptual theory. His inclusion in the same text of several alternative theoretical coding families should clarify the misconception of grounded theory as always being a basic social process. Forcing the use of a specific theoretical code, such as using a basic social process to organize and model a theory, often results in rather flat and thin theory and prevents the theorist from seeing a more interesting, novel, emergent theoretical code around which to integrate the theory. Similarly, preconceiving the study from the outset with a "skeletal framework . . . focusing the inquiry at an early stage . . . provid[ing] internal structure to the study" (Morse & Mitcham, 2008, p. 32) is another preempting of GT's emergent potential. Such strategies can be particularly problematic for an inexperienced theorist who lacks the confidence to stay open and reverts to the assurance of a structure in advance, especially under supervisor pressures to adopt the precepts of qualitative research.

Similarly, extensive literature reviews in advance of a study, often with the goal of identifying a gap in the literature, also present the potential for preconception—what Morse and Mitcham (2008) refer to as "the pink elephant syndrome." At best, identifying such a gap is a stab in the dark because the literature reviewed may not correlate to the emergent main concern and may even inhibit the researcher's ability to see the main concern. Such practices, however, are often encouraged by PhD supervisors unfamiliar with classic GT and can even influence standard requirements of the PhD thesis at many universities and of peer reviewer expectations for mainstream journal publication. As such, the undermining potential for GT studies is persistent and significant but can be overcome with a solid understanding and appreciation for emergence as foundational to GT development.

If, in accordance with classic GT precepts, the literature review is conducted after the core category has emerged and *around* this core category, the literature may be used as data. It may help in theoretical sampling for full saturation of emergent concepts as well as in theoretical coding for the emergence of relationships between concepts and overall integration of the theory.

CONSTANT COMPARATIVE ANALYSIS ●

The goal of GT is the generation of theory that conceptually explains latent patterns of social behavior:

> Conceptualization is the medium of GT for a simple reason: without the abstraction from time, place and people, there can be no multivariate, integrated theory based on conceptual,

hypothetical relationships . . . Because GT operates on a conceptual level, relating concept to concept, it can tap the latent structure which is always there and drives and organizes behavior and its social psychological aspects, all of which are abstract of objective fact. (Glaser, 2002, p. 24[1])

Thus, the conceptual abstraction of empirical data using constant comparative analysis is fundamental to doing GT. Constant comparative analysis is a strategy for directing the collection and analysis of data in tandem with theoretical sampling as a means of guiding the direction of further data sampling (Figure 3.1).

The analytical processes that underlie the constant comparative method have their roots in latent structure analysis as developed at the University of Columbia's School of Applied Arts under the leadership of Paul Lazarsfeld (Lazarsfeld & Henry, 1968). As a student at Columbia, Glaser saw the practical value in theory generation using empirical data that had been collected as preparatory to large-scale survey work. His own doctoral work employed secondary analysis of such data. As a student of Lazarsfeld, Glaser was exposed to Lazarsfeld's index formation process but saw the stripped-down, summing-up quality as a loss (Glaser, 1998, p. 23). One had an index but without meaning. Glaser's idea was rather than simply summing up indicators, he would instead compare indicator to indicator thereby generating conceptual properties and dimensions; this would be an index with

Figure 3.1   The Constant Comparative Analysis Process (Walsh, 2014c)[2]

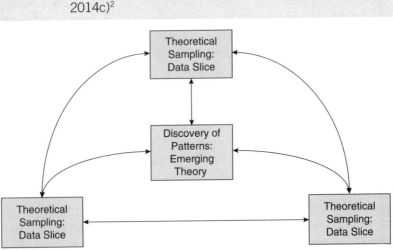

meaning (Glaser, 1998, p. 24). Another aspect of constant comparative method is *explication de texte*,[3] which Glaser studied at the Sorbonne. *Explication de texte* refers to "reading closely line by line to ascertain what exactly the author is saying without imputing what is said, interpreting it or reifying its meaning" (Glaser, 1998, p. 24). Glaser explains how *explication de texte* stirred his interest in latent patterns of behavior in social settings. Applying *explication de texte* to constant comparative analysis helps to generate concepts that closely fit what is going on in the substantive area without imputing meaning to the individual action; one simply names the concept as an abstraction.

The concept-indicator model requires that concepts and their properties and dimensions earn their way into a theory by systematic generation of data. GT's concept-indicator model begins with substantive coding in which empirical incidents are compared, incident to incident, to generate concepts. When many indicators become interchangeable, they lead to a pattern that is named (concept). Additional empirical incidents are compared to the emergent concepts, to build and substantiate these with property and dimensional definition. When further data yield no new concepts or additional elaboration of their properties and dimensions, **theoretical saturation** has been achieved. Then the concepts are related to each other to generate hypotheses. Constant comparison continues through theoretical coding whereby concepts are compared to other concepts to establish conceptual levels and their theoretical integration. Thus, the constant comparative analysis of data threads throughout the entire GT process, taking full advantage of the interchangeability of indicators to develop a broad range of acceptable indicators of concepts and their properties (Glaser & Strauss, 1971, p. 184), from the initial data collected through to the full integration of the generated theory that is "integrated, consistent, plausible and close to the data" (Glaser, 1965, pp. 437–438).

Glaser's (1965) seminal paper on the constant comparative method outlines four stages to the process—comparing incidents applicable to each **category**, integrating categories and their properties, delimiting the theory, and writing the theory—while reminding the reader that the process is not lockstep and linear but rather that the stages, once commenced, continue in tandem as the theorist cycles back and forth through the various stages. In addition, he specifies two defining rules of constant comparison: (1) "while coding an incident for a category, compare it with the previous incidents in the same and different groups coded in the same category" (p. 439), and (2) "stop coding and record a memo on your ideas" (p. 440). This latter rule establishes the central role of memoing in constant comparative analysis.

Memos are theoretical notes about the data and the conceptual connections between categories. By memoing throughout the constant comparative process, the researcher captures her emergent ideation of substantive and theoretical categories:

Bits of data and early codes are systematically examined, explored and elaborated on. Through memo writing, the theorist takes his emerging ideas apart, checks them and outlines further data collection . . . looks at the data from a variety of perspectives and analyzes them . . . The theorist gains further insights and creates more ideas about the data while writing. Hence, writing and rewriting are crucial phases of the analytic process. (Charmaz, 1990, p. 1169)

Later in the process, having achieved theoretical saturation of the core, its properties, and its related concepts, the researcher proceeds to review, sort and integrate the numerous memos captured along the way. The sorted memos generate a theoretical outline (a conceptual framework) for the full articulation of her grounded theory through an integrated set of hypotheses, thus achieving the final stage of the constant comparative process.

Constant comparative analysis shifts the theorist's attention from verification of facts to ideas generation, thereby enabling maximum creativity in following emerging theoretical leads, unconstrained by interview protocols or a preconceived theoretical framework. "Since no proof is involved, the constant comparative method requires only saturation of data" (Glaser & Strauss, 1967, p. 104). Comparing additional incidents in the data to emerging concepts has four purposes:

(1) It verifies the concept as a category denoting a pattern in the data. (2) It verifies the fit of the category nomenclature to the pattern. (3) It generates properties of the category. (4) It saturates the category and its properties by the interchangeability of indicators. (Glaser, 1998, p. 139)

As such, GT's verification is conceptual and propositional, not factual. Categories suggested are always tentative, and although they cannot be *disproved,* they can be modified by further data collection. Data collection continues until concepts are theoretically saturated, meaning that nothing new is being added to the elaboration of the concept or property. If conceptual ideas suggested in initial data do not pattern out with further data collection, then the theorist must decide whether the initial ideas have earned relevance in the emerging theory and decide what prominence, if any, they hold as the theory continues to develop. In so doing, the constant comparison method ensures the *earned relevance* of emergent conceptual ideas, helping to overcome what Morse and Mitcham (2008) refer to as "conceptual tunnel vision" in assigning more data to a category than actually belong.

Memoing in tandem with coding using Glaser's (1978, p. 57) questions[4] will control this tendency as the theorist must explain how the data indicate a concept or a property of a concept and how they relate to other concepts, and so on. Earned relevance and theoretical saturation of emergent concepts also help to control for "pink elephant paradox" (Morse & Mitcham, 2008) of thin data sets in which insufficient incidents fail to offer up enough conceptual indicators. The constant comparative method requires the theorist to keep moving through the data to see conceptual indicators over and over, constantly comparing and memoing her ideas and deciding what further data are needed to elaborate and saturate emerging conceptual patterns.

Different slices of data, including quantitative and qualitative slices, feed information into each other. If one uses mixed data, one should not analyze or interpret them in isolation but rather as data are collected and together with all previously collected data. As an illustration the reader may refer to Sections 1.2 and 1.3 in Appendix C and to Appendix D to see how all data (primary and secondary, qualitative and quantitative) were constantly compared in order to theorize. As one theoretically samples quantitative data to supplement qualitative data (or vice versa), one should not wait until all quantitative data are collected but keep analyzing the data set as new data are collected in order to systematically check for possible emerging new patterns and/or categories.

THEORETICAL SAMPLING ●

As noted earlier, the explicit coding and analytic procedures of constant comparative analysis work in tandem with the third foundational pillar of GT—theoretical sampling. In GT, theoretical sampling refers to the collection of data as guided by the emerging theory as opposed to some predefined sample or unit. In theoretical sampling, the theorist "jointly collects, codes and analyzes data and decides what data to collect next and where to find them in order to develop his theory as it emerges" (Glaser & Strauss, 1967, p. 45). Glaser (1978) refers to the process as deductive (conceptual) elaboration as opposed to logical elaboration found in hypothesis testing research. He defines conceptual elaboration as

> the systematic deduction from the emerging theory of the theoretical possibilities and probabilities for elaborating the theory as to explanations and interpretations. These become hypotheses which guide the researcher back to locations and comparative groups in the field to discover more ideas and connections from data. The data constantly check deductions that lead nowhere, as the analyst takes his directions from the emerging relevancies. Deduced hypotheses are not forced on the data when they fit poorly, they are discarded and others emerge in their place by constant comparative analysis. (p. 40)

Glaser and Strauss (1971) on selecting comparison groups:

The basic criterion governing the selection of comparison groups for generating theory is their theoretical relevance for furthering the development of emerging categories, properties, hypotheses, and integration of the theory. Any groups may be selected that will help generate these elements of the theory. (p. 183)

Theoretical sampling sharpens the definition of concepts, helps to define their properties, and tests tentative theoretical propositions (Draucker, Martsolf, Ross, & Rusk, 2007). Sampling is driven by conceptual emergence and relevance and limited by theoretical saturation, not by a preconceived theoretical framework or by statistical significance. Consequently, selection of data sources is neither random nor totally predetermined. Additional data are selected in service to the emerging theory as the theorist gathers additional data on emerging patterns by asking specific questions in subsequent data collection or by returning to data already collected and reviewing it, selectively sampling there for the emerging pattern. As Glaser (1978, pp. 37–38) explains, the deductive nature of theoretical sampling complements GT's overall inductive approach.

Theoretical sampling as a means of guiding the direction of the emerging theory has little efficacy if it is separated from the processes of coding and analysis. Memoing is part of the decision process around theoretical sampling, as it assists theorists to identify gaps in their analysis and points to possible new directions for further data collection, coding, and analysis. If the data are collected by theoretical sampling at the same time that they are analyzed, the integration of the theory is more likely to emerge by itself as this taps to the fullest extent the in vivo patterns of integration in the data itself. Questions guide the collection of data to fill in gaps and to extend the theory as a further integrative strategy. Theoretical sampling involves an iterative process (Figure 3.2) and requires time to learn.

Remaining analytical and flexible while also

> making theoretically sensitive judgments about saturation is never precise. The researcher's judgment becomes confidently clear only toward the close of his joint collection and analysis, when considerable saturation of categories in many groups to the limits of his data has occurred, so that his theory is approaching stable integration and dense development of properties. (Glaser & Strauss, 1967, p. 64)

Theoretical sampling also reduces the amount of data needed (Glaser & Strauss, 1967, pp. 109–111). At the same time, inadequate sampling will be evident in theory that is thin and not well integrated (p. 63). As Glaser and Strauss (1967) state,

> The basic question in theoretical sampling . . . is: *what* groups or subgroups does one turn to *next* in data collection? And for *what* theoretical purpose? . . . The possibilities of multiple comparisons are infinite, and so groups must be chosen according to theoretical criteria. (p. 47)

Figure 3.2 An Iterative Process

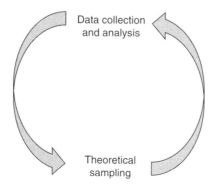

Data collection and analysis

Theoretical sampling

Comparisons provide diverse and similar indicators of conceptual categories and their properties. Discovering similarities and differences are important because they can indicate conditions under which categories and their properties vary and to what degree they may vary. Theoretical sampling encourages the theorist to employ multiple "slices of data" (Glaser & Strauss, 1967, p. 65) to explore a range of perspectives. Glaser (1978) offers a number of strategies for focusing data collection in theoretical sampling, including changing the location, participants, or interviewing style to elicit different slices of data; following up on emerging patterns in the data; and selectively sampling for additional data on specific concepts that appear to be significant to the emerging theory and, where possible, going back to key participants to ask for more information on these particular concepts. As Glaser and Strauss (1967) explain, the variety in data slices should be based on theoretical understanding of the conceptual category under diverse conditions and not simply on triangulated data types (p. 66). Sampling is determined only by the necessity of theoretical relevance and coverage. If the need to mix different types of data (quantitative and qualitative) emerges during the research process, the purpose is not to test or correct what has been found previously but to extend understanding of the phenomena under scrutiny and of the scope of the emerging theory, as well as to densify the concepts toward theoretical saturation: "Different kinds of data give the analyst different views or vantage points from which to understand a category and to develop its properties" (Glaser & Strauss, 1967, p. 65).

When theoretically sampling quantitative data, statistical validity may be set aside because data collection should be guided only by the emerging theory. All cases, including deviant minority cases, can be taken into account, as they are all potentially important and might require further qualitative analysis in order to discover unobserved variables and causal statements (Glaser, 2008). When software are used for some of the analyses, researchers can reflectively ensure that the mathematical algorithms in the software do not eliminate these *statistically insignificant* cases or groups of cases without investigating them, with the help of qualitative data previously collected or specifically collected for this purpose. Mixing quantitative and qualitative data whenever needed, and analyzing and interpreting them in an embedded manner, will allow researchers to identify whether or not so-called statistically insignificant results should in fact be taken into account. The reader may refer to Appendix C, Section 1.3 for an illustration of theoretically sampling mixed data.

DEVELOPING YOUR STANCE AS A GROUNDED THEORIST   ●

As mentioned at the outset of this chapter, many published accounts suggest that GT is a difficult methodology to master. Indeed, the expectation of joint collection, coding, and analysis of data with all three operations being done together, blurring and intertwining continually, from the beginning of the investigation to its end (Glaser & Strauss, 1967, p. 43) may seem a daunting quest to undertake, particularly for those trained in highly structured, linear, lockstep methodological approaches. What some may view as exciting and freeing can be seen by others as a terrifying jump into the abyss of endless and overwhelming data. Glaser (1992) cites the requisite skills for doing GT as the ability "to absorb the data as data, to be able to step back or distance oneself from it, and then to abstractly conceptualize the data" (p. 10). Glaser (1998) describes skill development in GT as a delayed action learning process (p. 220). He cites the importance of three attributes in the GT researcher: "an ability to conceptualize data, an ability to tolerate some confusion, and an ability to tolerate confusion's attendant regression" (Glaser, 2010, p. 4).

Glaser also repeatedly insists that GT is often best achieved by novice researchers, who are not as yet invested in a favored discipline perspective or theoretical code (e.g., power dynamics, social networks, etc.) but who are motivated and open to learning (Glaser, 2003). Over and over, in his writing, Glaser emphasizes the importance of *staying open* and not forcing preconceived ideas or frameworks upon data but rather fostering the emergence of conceptual theorizing from the empirical data. This dictum runs throughout all of his writings and must be seen as fundamental to developing the necessary frame of mind for doing GT.

Glaser and Strauss (1967) cite, as well, the crucial role of theoretical sensitivity in one's ability to develop good grounded theories. Much has been written about theoretical sensitivity; indeed, Glaser's second book is titled *Theoretical Sensitivity*, which may suggest its centrality to doing GT from his perspective. Glaser and Strauss (1967) describe theoretical sensitivity as the capacity to conceptualize and formulate a theory as it emerges from data; a continuous skill development process that involves both a personal and temperamental bent as well as the ability to "have theoretical insight combined with ability to make something of these insights" (p. 46). Suddaby (2006) also recognizes the subtle but significant interplay between technique and creativity in doing GT:

> Successful grounded theory research has a clear creative component. Glaser and Strauss were aware of this component

and the tension it would create with those who find comfort in trusting an algorithm to produce results. Glaser (1978) used the term "theoretical sensitivity" to describe the essential tension between the mechanical application of technique and the importance of interpretive insight. (p. 636)

Klag and Langley (2013) describe theoretical sensitivity as the capacity to generate conceptual leaps and suggest that "life events, background reading and unique training and work trajectories—may offer resources for insight" (p. 157). Glaser, however, warns not to allow personal perspectives and assumptions to taint one's openness to what may emerge in a GT study. Fundamental to one's theoretical sensitivity, he suggests, is the ability to "enter the research setting with as few preconceived ideas as possible—especially logically deducted, a priori hypotheses" (Glaser, 1978, pp. 2–3). Hernandez (2010) agrees with Glaser, suggesting that researcher preconceptions in the form of "personal beliefs or biases regarding a particular substantive area or ideas gleaned from published articles within this substantive area" (p. 154) are major blocks to developing theoretical sensitivity.

Glaser (1978) describes theoretical sensitivity as the ability to take a transcending view of data; to become a "non-citizen" (p. 8) by not privileging any particular perspective or view but rather letting the data speak for themselves. This is particularly the case with extant theory where Glaser suggests one need simply to footnote the work of others and integrate their ideas into one's emerging theory where relevant through "emergent fit" (pp. 8–9). Here, he is not suggesting that the theorist reject extant theory or that one must acknowledge and address all possible theoretical perspectives in one's analysis but rather that the theorist apply sensitivity and judgment in how to balance scholarship of extant theory and analysis of emergent conceptual ideas in service to theory with parsimony and scope (pp. 10–12).

From such statements we can see that theoretical sensitivity is not about bringing one's knowledge of extant theory into framing a GT study through theoretical frameworks and extensive literature reviews at the outset of a study. Glaser (1992) elaborates further on theoretical sensitivity by stating that it "refers to the researcher's knowledge, understanding and skill, which foster his generation of categories and properties and increases his ability to relate them into hypotheses, and to further integrate the hypotheses, according to emergent theoretical codes" (p. 27). Kelle (2005), however, complains that Glaser and Strauss have not provided sufficiently clear methodological rules for developing one's theoretical sensitivity suggesting that "it remains unclear how a theoretically sensitive researcher can use previous theoretical knowledge to avoid drowning in the data" (para. 9). McCallin (2006) suggests that the grounded theorist must embrace a particular style of thinking that is creative, inquisitive, critical, analytical, and comfortable with complexity—a style that is not necessarily inherent in all researchers and one that can be challenging to the novice.

Developing grounded theory—and one's stance as a grounded theorist—takes time and requires that the theorist is comfortable in tolerating confusion (Glaser, 1998, pp. 100–102), developing a rhythm of personal pacing as one cycles through the various analytic stages (Glaser, 1978, pp. 18–33), and assuming autonomy and ownership of one's emerging theory and its contribution to knowledge (Glaser, 1998, pp. 98–100). Perhaps most important to developing the stance of a true grounded theorist, Glaser suggests, is the ability to trust in GT's emergent power (1998, pp. 235–254).

IN SUMMARY

GT's three foundational pillars are exploration and emergence (i.e., concepts and relationships come from the data and are not preconceived or imposed on data), constant comparative analysis (i.e., data are continuously compared with previously collected and analyzed data, looking for similarities and differences to help toward conceptualization and theorization), and theoretical sampling (i.e., sampling is directed by the emerging theory and continues until theoretical saturation). Doing GT requires researchers to acquire and build up their theoretical sensitivity, which is the capacity to conceptualize and formulate a theory as it emerges from data and without any preconception.

TEST YOUR KNOWLEDGE

In the following questions one or several answers may be correct.

1. When you do GT
   a. You have to do a literature review before you start collecting data
   b. You analyze your data when you have finished collecting them

    c. If you use quantitative data, your sampling has to be statistically significant

    d. None of the above

2. Theoretical sensitivity is
   a. The capacity to adapt an existing framework
   b. The capacity to apply a theory
   c. The capacity to conceptualize a theory
   d. The capacity to formulate a theory
   e. None of the above

3. GT's foundational pillars are
   a. Emergence, constant comparative analysis, and sampling
   b. Emergence, content analysis, and theoretical sampling
   c. Verification, *explication de texte*, and theoretical sampling
   d. Emergence, constant comparative analysis, and theoretical sampling
   e. None of the above

4. Memos
   a. Are to be written at the end of the process of doing GT
   b. Should be written during the GT process
   c. Are important when you do GT
   d. Are not important in the GT process
   e. None of the above

FURTHER READING

Breckenridge, J. (2009). Demystifying theoretical sampling in grounded theory research. *Grounded Theory Review, 8*(2), 113–126.

Glaser, B. G. (1978). Theoretical sampling. In *Theoretical sensitivity: Advances in the methodology of grounded theory* (pp. 36–54). Mill Valley, CA: Sociology Press.

Glaser, B. G. (2013). *No preconceptions: The grounded theory dictum.* Mill Valley, CA: Sociology Press.

Glaser, B. G., & Strauss, A. L. (1967). Theoretical sampling. In *The discovery of grounded theory: Strategies for qualitative research* (pp. 45–77). Hawthorne, NY: Aldine de Gruyter.

Gynnild, A. (2006). Growing open: The transition from QDA to grounded theory. *Grounded Theory Review, 6*(1), 61–78.

Roderick, C. (2009). Learning classic grounded theory: An account of the journey and advice for new researchers. *Grounded Theory Review, 8*(2), 49–63.

ENDNOTES

1. The Creative Commons-Attribution-NonCommercial-ShareAlike License 4.0 International applies to all works published by the International Journal of Qualitative Methods. Copyright for articles published in the International Journal of Qualitative Methods remains with the first author.

2. The double arrows in Figure 3.1 illustrate the constant comparative analysis and "inextricable link between data collection and analysis" (Birks, Fernandez, Levina, & Nasirin, 2013, p. 3) leading to the discovery of patterns, which in turn guide further theoretical sampling until theoretical saturation is reached.

3. Literally translated, this French expression means "explanation of a text."

4. What are these data a study of? What category or property of category does this incident indicate? What is going on? What accounts for the main issue, and how is this issue processed or resolved?

4

Clarifying Common Sources of Confusion in Grounded Theory

After studying this chapter, you will:

- *identify, understand, and avoid common sources of preconception that limit emergent discovery in grounded theory*
- *differentiate between describing research findings and conceptualizing data*
- *differentiate between substantive and theoretical coding*

Most people carry assumptions about how to do research. These assumptions result from their university background and PhD training and sometimes prove to be a real challenge to reconcile with those of classic GT. Indeed, some might prove irreconcilable. Among the common assumptions are the need for a thorough literature review at the outset of a study to identify a gap that justifies pursuing the study, to establish a theoretical framework for data collection and analysis, and to formulate hypotheses to be tested or precise research questions developed ex ante to be answered in the study. Such assumptions are a major source of confusion and frustration for those wishing to follow a classic GT approach. In this chapter, we address three common sources of methodological confusion that will undermine your GT efforts: emergence versus preconception, description versus conceptualization, and substantive versus theoretical coding.

EMERGENCE VERSUS PRECONCEPTION ●

Research studies are often initiated to explore or confirm a specific research question or to test formulated hypotheses that are of interest to the researcher. GT's discovery stance, however, rejects the formulation of preconceived notions regarding the focus of a study in favor of exploring openly (i.e., without preconception) what is actually going on in the area under study rather than what we might decide at the outset should be the focus for inquiry. "GT listens to participants' own . . . concerns and then subsequently crafts questions from emergent concepts for subsequent theoretical sampling" (Glaser, 2003, p. 118). Remaining open to discovering what is really going on in the field of inquiry is often blocked, however, by what Glaser (1998) refers to as the forcing of preconceived notions resident within the researcher's worldview (i.e., ontological and epistemological perspective), an initial professional problem to be studied, or an extant theory and framework around which to focus the inquiry—all of which preempt the researcher's ability to suspend preconception. An experienced grounded theorist, Ólavur Christiansen describes professional research problems as

> problems "thought-out" and "thought-up" by the researcher, problems logically derived by the researcher and his/her seniors, problems found methodologically convenient and methodologically appropriate for the researcher, problems made apparently relevant by the availability of certain data (frequently quantitative data), problems made apparently relevant by fitting into some received concepts from preexistent theory, or problems made apparently relevant by fitting into some preconceived or spuriously drawn borders between subdisciplines. Such "professional problems" are typically not grounded in the underlying and essential agenda of those being studied. (Personal communication, July 19, 2004)

In GT the intention is to remain open to what emerges as a main issue in the substantive area of inquiry. To do so requires that the researcher be theoretically sensitive to discovering this main concern as opposed to pursuing a specific, predetermined research interest. "The first step in gaining theoretical sensitivity is to enter the research setting with as few predetermined ideas as possible—especially logically deduced, a priori hypotheses . . . to remain open to what is actually happening" (Glaser, 1978, p. 3). To be sure, a researcher's professional training and experience will often stimulate an initial research interest providing the motivation for pursuing a study, but a GT study must set aside the preconceiving practices of traditional training and established research methodology that condition the researcher to approach a study through an extant theoretical framework, ad hoc hypotheses, defined research questions, interview protocols, or precise coding schemes.

Preconception: A Classic Example!

Glaser recalls how meeting Alvin Gouldner (1920–1980) impressed upon him just how far off a preconceived interest can be from what is really going on in a research setting. He recounts Gouldner's using the example of a study in which a student was sent out to study risk-taking behavior among steeplejacks in New York City. The student was frustrated by the difficulty he had in getting the "jacks" to talk about risk taking in their line of work until one day, he observed them drawing straws before beginning a job and he was certain they were using the process to allocate the potential risk. To his surprise, the tactic had nothing to do with risk; rather, they were drawing straws for the best vantage points in terms of window peeping while on the job! The preconceived professional concern with risk taking was displaced with a focus on what was really taking place—a study in *strategic positioning*. (Holton, 2011, p. 213)

The fundamental premise of avoiding preconception has been dismissed by some scholars as naive and unrealistic (Dey, 1993, 1999; Kelle, 2007). Charmaz (2014) insists that "guiding interests, sensitizing concepts, and disciplinary perspectives" can serve as "points of departure for developing, rather than limiting, our ideas" (p. 31), but this is a slippery slope. When our inquiry is pre-framed through such heuristics, we can inadvertently shape how we approach our study and the resultant data that we use (see "Staying Open" in Appendix B, pp. 168). The adage "start as you mean to go" is particularly relevant to GT. The intention here is not to dismiss extant knowledge but rather to suspend its privileging in the initial design and framing of the study. "To preconceive relevance is to force data, not to discover from data what really works as a relevant explanation" (Glaser & Strauss, 1967, pp. 142–143).

Yet, to remain truly open to GT's principle of emergence can be one of the most challenging issues to those new to GT. This is a challenge that is often complicated by institutional requirements that routinely and without question require such pre-formulation at the study proposal stage. Such assumptions are so engrained in the scholarly community that they have become pro forma requirements in thesis proposals at many universities as well as in applications to ethics review boards and research funding agencies.[1] While compromises are necessary (Xie, 2009), all too often, mixing GT with other research approaches unfortunately reduces the outcome to conceptual description, presented thematically or evidentially, rather than as an integrated conceptual explanation. While such practices can render perfectly acceptable research findings, the absence of a core GT pillar (i.e., emergence) invalidates the claim of grounded theory.

A persistent preconception regarding GT is that it is a qualitative research method (Clarke, 2005; Goulding, 2002; Locke, 2001; Shah & Corley, 2006). We have already addressed this misconception in previous chapters. To reiterate, as a general research paradigm, GT can use any and all data and can adopt any philosophical perspective appropriate to the data and the ontological stance of the theorist. Consistent with the misguided assumption that GT is a qualitative method, many published guides to doing GT advocate the use of a preconceived theoretical framework (Goulding, 2002; Partington, 2002; Suddaby, 2006). Conducting an initial literature review is another dimension of preconception that is frequently advocated, but that again undermines the basic premise of classic GT, that is, that theory emerges from the conceptualization of data and not from extant theory. Such extensive review of the literature at the outset of a study can stifle a researcher's efforts to remain open to discovering what concepts are in the data regardless of what extant theories might suggest should be the focus of inquiry.

GT does not ignore extant literature, however. Rather, it simply holds review of the literature in abeyance until the core category of the grounded theory has emerged. Doing so avoids the possibility of forcing the theoretical direction of the study and instead enhances the potential to discover a true main concern in the area under study and to theorize from a new perspective and in rupture with existing literature.

Practically speaking, reviewing literature at the outset may simply result in the researcher spending valuable time on an area of literature that proves to be of little significance to the *discovered* grounded theory.

Indeed the analyst may be hard put to know *which* conceptual field [to invest in] until a theory [with its core category] emerges. If there is a particularly good theory in the field, one may . . . look for emergent fits. The result is usually extending and transcending the extant theory. (Glaser, 1978, p. 31)

Extensive engagement with the literature prior to data collection and analysis may also constrain the researcher's ability to remain open to theoretical ideas that may not have figured prominently in the literature. In classic GT,

the literature is just more data to be coded and integrated into the study through constant comparative analysis but its analysis and integration happens only after the core category, its properties and related categories have emerged, and the basic conceptual development is well underway, not in advance as is commonly presented in published research. Unless pre-empted by preconception, emergence is natural with the resultant grounded theory often charting new theoretical territory. (Holton, 2007a, p. 272)

• DESCRIPTION VERSUS CONCEPTUALIZATION

Some Firsthand Experiences of Novice Grounded Theorists

"At times I feel as if I am lingering on the 'ground level of description' waiting for the wings of conceptualization to pop up on my back and enable me to fly." ("The Conceptualization of Data," 2010)

"I have a lot of categories and relationships between them but I am afraid that I am using too much of the wording from existing theory." (E-mail excerpt from PhD student)

"My supervisor had her own preconceived ideas and was bent on full description. She kept asking me which group said what and to give percentages on the initial coding results." (E-mail excerpt from PhD student)

"Quite early in the research process, however, a 'story' presented by a participant was so compelling, and original, that just to 'code' the interview transcript without a full inclusion of this particular participant's story would have seriously diminished the research outcome." (Bryant & Lasky, 2007, p. 179)

As the comments in the previous box suggest, those new to GT often struggle to transcend the descriptive level. Transcending descriptive detail to achieve a conceptual explanation rather than simply describing research findings can be a particular challenge for those who are research-trained in evidence-based professional disciplines that value solely empirical detail. However, moving to explanation and the subsequent explanatory power of conceptual theory has much to contribute to these fields where GT's theoretical completeness offers a "powerful, predictive ability" (Guthrie, 2000, in Glaser, 2002, p. 34[2]).

Even though some studies might start with description before conceptualization is brought into play, unlike descriptive methods, the goal of GT is to discover and conceptually explain a main concern in a substantive area of inquiry and how that concern is addressed or resolved. Grounded theory is not about the accuracy of descriptive findings. It is about tapping into the latent structures in social settings. In abstracting these patterns to a conceptual level, GT theoretically explains rather than describes behavior that occurs generally in many diverse groups with a common concern (Glaser, 2003). While empirically grounded in one substantive area, the conceptual nature of a grounded theory offers general implications as theoretical propositions that extend beyond its empirical grounding.

In contrast, some qualitative research produces descriptive findings from which generalizations may be suggested but which are always limited by the sample (unit, case, etc.). At the other end of the spectrum, some quantitative research aiming at uncovering universal laws, considered as true until proved otherwise, overgeneralizes without taking structures, context, and human agency into consideration. "The concern is always accuracy, that is, the researcher has worrisome accuracy to constantly contend with. Generalizations are difficult to make from one unit to another and even within the unit studied" (Glaser, 2007, p. 42). Description bogs down conceptualization and reduces the level of abstraction with the concepts buried within the detailed description. As such, it is difficult, if not impossible, to see the simple elegance in the relationships between concepts that constitute the propositions or hypotheses that together integrate the (grounded) theory into a rich, multivariate conceptual theory (Glaser, 2003).

A further limitation of qualitative description is that it is confined to the unit studied, with emphasis on accurately depicting that unit but offering no claims to generalizing findings beyond the study sample. "The theory remains 'trapped' in the unit and is read as description" (Bigus, Hadden, & Glaser, 1994, p. 44). Description is also *stale dated* because as the unit of analysis changes over time, the description becomes less accurate and relevant. By contrast, GT's focus on latent patterns of social psychological and social structural processes, action, and interaction gives it an enduring quality, and its propositional (not evidentiary) presentation suggests general implications of the theory that apply beyond the unit(s) theoretically sampled (and more generally, with some modification based on further theoretical sampling, thus eliminating the risk of hasty generalization).

A certain mystery seems to surround the notion of conceptualization. Klag and Langley (2013) refer to the "conceptual leap" when theorizing from empirical data as "a consciously realized and abstract theoretical idea in an empirical study . . . beyond the specific context . . . connect[ing] situated particularities with conceptual understandings . . . grounded in abductive reasoning" (p. 150) and theoretical sensitivity as the capacity to generate such conceptual leaps (p. 157). Although they recognize GT's creative and iterative nature, they conflate GT with qualitative research and characterize the process as one of wading knee-deep in data while leaping from insight to insight. In so doing, they capture the qualitative researcher's experience of "data overwhelm" (Glaser, 2003, p. 24) but appear to miss the systematic methodology inherent in classic GT through constant comparative analysis, theoretical sampling (for core category emergence), and theoretical coding (for theoretical integration). GT's *full package* goes well beyond simply leaping from data to theorizing.

● SUBSTANTIVE VERSUS THEORETICAL CODING

Coding is a rather ubiquitous term, often applied to describe the iterative and complex procedures at the heart of GT's constant comparative method of analysis. In GT, coding refers to both the substantive coding of empirical data and, later, to the theoretical integration of emergent concepts through theoretical coding. While coding and memoing in GT proceed in tandem, substantive and theoretical coding do not. Theoretical coding is subsequent to substantive coding.

Substantive coding is the process of conceptualizing the empirical substance of the area under study, that is, the data in which the theory is grounded. Incidents in the empirical data are coded for indicators of concepts from which a grounded theory is then generated. Substantive coding begins with the initial open coding of data where the analyst codes each incident for as many concepts as possibly relevant. Open coding proceeds (in tandem with memoing) until the analyst perceives a pattern emerging that may indicate a potential core category. Once a core category has been tentatively identified, the analyst switches from open coding to **selective coding** by delimiting data collection and analysis to just the core category and any potentially related concepts. At this point, the analyst focuses on theoretically saturating the core category and related concepts and then proceeds to the final stage of GT coding: theoretical coding. Theoretical codes conceptualize how the substantive codes may relate to each other as hypotheses to be integrated into the final theory, reminding us that the essential principle of earned relevance in GT is not restricted to conceptual emergence but is equally important in the conceptual integration of the theory through the emergence of relevant theoretical codes.

In theoretical coding, the analyst constantly compares and questions the many analytic memos that have been generated through the earlier stages of substantive coding. This conceptual sorting (Glaser, 1978, p. 116) generates further memoing as the analyst explores the relationships among the core category and other categories. This process is done manually and thoughtfully with the analyst exploring connections and conceptual orderings among the concepts until a pattern emerges that organizes the concepts as a theoretical model with full explanatory power of the main concern. The underlying imperative, however, is that theoretical coding is not selected and imposed on the theory but that it must emerge and fit to earn its relevance as a theoretical integrator of the core category and related concepts.

Common misunderstandings regarding theoretical coding include (a) that it refers to the use of theoretical labels when coding empirical data and (b) that the analyst selects a specific theoretical code and applies it to the overall analysis of the data (Kelle, 2005). Various scholarly accounts of GT methodology have offered confusing and ultimately misleading advice regarding coding. Locke (2001), for example, describes GT coding as substantive and theoretical but then suggests that theoretical codes are discipline-related and applied by the analyst "through a kind of top down process" (p. 66). She goes on to suggest that while the general rule is that substantive coding occurs early in the study and theoretical coding at a later point, "these are not hard and fast rules . . . researchers will be working with a mix of in vivo and theoretical categories throughout their analysis" (p. 66). It would appear that she has not understood the transition from substantive coding to theoretical coding through core category emergence and theoretical saturation.

Gibson and Hartman (2014) offer a somewhat vague account of theoretical codes as selected and applied during selective coding, with their particular preference being the use of typologies to explore relationships between concepts. They make no mention of the hand sorting process in theoretical coding that Glaser has repeatedly emphasized as crucial to ensuring that theoretical codes are emergent and not forced (Glaser, 1978, pp. 116–127; 1998, pp. 187–192; 2005a, pp. 33–40). Dey (1999) suggests that the distinction between substantive and theoretical coding is unclear. He poses three questions that suggest his level of confusion is considerable: "Is theoretical coding an aspect of substantive coding or a separate activity? How do we select from among theoretical codes that all fit the data? Are the empirical cues guiding selection based only on observation?" (p. 109). Here again, such questions indicate that, while offering advice on GT, the author has not understood the progressive nature of GT coding or the emergence and appropriate fit of theoretical codes through hand sorting of conceptual memos.

Another common misconception regarding theoretical coding is that grounded theory is always a basic social process (Clarke & Friese, 2007). To be sure, the basic social process is undoubtedly the most widely used theoretical code in grounded theory. Glaser (2005a) acknowledges this popularity and frequency but at the same time notes, "I have seen many GTs that have no process in them, so process must be earned, NOT assumed" (p. 96). As another example of over-reliance on one theoretical code, Glaser (1978) notes the tendency of some theorists to conflate behavioral consequences with intentional strategies and to rely too frequently on the strategy family of theoretical codes (p. 76). He has offered a wide range of potential theoretical codes (Glaser, 1978, pp. 72–82; 1998, pp. 163–175; 2005a, pp. 17–30) and encourages researchers to read widely from theories in many disciplines as a means of identifying and adding new theoretical models to their repertoire. The purpose here is not to select (i.e., preconceive) a model but to simply enhance theoretical sensitivity by opening the researcher up to the numerous ways in which theory can be modeled.

IN SUMMARY

Common sources of confusion in grounded theory can be streamlined to three main areas: emergence (i.e., remaining open to what is actually going on in the data) versus preconception (i.e., forcing preconceived notions on the data), description (i.e., describing research findings confined to the unit studied) versus conceptualization (i.e., conceptually explaining how a concern is addressed and solved in a substantive area), and substantive (i.e., conceptualizing the empirical substance of the area under study) versus theoretical coding (i.e., conceptualizing relationships between substantive codes).

TEST YOUR KNOWLEDGE

In the following questions one or several answers may be correct.

1. When you conduct a research using classic GT
   a. You start with a research question
   b. You must use qualitative data
   c. You must conduct an extensive literature review ex ante
   d. None of the above

2. When you conduct research using classic GT
   a. Extensive description is necessary
   b. You must make theoretical propositions
   c. You should not read about theories in other domains
   d. None of the above

3. Substantive coding
   a. Includes open and selective coding
   b. Explains the main concern
   c. Is about searching the core category
   d. None of the above

4. Theoretical coding
   a. Helps the researcher to sort conceptually
   b. Explains the main concern
   c. Involves making propositions linking concepts
   d. None of the above

FURTHER READING

Gibson, B., & Hartman, J. (2014). *Rediscovering grounded theory* (Chapter 12). London: Sage.

Glaser, B. G. (1978). *Theoretical sensitivity: Advances in the methodology of grounded theory* (pp. 2–3, 31–33, 44–46). Mill Valley, CA: Sociology Press.

Glaser, B. G. (1998). *Doing grounded theory: Issues and discussions* (Chapters 5 & 6). Mill Valley, CA: Sociology Press.

Glaser, B. G. (2001). *The grounded theory perspective: Conceptualization contrasted with description* (Chapters 3, 4, & 6). Mill Valley, CA: Sociology Press.

Glaser, B. G. (2011). *Getting out of the data: Grounded theory conceptualization*. Mill Valley, CA: Sociology Press.

Glaser, B. G. (2013). *No preconceptions: The grounded theory dictum*. Mill Valley, CA: Sociology Press.

ENDNOTE

1. For some helpful advice on managing ethics review, see http://www .groundedtheoryonline.com/getting-started/ethical-review-irb.

2. The Creative Commons-Attribution-NonCommercial-ShareAlike License 4.0 International applies to all works published by the International Journal of Qualitative Methods. Copyright for articles published in the International Journal of Qualitative Methods remains with the first author.

5

Finding Your Data

After studying this chapter, you will:

- *understand grounded theory's use of data*
- *know how to collect data for a grounded theory study*
- *understand the iterative nature of data collection and analysis in doing grounded theory*

WHY "ALL IS DATA" ●

As grounded theorists, we have the wonderful freedom to identify and utilize in our analyses any and all data obtained from any relevant, available source. Doing so enhances the power of our theories to explain what is really going on. We use the data as we choose and find it to explain the pattern of behavior at issue. This explanatory power is a primary reason that many of us are drawn to GT. Its conceptual power renders GT valuable not only for theorists but also for practitioners and the participants in our studies through its focus on explaining "high impact main concerns" (Glaser, 1995, p. 4). The GT process ensures that our research, when finished, will be "actionable" (Schön, 1983).

In many methodological books, and as highlighted in Walsh (2014c), much is said about methods and techniques and little about data.

However, methods and techniques do not mean much without data, as "data is a necessary basis on which to build theories" (Evermann & Tate, 2011, p. 634) and, in most cases, you need good data to produce good theory (Lyytinen, 2009). Creswell (2014) describes qualitative data as text and images and quantitative data as numbers. The term *quantitative data* is mostly used to describe a type of information that may be counted or expressed numerically and is amenable to statistical analysis (Monette, Sullivan, & Delong, 2011), whereas *qualitative data* provide explanation for, and information about, something in the form of words that describe that phenomenon in depth (Monette et al., 2011). However, a researcher may choose to *quantitize* qualitative data (Sandelowski et al., 2009) or to *qualify* (Creswell, 2007) or *qualitize* (Sandelowski, 2000) quantitative data.

A researcher may also use secondary data in various ways, with different techniques, regardless of the methods used to collect these data. While many GT studies rely largely on qualitative data and interviews as a primary method for data collection, GT uses any and all data and data collection methods, including observations, visual and auditory media, or surveys from any sources (e.g., reports, newspapers, or questionnaires). As Glaser and Strauss (1967) explain,

> in field studies, theoretical sampling usually requires reading documents, interviewing, and observing all at the same time, since all slices of data[1] are relevant. There is little, if any, systematic interviewing of a sample of respondents, or interviewing that excludes observation. At the beginning of the research, interviews usually consist of open-ended conversations during which respondents are allowed to talk with no imposed limitations of time. Often the researcher sits back and listens while the respondents tell their stories. Later when interviews and observations are directed by the emerging theory, he can ask direct questions bearing on his categories. These can be answered sufficiently and fairly quickly. Thus, the time for any one interview grows shorter as the number of interviews increases, because the researcher now questions many people, in different positions and different groups, about the same topics. Although the time taken by most interviews decreases as the theory develops, the sociologist still cannot state how long all his interviews will take because a new category might emerge at any time; this emergence will call for lengthy open-ended conversations and prolonged observations within some groups. Also, theoretical sampling aimed at following an incident or observing over a period of time

requires sequential interviews, with no clear notion of when the sequence will be terminated. (pp. 75–76)

Furthermore, when developing emerging concepts/constructs that have not been extensively investigated in past literature, it is usually important to start your investigations with qualitative data. Additional slices of quantitative data may be needed to enhance theoretical saturation for generalizability purposes and for formal theory generation. A good example of this may be found in Leonardi and Bailey (2008). Although the authors never clearly state they conducted their research in a GT stance, an informal interview with the second author of this text confirmed that they had adopted a GT stance; they did not state this clearly in their work because the journal in which they wished to publish was not familiar with mixed data GT. You will find more about this issue of fulfilling research outlets' conventions, while not forfeiting your basic philosophical assumptions and methodological choices, in Chapter 9.

So this idea of "all is data" (Glaser, 2001) helps us to get away from an overemphasis on interview data and opens us up to fully exploring a wide range of data sources and slices. For example, one GT study of interagency working was completed by observing group meetings and using meeting minutes (Wood, 2009). Classic GT studies such as Jones and Kriflik (2006) and Sandgren, Thulesius, Fridlund, and Petersson (2006) explain their use of personal interviews, informal conversations, observation, and document analysis. Hämäläinen (2014) describes using opportunistic sampling to access entrepreneurs through his social networks and through chance encounters when traveling. Snowballing sampling through referrals led to further opportunities for data collection. His self-interviews and field observations over a period of years as a practicing entrepreneur provided yet more data. Glaser and Strauss (1965a) relied extensively on field observation and interviews from comparison groups across a range of hospital settings in their formulation of awareness theory, including geriatric, preterm birth, cancer, intensive care, pediatric, neurology, urology, and emergency wards. Walsh (2014a) used secondary qualitative data from a previously published GT and from the literature, primary quantitative data collected through a survey, and primary qualitative data collected through in-depth interviews (see Appendix C, Section 1.3). Focus groups are another valuable way to collect data from a number of individuals. They can be especially valuable for exploring a potential core concept as they allow you to gain the perspectives of a number of individuals at one time. Stjernsward and Ostman (2008) used both interviews and focus groups in their study of families living close to a depressed individual. Focus groups allowed them to capture data around mutual experiences and identities and to explore different perspectives through group interaction (p. 359). Focus groups can also allow you to gain a perspective by observing and noting the dynamics of the group conversation.

As with interviews, it is important not to preconceive the direction of the group's conversation by applying a set of preplanned questions; rather, open the group up with a "grand tour question" (Simmons, 2010). For example, if you were interested in exploring the impending status passage (Glaser & Strauss, 1971) of university students in their final year of study, you might open the discussion by saying, "I am supposed to be studying how students in their final year of study prepare for what's next, but I don't know what to ask you. What do you think we should talk about?" and then wait to see how individuals respond, how the conversation builds. You might probe by asking what they are doing to prepare for the next stage (job hunting, grad school, etc.), how it feels, and so on. Again, you can observe whether probing strikes a chord and generates a lively exchange or whether something else seems to be of more interest. Do different concerns emerge? What appears to be the main concern?

Helpful Hint: Focus groups are more challenging in that a lot can be happening at once given the number of individuals involved. Therefore, it is usually recommended to have a second person help you facilitate and make field notes.

While for grounded theorists, *all* can serve as data, in conceptualizing, it is important that we are able to recognize what kind of data we are getting. Here we are not referring to the methods of data collection (i.e., interviews, observations, surveys) but rather to the *intention* of the data—what Glaser (1998) refers to as types of data—baseline data (i.e., honestly describing what is), proper line accounts (i.e., filtered data where only what is considered proper or correct is revealed), professionally interpreted (i.e., a third-party *expertise* perspective), and vague responses (i.e., concealing or evading; p. 9). Recognizing the *type* of data that you are getting is also data and is important to discovering what is really going on in the situation at hand. Glaser's (1978) questions for coding data will help you to think about what types of data you are gathering; in particular, his question, *"What is actually happening in the data?"* (p. 57).

Memoing as you code your data will also help you to discover what is actually happening in the situation at hand; for example, is the interviewee offering an account of his or her own experience (baseline description), a reflection on that experience (vague or distanced), a projection of someone else's experience (professionally interpreted), or a *massaged* corporate version (proper line)? All are possibilities, and it is important to know what type of data you are getting and why you are getting this type of data. What is this really telling you about the phenomenon you are studying, and, more precisely, what may be emerging as the main concern?

For instance, in the focus group example presented earlier, you can observe who appears to dominate the conversation, how others react, what the tone is, and what the nature is of the interactions among group members; in other words, what is really going on with the group in their discussion. Is there a pattern in the way the group interacts? It is quite conceivable that using a series of focus groups, you might discover an interesting GT around, for instance, surfacing sensitive topics, silencing, or influencing and persuasion. If you are open to what emerges, you may have more than one GT study from the same focus group data.

Indeed, observation is an important source of data for doing GT. We are surrounded by data but often neglect to observe and note what is happening. As one student wrote, "I am a nurse on leave (50%) to do my PhD research. I have discovered, however, that when I go into work to pick up my mail or to just visit, I find myself observing what I see and hear and making note in my memos." Here is someone who has grasped GT's *all is data* dictum for leveraging valuable data about what's really going on; these are data that she may not have gained in a formal interview setting.

Perhaps You Are Wondering . . .

How many interviews do I need for a GT study?

There is no magic number of interviews required. While it is common for some qualitative or quantitative methods to specify sample size at the outset of the study, for a GT study the extent of data collection is governed by the emergence and theoretical saturation of a core concept. Students are often required, however, to state a specific number in their research proposals, and some supervisors may have a

(Continued)

> (Continued)
>
> specific number or range in mind to ensure adequate coverage of a population or sufficient data depth. So, how should you address this in your proposal? You might consider including a statement like this: *I expect my field work to involve approximately 30 participants. In accordance with classic grounded theory methodology, however, sample size cannot be definitively established in advance of the field work; rather, it emerges as the researcher engages in the constant comparison of conceptual indicators/incidents articulated by interviewees and proceeds through further theoretical sampling to theoretical saturation of emergent concepts.* Here, you've satisfied the requirement by offering a proposed sample size while also qualifying the specific number to allow for what emerges as necessary for theoretical saturation which you can later justify in the methods section of your research paper or thesis.

● OVERLOOKED SOURCES OF AVAILABLE DATA

A frequently overlooked source of data for doing GT is secondary data, that is, data that have been collected for some other purpose. Data collection can be expensive as well as time-consuming. Accessing extant data can accelerate and *densify* conceptual elaboration. As one example, Barney Glaser's doctoral research was based on the secondary analysis of survey data conducted by the Survey Research Center at the University of Michigan. Glaser explains that the data consisted of responses to 1,952 survey questionnaires completed by research staff at a large government medical research organization from which he selected a subset of 332 respondents and 100 questions that seemed relevant to his research interest of recognition in scientific careers (Glaser, 2008, pp. 34–35).[2] In addition, Glaser and Strauss (1967) devote a full chapter to the use of available qualitative data for generating theory. Furthermore, in our times of *big data*, the Web is also a valuable source of already collected data (secondary data, both qualitative and quantitative) that are mostly free and available to all, through data mining. Thus, readily available data can be a rich source for theoretical sampling as a GT study progresses.

Analysis of secondary data can yield unexpected emergent core concepts that trigger theorizing. As one example, while conducting a qualitative thematic analysis to assess leadership development needs in an organization, one author of this text was struck by what she observed to be a persistent disconnect between what managers expressed about the organization's efforts to enhance healthy workplace practices (proper line data) and what they shared about their own experiences of the organization's culture (what was really going on). This disconnect emerged in interviews as an unexamined *inner dialogue* where managers struggle to resolve the tension they experience while still attempting to honor espoused organizational values (Holton & Grandy, 2015). While this emergent concept of an inner dialogue was outside the objectives of the original research project, it offered important insight and explanation as to how middle managers in organizations struggle to process conflicts in attempting to honor and reconcile personal and organizational values.

Of course, extant literature can also be used as data, particularly if the literature is empirically grounded. A major issue in using literature as data for a GT study is when to use it. While it is common in many research methodologies to initiate a study with a literature review, as discussed in Chapter 4, in a GT study we suspend our engagement with extant theory so as to avoid the risk of preconceiving our work, thereby missing important concepts that may emerge from our data simply because we are too focused on what the literature has deemed as important. In GT, we start with empirical data and remain open to what emerges rather than being influenced by what comes from the literature. Once our core concept has emerged, we can use the literature as an additional data source to theoretically sample and constantly compare concepts from the literature with emergent concepts. As such, literature based on empirical data can help to elaborate our emerging concepts and assist us in knowing where to direct our attention in further theoretical sampling.

Perhaps You Are Wondering . . .

My university (or funding agency) requires that I do an initial literature review as part of my research proposal. How do I manage this without undermining my GT study?

Standardized approaches to research proposals frequently follow the traditional hypothetical-deductive approach where extant literature is searched and assessed so that the proposed study can be situated within, and contribute to, that body of knowledge. The literature review is intended to point to a gap in that knowledge and the proposed study

(Continued)

(Continued)

to contribute to addressing that gap. One strategy for addressing this requirement is to keep the initial literature review broad in scope, perhaps by offering a contextual or thematic overview of the substantive area of research interest, setting the stage for an exploratory study rather than focusing on a specific gap to be addressed. The latter assumes a focus that may not be relevant to the proposed GT study and, as such, not only consumes researcher time and energy but may well derail the potential to discover an emergent grounded theory.

● COLLECTING YOUR OWN DATA

Gaining Access

GT studies that rely on qualitative data often feature interviews as a primary source of data. Individuals, however, often exhibit reticence to be interviewed, especially if you wish to tape-record the interview. Some may politely agree but then guardedly engage. It is often much easier to engage in informal conversations with participants, simply making note of key points, incidents, and responses that you can later write up, code, and memo. It is often enough to simply capture a few key words during the conversation; you may not even need to write them down at the time but simply store key words or phrases in your memory. They will serve as triggers for you to sit down as soon as possible after the conversation to elaborate in a more extensive field note that you can then code and memo.

Audio taping often sets up a completely different dynamic between the researcher and participant. Taping can change the data as the researcher relies on the assurance of a taped interview that can be consulted later and, as such, the researcher may relax his or her listening rather than staying fully engaged in capturing key words and thoughts in situ. In addition, interviewees may respond very differently to questions when they know their answers are being taped. Many become nervous at the prospect of being formally interviewed and taped. Such nervousness can be a form of performance anxiety (e.g., *Will I be able to answer the questions? Will I be asked something I prefer not to answer? If so, how do I handle the situation without feeling embarrassed? What if I make the researcher unhappy? And so on . . .*).

Researchers often worry that by not taping, they will miss important data. What you are discovering in a GT study is a pattern that is going on all the time, so there are endless opportunities to capture it;

no one interview is that precious. If something is relevant to your theory, you will find multiple indicators in subsequent data as your study progresses. Furthermore, taping and then later transcribing leads to a volume of data that may render little of relevance in terms of identifying a core concept. Researchers are often required, however, to tape interviews as a condition of ethics review or, in the case of doctoral students, to demonstrate competence in interviewing. The experience of Sandgren, Thulesius, Petersson, and Fridlund (2007) describes an approach that accommodates such requirements without unduly undermining the GT research approach:

> The first ten interviews were tape recorded and transcribed, but for the later interviews, only field notes were taken according to classic grounded theory (Glaser, 1998, 2001). Interviews lasted between 45 and 90 min. By the end of the study, interviews were shorter owing to the delimiting properties of grounded theory. (p. 228).

Conducting a research study within an organizational context can carry its own challenges to gaining access and can take considerable time. There are, of course, the ethics review requirements of universities and granting agencies that must be met in terms of full and informed consent and voluntary participation of the individual participants. To gain access to individual participants within an organizational context, however, also necessitates determining the appropriate organizational *gatekeeper*, ascertaining their concerns with your request and considering what you may be able to do to address these concerns.

One way to initiate the relationship is to request a meeting to discuss your research project and to seek their advice in how their organization might be involved in your study. Be humble, polite, and respectful in your interactions with the organization and the gatekeeper, as you will most certainly be shut out if you respond otherwise. Once you have been able to allay, or at least reduce, any apprehension through an open discussion, you will have a better chance to gain the desired access. The more prepared you are to allay any concerns, the more likely your chances will be to proceed with data collection without undue delays.

Helpful Hint: Be sure to make notes during the conversation with the organizational gatekeeper, as your notes may reveal early indicators of a main concern within the organization.

Of course, there will be times when you simply will not be granted access or your access will be restricted in such a way that you may not gain the data you had hoped for. In such situations, what you gain may be proper line data, where the individuals you are permitted to interview and the situations you are permitted to observe will be carefully selected and controlled to present the organization in a favorable light. These are still data that you can code and memo, but it is important to remember what these data are and to capture this in your memos. *What are you really hearing in these data? What is the context in which you have gained these data? What data are you not being given access to? What's really going on in this situation?* One way to encourage a breakthrough when you think you are being proper-lined is to probe with questions such as *What do you mean by that? I hear a lot of managers say that, but I'm not sure what they really mean. What does it mean to you? Why is that important?*

Collecting Quantitative Data

While doing GT, you may feel compelled to use quantitative data slices and wish to collect these through a survey, for instance, in order to theoretically saturate your concepts. Then, it is often essential during pretests to also interview some of the respondents in order to investigate how the questions asked in your survey are understood and if they address the category that you are trying to saturate. While administering the final survey, it is often necessary to informally reassure participants and confirm that anonymity will, indeed, be maintained and that they will not be traced through their answers. Beyond ethical issues, if respondents are convinced you will keep their information confidential, it will increase the chances that you are collecting *baseline* data as opposed to *proper-line* data, more especially if data are self-reported by participants and hence subjective. (See Appendix C, Section 1.4 as an illustration of the careful choice of measures in a quantitative survey within a GT study.)

While collecting data for a survey, it might also be important to carefully note the context of the survey administration. (As an illustration, you may refer to Appendix C, Section 1.3.) For instance, if students are respondents to a questionnaire, one could legitimately inquire and note if both the questionnaire administered and the research core investigations are related to a course attended by participants. Along the same lines, it might also be necessary to note if student participation to the survey is mandatory as a required part of a course, based on partially voluntary participation (extra grades for those who answer the questionnaire) or totally voluntary participation (no specific incentives). Your emergent theory may vary with the social structural conditions under which the data are collected.

In GT, it is also often helpful to reinterview some participants as your study progresses. Reinterviewing is a form of theoretical sampling that can add important *depth* to your emerging conceptualization and can be as important as the *breadth* offered by interviewing a range of individuals. Reinterviewing can be especially helpful where your access to data may be limited to a very specific population or a sensitive area of research interest (e.g., transgender youth, marathon runners over the age of 80, illegal immigrants seeking health care, etc.). In particular, once your core category has emerged, you may wish to theoretically sample by returning to earlier interviewees and probing more specifically around the emergent core. You might say something like *"I recall when we chatted previously that you mentioned . . . (core concept). . . . I've heard from others some similar experiences so I'd like to know more about what you experienced."* Or you might say, *"In some of my conversations with others, they have mentioned. . . . Has this been your experience? Can you tell me more about what happened?"* Given that reinterviewing is so often a valuable way of theoretically sampling to elaborate the properties and dimensions of your emergent core concept, it is important to identify your intention to employ multiple interviews for theoretical sampling purposes as part of your research ethics proposal.

Helpful Hint: In preparing your research ethics proposal, be sure to consider potential issues related to gaining access and articulate how you plan to address each to ensure the key principles of ethical conduct in research (i.e., free and informed consent, voluntary partici-pation, confidentiality, etc.). It is much easier to address these issues at the outset rather than having to later return to the ethics review board with amendments. Addressing potential issues at the outset of your study forces you to think through what you intend to do and, as much as possible, problem solve in advance. It also demonstrates to the review board that you have thought through the research process and can conduct your study in a scholarly and ethical manner, thereby enhancing the confidence of the review board in your overall proposal.

Instilling a Spill

In other research approaches, it is generally researcher interests that shape a study. Researchers explore and answer questions that come from their own professional interests or, as is often the case with novice researchers, topics that have been suggested by a supervisor

based on their knowledge of the research field and the related literature. As we have previously explained, in classic GT the research aim
is to discover a main concern that is being processed, managed, or
resolved in the substantive area under study. The best way to discover
this main issue is to avoid, as much as possible, any preconceptions
regarding what the main issue may be. As Nathaniel (2008) explains,
"the researcher must be open to hearing the story from the informant's
perspective" (p. 61). This means setting out to collect your data without
a theoretical framework or specific research questions, interview protocols, or predetermined coding schemes.

In collecting interview or informal conversation data for a GT study,
all that is needed is one "grand tour" question (Simmons, 2010),
something as simple and open as *"Tell me about your job/family/hobby/what
it's like to work here, etc."* Sandgren et al. (2006) opened their interviews
with palliative care nurses by asking, "Tell me what it is like to care for
palliative cancer patients" (p. 81). Jones and Kriflik (2006) used two
broad questions to open their interviews: "Tell me what leadership
means to you," and "How do you feel about your job?" (p. 160).
Hämäläinen (2014) found that, in many instances, simply starting the
conversation with, "Hi. I'm doing [a] PhD about entrepreneurship"
(p. 17) was all that was needed. Questions such as these open the space
for interviewees to tell you what they want to talk about. As the researcher,
your challenge is to wait to see where they wish to take the conversation
and then to ask follow-up questions that sustain the openness while
probing enough to have the interviewees elaborate on what they have
raised. Sandgren et al. (2007) describe using more specific questions such
as "Tell me about a difficult caring situation," "How do you handle
difficult situations?" and "Tell me about a caring situation that went well"
to encourage interviewees to elaborate on the range of their caring
experiences (p. 228). As Glaser (1998) points out, the goal in GT is to
"instill a spill" (p. 111) to find the trigger that starts the person talking
naturally and exhaustively about what concerns or interests him or her.

Perhaps You Are Wondering . . .

Can my opening question be too broad?

One novice researcher asked My field of interest is to research emotions in organizations. I have conducted 10 interviews so far asking
people how they are feeling about their work. I have coded and memoed
after each interest. The only issue is that I do not seem to derive

> common patterns or processes or even indicators thereof.... I am find-
> ing that the variables for feelings are endless and are so tightly coupled
> with the individual. I was wondering if this has to do with the fact that
> my inquiry is too broad.
>
> Here we have a novice who is trying to stay open to emergence of
> a main concern but feeling worried as no potential core category (pat-
> tern or process) is emerging. What should he do? Well, his area of
> interest—emotions in organizations—is clearly a broad topic. There are
> several options that he might consider: First of all, he might narrow his
> population to a certain type of organization (public service, communi-
> cations, health care, etc.) or to a certain occupation (auditors, recep-
> tionists, nurses, etc.) across organizations. He might also narrow his
> opening question somewhat; for example, *"How did you feel when you
> arrived at work this morning?" "Tell me about a time when . . . ,"* or *"What
> feeling would best describe how you feel about your job?"* Offering a little
> context for your question should help to elicit focused responses from
> your interviewees without preconceiving and encouraging responses
> around a suggested emotion. Be patient with the first few interviews.
> Stay open and permit your interviewees to decide where they wish to
> take the conversation. Follow their lead with more probing questions.

Try to set the climate for the interview as one between equals and
not one of interviewer and interviewee. Your goal is to set the *tone* for
the conversation so that your interviewee feels comfortable in opening
up and sharing with you. Use your intuition; you'll get a sense from the
energy in the conversation when the interviewee is finished spilling.
Continuing to probe may render little of value. Remember, you are not
seeking to capture descriptive detail; rather, your data are in service to
identifying concepts.

It may be helpful to begin by talking about yourself and by swap-
ping stories to reduce the sense of formality. However, it is important
not to dominate the conversation. The less you talk, the more likely you
are to get to their main concern. If there is a pause in the conversation,
don't panic and attempt to fill the void. Offer soft encouragement for
the individual to continue, for example, a nod or a smile and a simple
"Please go on." You might also just repeat the last few words the individual has said and then wait. Give the interviewee time to process his
or her responses. Be patient. As Glaser (2001) says, be a "Big Ear"
(p. 175), an active and engaged listener. Probe and encourage your
interviewees to tell you more. Don't rush them or they may shut down,

assuming you are in a hurry or simply not interested in what they want to share. This is especially important if what is being shared is in any way sensitive. Ensure that your interviewees have time to feel comfortable in opening up to you. As one researcher wrote, *"I have found that once you break the ice with them, they go on and on—literally! They want to talk and they want to tell you their experience."*

Staying Open

Glaser (1978) offers useful ideas for staying open during field work. These include changing the style of your interviewing (e.g., sharing a walk with the interviewee rather than sitting down to converse, etc.) and the place(s) where, or time of day when, you normally do interviews (e.g., a park rather than a coffee shop; weekends rather than weekdays, etc.). Hans Thulesius, a medical doctor and experienced grounded theorist, draws on the advice of famous Canadian physician William Osler for assessing patients in offering the following:

As a GP, I've learned that listening to the patient will give you the diagnosis in most cases. One of the worst mistakes a doctor can make is interrupting the patient too early because they are already busy formulating a hypothesis about the patient's problem. So in GT interviewing, if you're doing the same things as doctors, you want to go from one part of the story to the next so you're busy thinking about the next question to move the interview along but you're not focusing on what the interviewee is saying. If you just wait, almost always the interviewee will give you the rest of the story, the explanation you were looking for, so your "thinking up" energy is just wasted. Let your interviewee talk. Listen carefully and just give encouraging nods or hums, keep eye contact, and eventually repeat the last word in what he just said to encourage him to go on with his story—[it] almost always works! (Personal communication, October 20, 2014)

Field Notes

GT does not require capturing the type of detailed descriptive data that may be considered as important in some circles. However, you may find that these descriptive details may be required in order to publish your theories in some top tier research outlets (see Chapter 9). As far as GT methodology is concerned, however, field notes suffice as GT is a concept-indicator methodology that relies on the patterned presence of conceptual indicators through multiple incidents as captured across your data. What you are attempting to do is capture incidents (experiences, stories, gossip, confessions) that may suggest a concept (i.e., a pattern of behavior) that helps to explain what is going on (i.e., a main concern) in the situation that you are studying.

Novice researchers will often ask about the *right way* to do field notes, but there is no one right way. Variations on field notes are common to many professions; for example, the proceedings of a business meeting may be captured as minutes, journalists will make notes during interviews, lawyers keep case notes, and doctors and nurses observe and make note of a patient's symptoms. Field notes in GT are not intended to serve as detailed evidentiary notes as is common to the health or legal profession; instead, GT field notes are simply *in the moment* reminders of incidents that may indicate potential concepts. There is no need to try to capture detailed descriptions. You need only capture enough detail about the incidents being shared or observed so that you will be able to later code your notes for those concepts and elaborate your ideas in memos. For instance, when you are interviewing, simply jot down key words as you listen and complete your field notes as soon as you have an opportunity to code and memo your ideas (see Figure 5.1 for a sample of quick notes taken in the field). Or, when you are developing a questionnaire based on verbatim data where exploratory factor analysis points at an item as double loading on two categories previously identified as different, take some brief notes as you go along, until you have time to go back to your qualitative data and investigate further. Waiting too long, however, may mean that you lose some of the insights that triggered the initial note.

Figure 5.1   Field Notes Taken During an Interview

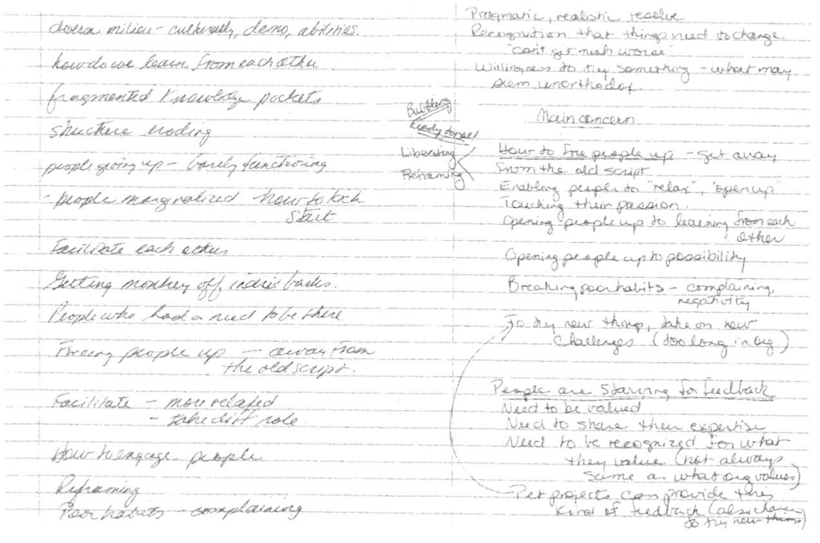

Perhaps You Are Wondering . . .

Will I miss important data if I use field notes rather than tap-ing and transcribing interviews?

One novice researcher wrote, "I know that using field notes helps to delimit the data for analysis. My supervisor is worried, however, that this leads to important things being left out. Also, what determines what I remember to include in the field notes? We compared one field note that I had done with the transcript for that interview and found that some of the subtleties and nuances from the interview had been lost in the field note. So, should I rely solely on the field notes or start selectively coding sections of the interview transcripts to complement them?"

This researcher is worried about missing something important by relying on field notes. It is important to remember that GT is the study of a concept, that is, a pattern of social behavior. Any social setting will contain many patterns, but the goal of GT is *not* to identify and explain *every* pattern in the data but, rather, just one pattern that appears to account for much of what is going on. As such, worries about ensuring full and accurate coverage in data collection are inconsistent with GT methodology. The full scope of social behavior in any substantive set-ting is simply too complex to be fully captured in any one grounded theory study. Anything that is relevant to that pattern will surface in several incidents (i.e., interchangeable indicators), so there is really no need to worry about missing something in a transcript.

● DATA COLLECTION AND ANALYSIS AS AN ITERATIVE PROCESS

While doing GT, "any data (qualitative and/or quantitative), films, pho-tographs, literature etc. may be used. They may be collected by methods, and analyzed with the help of techniques that appear suitable . . . to facilitate theory emergence, while congruent with . . . [your] philosophi-cal stance" (Walsh, 2014c, p. 19). Whether you begin data collection with interviews, focus groups, observations, social media accounts, organiza-tional documents, or newspapers, it is important to remember that data collection is incremental and iterative. GT enables the stimulation of parallel processes of analysis, synthesis, and conceptualization of data. Data are coded as they are collected, and memos are written in conjunc-tion with coding. Memoing opens up the data to reveal subtle patterns of social behavior. It is also very important not to hinder the emergence of theory but rather to allow your creativity some freedom, while at the same time following classic GT's essential guidelines.

Adhering to the simultaneous and sequential nature of data collection, coding, and memoing is fundamental to classic GT and will save you in so many ways! GT's constant comparative analysis and theoretical sampling will save you time as you only need to collect the data necessary to discover and elaborate your theory. Doing so will save you from that overwhelming feeling that so many novice researchers experience when they have spent considerable time collecting mountains of data "because it was there" and then have no idea where to start in making sense of what they have collected. Instead, collect your data one opportunity at a time and focus your efforts on coding and memoing as you go, building up your memo bank. Doing so will reveal the subtle patterns that begin to emerge from your data to explain what is really happening in your area of research interest. If you need quantitative data to help you make sense and see more clearly the emerging patterns, then you should not hesitate to collect these data as well.

Remember also that GT is a delayed action phenomenon (Glaser, 1978, p. 34; 1998, p. 6). Frequently, several days after you have collected a slice of data, coded it, and written memos, new thoughts will arise in your mind that bring moments of clarity to what is emerging from your data. Glaser (1978) calls this **preconscious processing** (p. 23). At such moments, stop and capture your thoughts in another memo! You may want to explore these new insights by theoretically sampling; you may want to go back to the last interviewee and ask more questions about this issue, review earlier data to see if there are indicators of this new idea, or pursue it in your next interview. The goal is to develop more understanding of conceptual ideas as they emerge in your analysis.

IN SUMMARY

GT is based on a concept-indicator model of theory building. Conceptual indicators can be found in any and all types of data. The cardinal rule in GT is not to undermine the discovery of latent patterns in data by preconceiving what to look for or what type of data to use. The goal when initiating your research is to remain open to what emerges as a significant concern in the area under study and to then build an empirically grounded theoretical explanation of how that main concern is handled. In GT, data are analyzed as they are collected. Additional data are theoretically sampled based on emerging conceptual ideas as captured in field notes and analytic memos.

TEST YOUR KNOWLEDGE

In the following questions one or several answers may be correct.

1. While doing classic GT
   a. You have to use only qualitative data
   b. You have to use qualitative and quantitative data
   c. You may use quantitative data
   d. You may use any data
   e. None of the above

2. In classic GT, primary data
   a. Are the data that are the most important
   b. Can only be used once
   c. Are the data specifically collected for your research
   d. Should be used first
   e. None of the above

3. While conducting interviews in a classic GT stance
   a. You must tape all interviews
   b. You should never tape interviews
   c. You can tape some or all interviews
   d. None of the above

4. In classic GT
   a. Detailed description is essential
   b. Field notes are essential
   c. Capturing incidents to identify patterns is essential
   d. None of the above

FURTHER READING

Andrews, L., Higgins, A., Andrews, M. W., & Lalor, J. G. (2012). Classic grounded theory to analyze secondary data: Reality and reflections. *Grounded Theory Review, 11*(1), 12–26.

Glaser, B. G. (2001). *The grounded theory perspective: Conceptualization contrasted with description* (Chapters 11 & 12). Mill Valley, CA: Sociology Press.

Nathaniel, A. (2008). Eliciting spill: A methodological note. *Grounded Theory Review, 7*(1), 61–65.

ENDNOTES

1. For an excellent discussion of "slices of data," see Gibson and Hartman (2014), pages 125–131.

2. For a full elaboration of Glaser's secondary analysis of data, see Glaser and Strauss (1967), Chapter 8.

6

Analyzing Your Data

After studying this chapter, you will:

- *appreciate the distinction between descriptive analysis and conceptual analysis*
- *articulate how to employ constant comparative analysis*
- *distinguish between the various types and stages of coding used in GT*
- *appreciate the key role of analytic memoing in GT analysis*
- *articulate how to identify a core category*
- *appreciate the iterative nature of data analysis in GT*
- *evaluate the impact of software applications on GT analysis*

In this chapter we focus on the techniques of data analysis as employed in classic GT. The conceptualization of data through coding and memoing is the foundation of GT analysis, the goal being the discovery of a latent pattern of social behavior that explains a main issue or concern within an area of research interest. This latent pattern analysis approach unravels the complexity in a social setting to reveal a main concern motivating predictable action. Such patterns of behavior are often subtle and deeply embedded, requiring careful attention to what is revealed in the data. GT focuses on one issue—a main concern—and the pattern of behavior that explains how that concern is perpetually processed, managed, or resolved.

This pattern—the core category—emerges as data are open coded and conceptualized. Once the pattern emerges, the analyst shifts attention to concentrate on theoretically sampling and selectively coding further data to elaborate, and eventually saturate, this core category and any concepts that appear to have some relationship to the core. As a pattern, the core is modeled via theoretical coding to organize and integrate the relationships between and among the core and related concepts. This theoretical coding is not selected but rather emerges through intensive hand sorting of analytic memos, aided by creative insights through the analyst's preconscious processing of analytic ideas that have percolated outside conscious efforts to analyze the data— what Glaser (1998) calls the drugless trip.

Incidents can be described as indicators of phenomena or experiences as observed or articulated in the data. These are labeled and analyzed using the constant comparative method to generate initially substantive, and later theoretical, codes. The process begins with substantive coding through careful reading of the data to identify incidents as indicators of concepts emergent within the data. As the theorist proceeds to compare incident to incident in the data, then incidents to emerging concepts, a main issue or concern surfaces across the coded data, and a category, which appears to account for most of the variation around this issue or concern, becomes the focus of the study. This category is referred to as the **core category** and becomes the focus of further selective data collection and coding efforts until the theorist has sufficiently elaborated and integrated the core category, its properties, and its theoretical connections to other relevant categories. At this point, the theorist has achieved theoretical saturation of the core concept and is ready to articulate the emergent theory.

Worth Noting: Study participants may not specifically articulate a main concern in your collected data. The main concern is a latent pattern that they simply act on without consciously identifying. The grounded theorist sees the concern emerge as a latent pattern through systematic coding and memoing.

As Suddaby (2006) suggests, GT is not simply the routine application of formulaic technique to data but has a clear creative component. This creativity is particularly evident in the memoing of conceptual ideas that parallels the coding process. Indeed, without this parallel processing, key conceptual realizations will be lost and the resulting analysis flat. It is this *grab* that offers such explanatory power.

• CONCEPTUAL ANALYSIS AS DISTINCT FROM DESCRIPTIVE ANALYSIS

Barney Glaser has been known to comment that description runs the world, with conjecture a close second. His point is that while empirically descriptive and hypothesized research studies outnumber grounded theories, they often fail to offer high-impact explanatory variables in the same way that a good grounded theory can offer. As we have discussed in Chapter 4, description captures a moment in time, but the essentially linear nature of descriptive writing hinders the theorist's ability to produce a complex yet parsimonious multivariate theory. Concepts remain buried amid detailed empirical accounts, and it is difficult if not impossible to see the simple elegance in the relationships between concepts that together integrate a grounded theory and provide its explanatory power. GT provides a systematic way to conceptualize and integrate a theory to achieve that full explanatory power.

As discussed in Chapter 3, constant comparative analysis is a foundational pillar of classic GT. After first discussing here the various types of coding in GT, we explore constant comparative analysis, memoing, and core category emergence and development. Next we discuss some cognitive attributes of the classic GT approach that enhance theorizing. While we touch on theoretical sampling and theoretical coding in this chapter, we reserve their full discussion for Chapter 7, as both are key techniques in *shaping* a grounded theory.

• USING CONSTANT COMPARATIVE ANALYSIS

Conceptualization is fundamental to GT for "without the abstraction from time, place and people, there can be no multivariate, integrated theory based on conceptual, hypothetical relationships" (Glaser, 2002, p. 26[1]). Coding and memoing are the key heuristic techniques in constant comparative analysis. While initial attempts at data analysis may very well be more empirically descriptive than conceptual, the classic grounded theorist moves past description to fracturing the data for their conceptual essence through constant comparative analysis. The purpose of constant comparison is to see if the data support and continue to support emerging concepts. Moving through the data to see incidents over and over, constantly comparing and conceptualizing, forces the theorist into

confronting similarities, differences and degrees of consistency of meaning between indicators which generates an
underlying uniformity which in turn results in a coded category and the beginnings of properties of it. From the comparisons of further indicators to the conceptual codes, the
[conceptual] code is sharpened to achieve its best fit while
further properties are generated until the [concept] is verified
and saturated. (Glaser, 1978, p. 62)

By moving through the data to see conceptual indicators repeated
in incident after incident and constantly comparing these, concepts are
developed and their properties and dimensions elaborated.

Concept validity is established through the interchangeability of
indicators in multiple incidents. This means that although incidents are
different, they indicate the same concepts. As such, GT's constant comparative analysis is a gradual building up of conceptual codes into
concepts and then concepts into categories.[2] Doing so requires the theorist to grapple with both chaos and control. The chaos is in tolerating
the uncertainty of not knowing in advance but remaining open to what
emerges through the diligent application of constant comparison for
interchangeability of indicators and theoretical sampling for core emergence and saturation. At the same time, constant comparison helps
alleviate the "data overwhelm" (Glaser, 2003, p. 24) that results from
simply collecting data in a linear fashion without taking the time for
analysis and shaping further data collection through theoretical sampling. Used in conjunction with theoretical sampling, constant comparison generates theory that is "integrated, consistent, plausible and
close to the data" while also "allow[ing], with discipline, for some of
the vagueness and flexibility that aid the creative generation of theory"
(Glaser & Strauss, 1967, p. 103).

The constant comparative approach begins with the first data collected and continues throughout the analytic process through to theoretical saturation and integration, illustrating the nonlinear, spiraling
nature of GT with the boundaries between the various steps not clearly
delineated. Glaser (1998) describes the GT process as "subsequent,
sequential, simultaneous, serendipitous and scheduled" (p. 15). The
process begins with the analyst first coding and comparing incidents in
the data—first, incident to incident; later, incidents to concepts (i.e.,
emergent concepts from earlier comparisons) whereby concepts and
the **properties** and **dimensions**[3] of those concepts are elaborated and
eventually saturated (i.e., no new properties or dimensions are emerging from additional data); and then, concept to concept to establish

conceptual levels between relevant concepts in relation to the core category.

Glaser uses the phrase **interchangeability of indicators** to describe the process of comparative analysis of conceptual indicators in data. The phrase comes from his background in quantitative analysis and the work of Paul Lazarsfeld in index formation:

> Lazarsfeld used the traditional psychological index formation approach. He would take questions that bore on the same topic and sum up their aggregate values for a group. Then he cuts the range of values in half or thirds to construct an index with various values. For example several indicators on degree of recognition produced an index of high, medium and low recognition. Then every person in the sample got a value. What was *not* done was to compare with its meaning each indicator to each indicator . . . When the comparison is made . . . a category is generated (an index with meaning). To continually compare each incident to incidents and categories generates meaningful properties of categories. This constant comparison is a far richer yield of concepts and relationships . . . than is the yield from just summing. (Glaser, 1998, pp. 23–24)

Constant comparison requires concepts to earn their way into a grounded theory through this interchangeability of indicators. This *earned relevance* through emergence is a fundamental premise of GT and is grounded in the coding of data. (See Appendix B for an illustration of the constant comparative method.)

● TYPES AND STAGES OF CODING IN GROUNDED THEORY

All coding in GT is in aid of conceptualization. There are, however, two distinct types of coding: substantive and theoretical. By substantive coding we are referring to the process of conceptualizing the empirical substance of our data. Theoretical coding refers to the integration of our emergent concepts as a model that explains the pattern of relationships between the core category and related concepts. Substantive coding begins with the first data collected, whereas theoretical coding is reserved for the later stage of the GT process once a core category has emerged and been fully developed (saturated) and any concepts that have a relationship to the core category have been fully saturated. At this stage, it is time to explore the modeling of those relationships as a fully integrated grounded theory.

Open Coding

The substantive coding process begins with open coding of empirical data. **Open coding** means to identify **incidents** in the data that appear to indicate one or more concepts and labeling these using one or two salient words per code—preferably verbs to capture the action in concept(s) indicated. Glaser (1978) refers to two types of substantive codes: in vivo and analytic. He describes in vivo codes as capturing exactly what is going on in the incident (e.g., remaining composed) and analytic codes as explaining theoretically what is happening (e.g., identity maintenance). As such, in vivo codes are a first effort at concept identification, and analytic codes raise the level of conceptual abstraction.

Descriptive labeling of incidents is fairly straightforward, but it can be a challenge for some to move from the descriptive to the conceptual level. In close reading of the data, concepts are identified and eventually saturated. Close reading also ensures that no important concepts are overlooked and that concepts *earn* their relevance rather than being accorded an *assumed* importance based on extant theory. It is important here to avoid numerous *one incident* codes. Constant comparison of incidents, noting similarities and differences among incidents and looking for patterns emerging in the coded data, will help to reduce the potential for drowning in one incident codes. The more you code, the more you begin to see the same conceptual indicators (codes) across your data—a pattern emerges, raising the conceptual level of your coding.

A common source of confusion for novice grounded theorists, especially those familiar with qualitative methods, arises with Glaser's (1978) reference to line by line coding (p. 57). Many novice researchers— particularly PhD students—are required to tape and transcribe interviews as a demonstration of research skill development and possibly as a condition of graduate studies or research ethics approval. However, in most instances, coding this type of data may not lead the researcher beyond description due to the volume of data produced in transcripts. However, Glaser (1978) is not referring to the line-by-line coding of interview transcripts but rather to the coding of field notes— abbreviated notations captured during periods of field observation, interviews, conversations, focus groups, and so on. Field notes help the researcher to begin the conceptualization process while *in the field* as she listens for the main concern and notes indicators of how that concern is processed or resolved. Quick notes can then be written up in more detail and then coded and elaborated through memoing. (See Figure 6.1 for a sample of coded field notes.) Coding of field notes, in comparison to lengthy transcripts, helps the analyst to stay focused on what is really happening in the substantive area—what appears to be the main concern— while the absence of detailed conversational or descriptive passages facilitates coding and memoing on a higher conceptual level.

Figure 6.1   Coded Field Notes

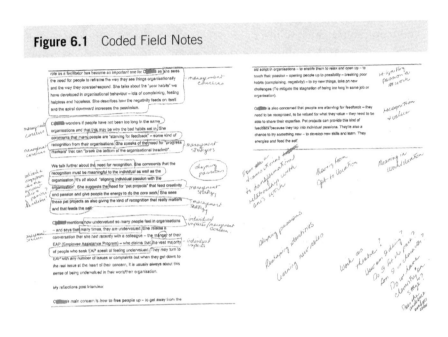

It goes without saying that a grounded theorist must code her own data. Coding unlocks the conceptualization of data and initiates theory generation. A fundamental criterion for coding is the suspension of any preconceived notions about what the data should reveal. Accordingly, a grounded theorist doesn't employ a predefined set of codes assumed to be relevant. As Glaser (1992) suggests, "the analyst should just *not know* as he approaches the data" (p. 50). Instead, the goal is to fracture the data conceptually by posing questions such as the following:

What are these data a study of?

What category does this incident indicate?

What is actually happening in the data?

What is the issue facing the participants?

What is their main concern, and how do they manage or resolve it?

Asking these questions of the data as you code incident by incident facilitates the generation of a core category (Glaser, 1978, p. 57).

Labeling incidents with conceptual codes and, later, with categories "help[s] the theorist to build an *analysis* of the data rather than remain at the level of ethnographic description" (Charmaz, 1990, p. 1167). Glaser (1992) reminds us that in open coding we must guard against "slipping into preconception instead of listening carefully to each incident in order to figure out what the research is truly a study of" (p. 45). Open coding incident by incident in the data with the list of previously presented questions keeps the analyst close to the data rather than lapsing into ungrounded theorizing and corrects any forcing of "pet" themes on the data by requiring "the analyst to verify and saturate categories, and minimiz[ing] missing an important category, produc[ing] a dense, rich theory, and giv[ing] a feeling that nothing has been left out" (Glaser, 1978, p. 58).

Keep moving through the data rather than pondering too long on any one incident. Doing so will facilitate your seeing emerging patterns in your coding. As concepts begin to take shape, additional constant comparisons help to clarify the logic in emerging concepts and their properties as well as reducing the emerging theory through a smaller set of higher-level interrelated concepts. Given this constant, emergent refinement of concepts and categories, it is important not to fret about the specific labels at the open coding stage. Use labels that help to capture the idea while keeping in mind that there will be time later in the process to refine the labels of your concepts and categories.

Glaser on Data Collecting

Glaser (1978) suggests that staying too long "in the field" collecting data is a common problem. He recommends no more than half a day at a time in data collection. He also reminds us that while open coding can generate many codes very quickly, it is important to interrupt coding to memo ideas. Coding and memoing as data are collected is important because this is when ideas about the data are freshest in your mind. Doing so also facilitates theoretical sampling by allowing you to see where you need to go next to elaborate on ideas that emerge through your coding and memoing.

Selective Coding

In **selective coding**, the analyst delimits coding to only those concepts (i.e., variables) that relate to the core category in sufficiently significant ways to produce a parsimonious theory. If a concept, regardless of its novelty or the personal preference of the analyst, does not have relevance in relation to the core category, it is dropped from subsequent analysis and theoretical elaboration. In this way, the core category becomes a guide to further data collection and theoretical sampling. During the initial open coding, the analyst will have coded many incidents with many of these being coded for more than one concept. Once a potential core category is selected, the coding technique shifts from open to selective. Because not all data pertain to the core category (or related concepts), it is necessary to "delimit" coding to just that which pertains to the core and related concepts.

Initiating Selective Coding

Delimiting occurs at two levels. First, as the theory integrates, it solidifies with fewer modifications needed as the researcher compares the next incidents of a category to its properties. Later modifications are mainly about clarifying the logic of the theory and integrating elaborating details of properties into the major outline of interrelated categories. As the researcher begins to discover an underlying uniformity in the categories and properties, the theory is reformulated with a smaller set of higher level concepts. This second level of delimiting the theory reduces the original list of categories for coding.

As the theory develops, becomes reduced, and increasingly works better in ordering a mass of data, the researcher becomes committed to it. This allows for a delimiting of the original list of categories for subsequent collecting and selective coding of additional data, according to the newly established boundaries of the theory. By delimiting the focus to one category as the core variable, only those categories related to that core are now included in the theory. This list of categories, now delimited for additional selective coding, is subsequently (and continuously) delimited through theoretical saturation of each category. (Holton, 2007a, pp. 280–281)

Any incidents that have been coded for several possible concepts are reviewed and their relevance and relationship to the core category affirmed in memos. As concepts are saturated (i.e., additional data fail to yield any new properties or dimensions of the concept), additional data collection and coding are further delimited as the fully saturated concepts are set aside while the analyst continues to theoretically sample and saturate the remaining concepts. Delimiting speeds up the analysis by focusing theoretical sampling and constant comparison on just the core category and related concepts and reduces the potential for the analyst to be overwhelmed with excessive caches of data that bear no relevance to the emerging theory.

Another Aspect of Delimiting

In studies with a heterogeneous *sample* (e.g., senior managers, middle managers, and frontline staff), in which each segment of the sample appears to have a different main concern, the analyst should consider delimiting the study to focus on one subset of the sample at a time. Subsequent stages of analysis can focus on the other subsets with the potential for different core categories emerging from each subset analyzed. A good example is Sandgren (2010). The author undertook three separate GT studies in the same substantive area (palliative cancer care): (1) acute care nurses' *striving for emotional survival*, (2) home care nurses' *doing good care*, and (3) patients' and relatives' *living on hold*. Sandgren then used data from the three grounded theories to generate an overarching grounded theory of *deciphering unwritten rules*. These rules explain how patients, relatives, and nurses deal with the uncertainty of how to act and behave within the sensitivities associated with a palliative care setting.

When doing open and selective coding, researchers sometimes feel the need to collect quantitative data. They have done some open coding of collected qualitative data and have identified the core category and some related categories through further selective coding. However, some categories are not saturated, and some data are double coded. To help produce parsimonious results and fully saturated categories, quantitative data may be collected. A questionnaire may be developed with items grounded in the qualitative data previously collected. Exploratory factor analysis of resulting quantitative data may then help the researcher to achieve parsimony and reach theoretical saturation of the various categories previously highlighted with qualitative data. The process of selective coding is sometimes limited by the researcher's interpretation of the data and capacity to synthesize parsimoniously all the data obtained. In some instances, this drawback may be considerably lessened by using quantitative data and techniques.

Mixed Methods Example

The theory of information technology (IT) culture creep (Walsh et al., 2010) was grounded in qualitative data. Using qualitative data in a Straussian approach to GT helped provide rich descriptions of IT user ideal types and the 18 possible dimensions of the explanatory second-order IT culture construct. However, some of the 18 dimensions we had qualitatively identified for the IT culture construct appeared redundant, as many items from our qualitative data were double-coded within two subcategories. With our qualitative data, we had not been able to eliminate the redundant dimensions among the 18 identified qualitatively. We therefore decided to collect quantitative data and use quantitative techniques to help us solve this issue (Walsh & Gettler-Summa, 2010). With a diversified population, we thus investigated further our core category, the users' IT culture, while linking it to user ideal types and eliminated correlated redundant dimensions. At the same time, we aimed to assess the relative importance of each first-order construct (the IT culture dimensions) used to describe the ideal types. To sum up, mixing data and methods helped us conceptualize with parsimony; it allowed us to densify the IT culture concept through dimension reduction (from 18 to 8).

Theoretical Coding

As discussed earlier, **theoretical coding** refers to the modeling of the relationships between and among the core category and related concepts as a fully integrated theory. It is the final stage in the coding process and is largely responsible for the overall "shaping" of the theory. We turn to a more extensive discussion of theoretical coding in Chapter 7.

The different types of coding in classic GT, which we described earlier, are summarized in Table 6.1.

Table 6.1   Coding in Classic GT

Types of Coding		Description	Purpose
Substantive	Open	In vivo codes: Capturing what is going on Analytic codes: Conceptualizing what is happening	To identify *incidents* in the data that appear to *indicate* one or more concepts
	Selective	Coding around the core category	To identify properties and dimensions of the core category
Theoretical		Coding to model the relationships between and among the core category and related concepts	To shape and integrate the theory

CORE CATEGORY EMERGENCE   ●

> **One Student's Experience**
>
> "When I let go of what I wanted the problem to be, I actually found some of the answers to what the problem really was, and I actually found something much bigger—a theory of who, how, and why."

Data collection in GT focuses on a general area of interest. Then, as coding and memoing proceed using the questions listed earlier, the analyst begins to discern a latent pattern that focuses attention on a main issue or concern in the area under study. As the analyst memos ideas around this main issue, a core category emerges that seems to explain the most variation in the social behavior around the central issue or concern and how the issue is processed or addressed. This core category will relate to several other concepts, providing a focus for theoretical integration through elaboration of the relationships between and among the emergent core and related concepts. Indeed, this theoretical integration is the "prime function" (Glaser, 1978, p. 93) of the core category, ensuring that the resultant theory is both conceptually dense and theoretically saturated through the increasing development of conceptual interrelationships that organize the theory. Without a dynamic core variable that cuts across empirical units, theoretical linkages may not be seen and the theorist may opt to simply link up largely descriptive comparisons (Bigus et al., 1994).

Differentiating Between a Main Concern and a Core Category

Novice grounded theorists will often confuse the main concern with the core category. The distinction is that the main concern highlights the issue or problem that occupies much of the action and attention in the research setting, whereas the core category *explains how* that concern or problem is managed, processed, or resolved. As such, the main concern and the core category are tightly coupled but distinct conceptualizations. As one example, in Holton (2006, 2007b) the main concern of knowledge professionals was coping with persistent and unpredictable change in their workplaces. The core category that emerged was rehumanizing, a three-stage process, whereby knowledge professionals engaged in fluctuating support networks that served as informal psychic softeners in countering dehumanizing workplace climates.

As another example, in Walsh, Kefi, and Baskerville (2010), the main managerial concern was dealing with different types of IT usage within firms, and the core category that emerged was the IT acculturation process investigated through IT culture ideal types.

A core category is tentatively identified, often fairly early in the open coding stage, following which the analyst considers which other coded concepts appear to have some relationship to the core category. The core category, as a theoretical code, can be organized or modeled in numerous ways. It is often a process with two or more stages (e.g., "status passage"; Glaser & Strauss, 1971), but it can also be a typology (e.g., "awareness contexts"; Glaser & Strauss, 1965a; Walsh et al., 2010), a continuum (Giske & Gjengedal, 2007), strategies (Sandgren et al., 2006), a cycle (Higgins, Barker, & Begley, 2008), or dimensions (Pergert, 2008).

Glaser (1978) and Glaser and Holton (2004) offer criteria for selecting and confirming a core category: centrality (i.e., it appears central to the main concern), frequency (i.e., it reoccurs frequently in the data and can be seen as a stable pattern), relevance (i.e., it relates meaningfully and easily with other categories), grab (i.e., imagery and explanatory power with general implications[4] beyond the substantive area), and variability (i.e., although conditions vary, the essential meaning remains constant; see Figure 6.2).

Figure 6.2 Core Category and Main Concern

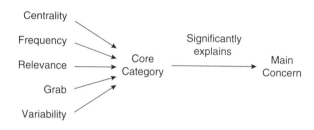

As previously discussed, once a core category has emerged, the analyst considers other concepts that have patterned out in open coding to determine their relevance in relation to the core category. Further data collection, coding, and memoing are delimited to theoretical sampling for additional conceptual indicators of the core and these related concepts, moving the analyst in the selective coding stage. Given its centrality and significance for ensuring full explanatory power, it does take longer to saturate the core category than related concepts.

One Student's Experience

"I think I've got it . . . one word that has come from my analysis of the data . . . it fits with so much data that I am amazed. It accounts for differences in emotions in a wide variety of situations; attitudes towards a wide variety of shopping types and explains very diverse shopping behaviors. And it makes sense. It did not come from me; it came from the data."

THE KEY ROLE OF ANALYTIC MEMOING IN GT ANALYSIS ●

Memoing is the core ideational processing of theoretical ideas as they emerge through coding and constant comparative analysis. Memos are the researcher's theoretical notes about the data and the conceptual connections between categories. Memo writing is a continual process that helps to raise the data to a conceptual level and develop the properties of each category. Memos present hypotheses about connections between categories and/or their properties/dimensions and begin the integration of these connections with clusters of other categories to generate a theory. The constant comparative reasoning captured in memos debunks preconceived notions about what the data should reveal (Glaser, 1978). As Glaser (1978) suggests, the goals in memoing are to stimulate and capture conceptual ideas that emerge from coding and constant comparative analysis, to do so with complete freedom from the usual constraints of proper writing (i.e., grammar, syntax), and to build up a rich fund of captured ideas in a highly sortable format that facilitates theoretical integration of a rich, dense yet parsimonious theory.

Memoing your ideas—*AS YOU CODE*—is essential to transcending descriptive analysis. Glaser (1998) notes that "falling out" (p. 177) at the coding stage is the downfall for many who wish to do GT. Without theoretical sensitivity and persistence in using memos to capture ideas as they emerge, such work defaults to conceptual description where concepts and their properties are simply identified and described without any integrative theoretical explanation. As Klag and Langley (2013) suggest, "it is often in the very act of writing that productive conceptual ideas develop and crystallize" (p. 161).

One Student's Experience

"I read the transcripts line-by-line, asking all the time 'What is the participant trying to do?' and making notes on the margins. Curiously these notes were less important than the memos that this exercise generated. It was as if writing memos allowed me to better understand what was going on—to gradually increase my knowledge of the situation. To see what the participants were trying to do and how they did it. After some time I had so many memos that I was curious to see the whole picture. It takes time but if you are constantly analyzing the data and looking carefully at it, there's no way you can escape learning more and more about the situation. And the memos are the tool that will allow you to put everything together so you don't have to worry about keeping it all in your mind all the time."

Locke (2007) suggests that capturing theoretical ideas in GT necessitates dual modes of thinking whereby we acknowledge the tension between the irrational free play of ideas as our minds wander and explore and the rational control required in diligently pursuing those ideas in a systematic way: "Thus, staying firmly and single-mindedly in touch with what it is we are trying to understand at the same time as we open and loosen up our thinking to roam freely defines thinking in these dual modes" (p. 570).

Fine and Deegan (1996) describe *serendipity* as a unique and contingent mix of insight and chance, whereas Klag and Langley (2013) contrast serendipity with deliberate application of heuristics to stimulate variety in theorizing, suggesting that both play an important role in facilitating conceptual leaps. While acknowledging that GT entails both the serendipitous and the systematic, Glaser does not view logic and intuition as diametrically opposed but rather as twin foundations for theory generation. The theorizing process in GT operates at both a conscious and a preconscious level to process and organize empirically grounded, analytically induced concepts.

Skill in memoing, and therefore the conceptual depth of the memos, is part of the experiential learning curve in GT skill development. Memos are works in progress, intended to capture ideas as they emerge without the worries of writing style, grammar, and spelling that can cause some writers to freeze their thinking. Many memos written early in the constant comparison process may never find their way into the final theory because they may not relate to the core category; thus, to spend time perfecting these memos is to waste research time. Time is better spent in letting the ideas flow and capturing them as they emerge. There will be time later in the writing process to polish them.

Early in the GT process, writing several short memos on each category facilitates **theoretical sorting** of ideas from which more substantial memos will be written as the process moves toward conceptual elaboration and, later, integration. (See Appendix B for an illustration of the maturation of early shorter memos into more substantial memos as conceptual ideas develop.) Glaser (2014) advocates "free style" memoing:

> Hans Thulesius, a well-known grounded theory researcher and teacher, confirms my dictum of free style memoing. Hans says "Memoing is very important in GT research, but you can memo in whatever way you like. Hand writing, typing or drawing diagrams but keep them private. When you have a

big stack of memos you can begin hand sorting them, placing them in smaller piles on a big table. Then writing more memos are triggered by the sorted memos which when you reach saturation will eventually lead to a working paper." Hans continues about free style memoing: "Every person finds his or her own way of writing and organizing one's memos. The most important thing about memos is that you get out your ideas onto paper. Glaser warns against rules for memos since they can stifle the creative memo writing. Memos should be written at any time to capture the ideas that come when you compare and code data. And stay open to whatever emerges and memo it at all stages of doing GT" (p. 26).

Preconscious processing means that ideas can come to mind at any time. Glaser (2014) urges the GT theorist to write continually, memoing thoughts and ideas as *analytic bits*. Charmaz (2014) describes writing and rewriting as crucial phases of the analytic process. Having confidence in your memoing is critical, especially early in the GT process when it is unclear as yet where theorizing may be headed. Grounded theorists learn to trust in whatever ideas occur as they are reading through their data and trying to find patterns to explain social behaviors in the data. The delayed action nature of GT requires continuous memoing of ideas, comparing them to earlier memos to continually build a bank of memos. Just as with a bank, your investment grows as you continue to deposit and build your account, promising a profitable return. As Breckenridge (2013) describes,

As my memo bank grew, my confidence increased and my pace quickened as I became less worried about getting the coding right and more excited by the number of possibilities emerging in the data. The more I analyzed, the longer my memos became as I was able to see more theoretical connections and identify further questions for theoretical sampling. This in turn slowed my pace, as I moved back and forth between coding, constant comparison and memo writing. At times I found the systematic approach to coding and constant comparison rather tedious. Thankfully, however, moments of tedium were only ever temporary and frequently gave way to excitement as new concepts emerged, reigniting my motivation as memos became more full and vibrant with new ideas and connections. (p. 9)

Some Advice for Productive Memoing

While emphasizing that memoing is a highly personal process, Glaser (1978) does offer a number of *rules* for memoing, including the following:

1. Keep data and memos separate. Reference memos to field notes from where they emerge. Use incidents as illustrations of only one code (as much as possible).
2. Always interrupt coding to memo whenever an idea arises.
3. Bring on memoing by starting to write on a code—such writing will open up the output stage of creativity.
4. Modify memos as growth and realizations occur.
5. Keep a list of emergent codes at hand.
6. If too many memos on different codes seem the same, compare codes or their dimensions for differences that are being missed between the codes. If they are still the same, collapse the two into one code.
7. Problematic digressions should be followed through on a conceptual, not logical, elaboration basis for the purpose of theoretical sampling for indicating an area for future research. In such cases, memos should make clear distinctions between data and conjecture.
8. Run memos open as long as possible to enable development of rich diversity.
9. When writing memos, talk conceptually about the substantive codes as they are theoretically coded (do not talk about people), and write about the conceptually generated patterns that people engage in (and not about the people per se).
10. If analyst has two burning ideas, he should write them up one at a time to keep them straight and avoid confusion.
11. Indicate in memos "saturation" when analyst thinks he has saturated a category.
12. No matter how well memoing techniques are working, always be flexible with them.

A common concern expressed by novice researchers is how to illustrate (i.e., *verify*) the empirical grounding of their concepts and categories, as would be expected in a qualitative study. One way to achieve this is by creating an audit trail that links memos to the data from which they were generated. Then, using a simple labeling scheme, footnotes can be used to record the connections (from data to memos) in the final memo sorting and writing up of the theory.

An Example of Labeling to Create an Audit Trail

A memo labeled "Memo AU 0904-4" (indicating that it is one of four memos written on August 9, 2004) and including references to data from interviews collected on four occasions (October 23, 2001; September 10, 2003; November 12, 2001; and November 26, 2001) is footnoted in the final write-up of the theory as "Field Interview O 2301-2, S 1003, N 1201, N 2601; Memo AU 0904-4."

While such evidentiary detail is not relevant or required as part of the GT process, it may be important—and expected—to satisfy thesis advisers or journal reviewers accustomed to full data displays. Initiating a similar labeling scheme for all data and memos at the outset of a study offers the analyst an opportunity to keep the data-memo connections clear as the study progresses as well as offering an *audit trail* option for later thesis defense or publication.

THE ITERATIVE NATURE OF DATA ANALYSIS IN GROUNDED THEORY

Earlier in this chapter we make reference to Glaser's (1998) description of GT as "subsequent, sequential, simultaneous, serendipitous and scheduled" (p. 15). Glaser's description is an apt one, and our challenge in writing this chapter has been to attempt to relate *linearly* a process that is anything but linear! Glaser (1978) describes the importance of personal pacing, creativity, and cycling in doing a GT study. The iterative nature of GT, coupling a rigorous and systematic analytic approach with an open and flexible embrace of creative insights through preconscious processing—wherever and whenever they emerge—requires the grounded theorist to be comfortable with both chaos and control:

> The chaos is in tolerating the uncertainty and subsequent regression of not knowing in advance and of remaining open to what emerges through the diligent, controlled, often tedious application of the method's synchronous and iterative processes of line-by-line coding, constant comparison for interchangeability

of indicators, and theoretical sampling for core emergence and theoretical saturation. This discipline is simultaneously complemented by requiring the theorist to remain open to the innate creativity in preconscious processing of conceptual ideation and theoretical integration. (Holton, 2007a, p. 273)

Fortunately, GT has *built-in* motivational phases that carry the theorist onward with energy and the excitement of discovery. Eureka moments (Glaser, 1998) that emerge from preconscious processing of a study in progress are an important motivator. As Breckenridge (2013) describes,

Theoretical realizations sometimes take a while to emerge. Glaser has called this preconscious processing. Although I was not convinced about this idea at first, reflecting on my own experience, I can remember clearly those occasions where I had given up only to find that clarity of thought emerged when I least expected it: as I was cooking, out walking, on the train and even waking in the middle of the night to scribble down memos in the dark. (p. 11)

Such experiences are commonly shared among grounded theorists! Yet, those new to GT often seek specific procedures or templates for analyzing their data. There is no one *correct* way to code and memo. The choice is a personal one that will evolve as your GT skills develop. Some experienced grounded theorists have shared their approaches (Breckenridge, 2013; Holton, 2007a; Scott, 2009). You may find these interesting and possibly helpful in developing your own approach. The best advice is to keep it simple but organized and do whatever you can to stimulate *hand-eye-brain* cognitive and preconscious processing through manual coding, memoing, and sorting procedures. And finally, the grounded theorist must be able to trust in the process every step along the way and to trust that following the GT methodology will yield a theory that is rich in explanatory power and relevant to the area under study.

TO SOFTWARE OR NOT TO SOFTWARE   ●

Computer-assisted data analysis is now commonplace in the research world and novice grounded theorists are often tempted to adopt software for data analysis. Bringer, Johnston, and Brackenridge (2004) suggested that QSR*NVIVO is compatible with doing GT; however, in doing so, they conflate GT with qualitative research methodology for which detailed transcription of interview data is the norm. While software programs are excellent for searching and sorting through such data, they tend to do so in a structured linear and hierarchical manner that is more appropriate to what Glaser would refer to as the *full coverage* nature of qualitative data analysis. GT quickly leaves the data behind through constant comparison to conceptualization, a process that relies on lateral thinking (de Bono, 1968) through the conceptual sorting of ideas and creative realizations through preconscious processing.

GT is about the sorting of theoretical ideas captured in memos. The danger in using qualitative software applications is that the analyst slips into mechanically coding large volumes of data and sorting codes without engaging systematically in constantly comparing incidents within the data and memoing conceptual ideas that, over time, surface the subtleties in realizations and relationships between and among incidents and emergent concepts. As Breckenridge (2013) explains,

> It was easy to code the data—too easy perhaps—and I quickly amassed a long list of codes with no idea how they might be connected to one another. Sitting at the computer "dragging and dropping" sections of data became automatic and unthinking. I was simply organizing my data into a fractured list, without comparing incident to incident or stopping to write memos. (pp. 8–9)

The result of such mindless coding may, at best, lead to a drift into conceptual description without the capacity to generate a conceptually dense and fully integrated grounded theory.

A further danger to employing software for data analysis is that the analyst may be lured into indiscriminate data collection, collecting more data than is necessary simply because it is there. Practically speaking, employing qualitative software entails a significant learning curve; it is not only time consuming but holds the potential for stifling analytic creativity. Both authors of this book, who have been trained very differently, find NVIVO software useful for archiving coded qualitative data and for linking memos to incidents in the data and linking memos as they cumulatively build ideas. This archiving capacity is particularly useful in later writing up for publication.

IN SUMMARY

When doing classic GT, you have to go beyond descriptive analysis and reach conceptual analysis. All data—whether qualitative, quantitative, or both—must be constantly compared and analyzed as they are collected through iterative cycles and memoing effected alongside this process, as ideas emerge. To help analysis, various steps in coding of data are applied: Open coding of all data is done until core category emergence, then selective coding around the core category, and, finally, theoretical coding to highlight causal relationships between concepts. Memoing plays a key role in the analytic process. Memoing begins as soon as the first data are coded and continues throughout the process to the final write-up of the theory. Despite its popularity, grounded theorists are cautious in their use of analytic software, reserving its use for archiving (and later retrieval) of manually coded and sorted data.

TEST YOUR KNOWLEDGE

In the following questions one or several answers may be correct.

1. In classic GT
   a. You first have to collect all data and then analyze them
   b. You analyze your data as you collect them
   c. You must decide which data to collect next before you start analyzing collected data
   d. You should constantly compare all collected data
   e. None of the above

2. In classic GT, coding is
   a. Open, axial, and selective
   b. Open, selective, and theoretical
   c. Substantive and theoretical
   d. None of the above

3. The core category
   a. Keeps recurring in the data
   b. Has grab
   c. Emerges while you are open coding
   d. Must emerge before you start selectively coding
   e. None of the above

4. While doing classic GT with qualitative data,
   a. You must code every word
   b. You must code every sentence
   c. You must use software to help you code
   d. None of the above

FURTHER READING

Glaser, B. G. (1965). The constant comparative method of qualitative analysis. *Social Problems, 12*, 436–445.

Glaser, B. G. (1998). Generating concepts. In *Doing grounded theory: Issues and discussions* (Chapter 9). Mill Valley, CA: Sociology Press.

Glaser, B. G. (2001). Constant comparison and core confusion. In *The grounded theory perspective: Conceptualization contrasted with description* (Chapter 13). Mill Valley, CA: Sociology Press.

Glaser, B. G. (2014). *Memoing: A vital grounded theory procedure*. Mill Valley, CA: Sociology Press.

Holton, J. A. (2007a). The coding process and its challenges. In A. Bryant & C. Charmaz (Eds.), *The SAGE handbook of grounded theory* (pp. 265–289). London: Sage.

ENDNOTES

1. The Creative Commons-Attribution-NonCommercial-ShareAlike License 4.0 International applies to all works published by the International Journal of Qualitative Methods. Copyright for articles published in the International Journal of Qualitative Methods remains with the first author.

2. Glaser has a tendency to use the terms *code, concept,* and *category* interchangeably. Here we wish to clarify our use of the terms. By code, we refer to the labels attached to incidents during the substantive coding stage of analysis. Codes are often descriptive, particularly in the initial stages of data analysis. By concept, we refer to the resultant naming of a higher level abstraction of a conceptual idea as indicated through the cumulative comparison of codes. Similarly, a category denotes the further abstraction of individual concepts as a latent pattern. As an example, we might note the following codes in data: *being myself, being heard, authentic connecting, quiet voices, comfortable with each other, trusting my own voice, being genuine.* These, along with other codes, are later incorporated into the concept *authenticity,* which later emerges as a property of the core category of *rehumanizing.*

3. We differentiate here between *properties* as latent, qualitative characteristics (e.g., authenticity, trust, healing) and *dimensions* as the measurable component of a concept (e.g., space, time, size).

4. It is the general implications of a core category that lead to formal theory development (Glaser, 2007, p. 4)

7

Shaping the Theory

After studying this chapter, you will be able to:

- *articulate the role of theoretical sampling, theoretical saturation, and theoretical coding in shaping an emerging grounded theory*

- *utilize theoretical sampling and theoretical saturation to build emergent concepts and categories*

- *utilize theoretical coding to integrate a grounded theory*

Our purpose in this chapter is to explain key techniques for giving shape to the theory as it emerges and develops. As we have set out in earlier chapters, GT is an elegant and intricate approach to capturing and conceptualizing latent patterns in social settings. While too complex to be approached in a linear fashion, GT is readily embraced by our innate capacity for pattern recognition through preconscious processing (Glaser, 1998, p. 50). In this chapter, we will explore the techniques of *theoretical sampling, theoretical saturation,* and *theoretical coding,* which enable the analyst to explicitly build and shape the emerging theory and to present it as an integrated conceptual explanation.

● THEORETICAL SAMPLING

Theoretical sampling is the process whereby the analyst decides both what data to collect to develop emerging concepts and where those data may be available. The purpose of theoretical sampling is to discover categories, properties, and interrelationships suggestive of a theoretical *whole*. As such, theoretical sampling is theory-driven sampling, controlled by the emerging theory and not determined in advance based on a preconceived theoretical framework. Glaser and Strauss (1971) note that

> no one kind of data on a category nor any single technique for data collection is necessarily appropriate. Different kinds of data give the analyst different views or vantage points from which to understand a category and to develop its properties. (pp. 183–184)

Glaser and Strauss (1967) speak of these different views or vantage points as slices of data and suggest that "theory generated from just one kind of data never fits, or works as well, as theory generated from diverse slices of data on the same category" (p. 68). Gibson and Hartman (2014) distinguish between data slicing and theoretical sampling:

> Data slicing, in keeping with Glaser and Strauss (1971), refers to the use of an individual comparison between different substantive groups or different social units for the purposes of developing theory, usually in the form of refining categories. Theoretical sampling refers to a process of combining several different slices of data for the purpose of developing theory. (p. 128)

Theoretical sampling of different *slices*, in parallel with constant comparative analysis, assists conceptual elaboration with the overall integration of the theory more likely to emerge *organically*. By employing a range of data slices, the analyst discovers similarities and differences that bring forth the variability of concepts and their properties in various contexts and under varying conditions, thereby enhancing the conceptual density of the emerging theory. The comparisons are ideational, not population-specific. As such, "there are no limits to the techniques of data collection, the way they are used, or the types of data required" (Glaser & Strauss, 1971, p. 184), provided that GT's foundational principle of emergence is respected.

As an illustration of theoretical sampling of different slices of data in different substantive groups and in different social units, you may refer to Walsh, Kefi, and Baskerville (2010). Sampling was first done in a corporate setting, within different firms (different substantive groups) and then in a societal setting (different social unit).

During the open coding stage, sampling proceeds in all directions that seem relevant and add to the emerging concepts. Once a potential core category has emerged, theoretical sampling becomes selective as the analyst focuses on developing central issues related to the emerging theory "guided by the logic of the emerging analytic framework" (Glaser & Strauss, 1965a, p. 289). There is a deductive element to theoretical sampling as the analyst memos by probing and questioning emergent theoretical ideas and deciding where to go next to get the data to fill gaps and elaborate on emerging ideas, but this deduction is in service to further inductive analysis as the theory develops. The analyst may go back to existing data to sample for emerging ideas as well as generating new data from new slices of data. This deductive (conceptual) elaborating is essential for the systematic generation of theoretical possibilities, as propositions or hypotheses, to build and explain the emerging theory. Fresh data from new populations and samples assist in extending the scope and coverage of the emerging theory, thus driving toward substantively formalized theory and a less idiographic, contextualized perspective. The possibilities for multiple comparisons through theoretical sampling are endless and so the grounded theorist selects comparison groups according to theoretical criteria. "Groups are, from a theoretical viewpoint, clusters of variables, which are not readily apparent, and many of which are to be discovered by comparison" (Glaser, 1978, p. 42).

> The criteria of theoretical sampling are designed to be applied in the on-going joint collection and analysis of data associated with the generation of theory. Therefore they are continually tailored to fit the data and are applied judiciously at the right point and moment in the analysis. The analyst can continually adjust his control of data collection to ensure the data's relevance to the impersonal criteria of the emerging theory. (Glaser & Strauss, 1967, p. 48)

Sampling strategies also control the scope of the theory by consciously choosing to limit or extend the population sampled. Glaser and Strauss (1967) suggest that at the outset, the process is to establish the basic categories and their properties by minimizing differences (i.e., maximizing similarities) in theoretically sampling comparative groups so as to verify the relevance of emerging categories, generate their properties, and identify the conditions and fundamental differences under which they vary. Once this basic work is achieved, the analyst turns to maximizing differences among comparison groups as a means of identifying the scope of the emerging theory and stimulating the theoretical density so as to saturate conceptual properties once the basic conceptual framework has emerged (p. 58).

Skill in theoretical sampling develops over time. It requires the ability to be both analytic and flexible. There is no precise formula to be applied and no limitations on the techniques for data collection; rather, sampling requires sensitive judgments as to the best places to go next to find the data needed to answer key questions as they emerge in advancing and satisfying gaps in the emerging theory. Comparing data as it is collected produces a "cumulatively *intensive theoretical sensitivity*" (Glaser, 1978, p. 36) as the analyst gradually sees more and more of theoretical relevance in the data, creating more abstract levels of theoretical connections as the theory is gradually built up inductively through progressive stages of analysis.

Jørgensen, Dahl, Pedersen, and Lomborg (2013) explain the theoretical sampling approach in their grounded theory of coping with COPD (chronic obstructive pulmonary disorder):

The aim was to secure data that could capture the multidimensionality of coping ... Data collection and analysis guided the theoretical sampling phase. For example, the coping behavior of the first included participant with moderate COPD persistently deviated from the behavior of the following five included participants with severe or very severe COPD. Several possible reasons for this deviation were looked for in the data. In the ensuing data collection and analysis process, this heterogeneity led us to obtain an equal distribution of male and female participants with differing degrees of COPD. Additionally, data revealed that spouses constituted a significant extra-personal and interpersonal resource, playing a vital role in how participants handled a life influenced by breathlessness. Therefore, spouses were invited to participate in the following interviews with the intention of enriching our understanding of the participants' coping strategies. These discoveries on equal terms with other preliminary findings resulted in an ongoing alteration of guides for interview, video observation, and selection of video sequences. (p. 5)

Theoretical sampling generally means that the researcher may well spend a longer time *in the field* but will be collecting fewer data as the direction of data collection is more intentional and focused, thereby giving the researcher momentum, purpose, and confidence in the categories that are emerging from the data (Glaser & Strauss, 1967, p. 76). The adequacy of the analyst's theoretical sampling will vary with the level of theory proposed; the more formal the theory is, the greater the scope and range of data sampled will be.

Perhaps You Are Wondering . . .

Early in the research process, theoretical sampling may involve asking an interviewee about a concept that has emerged in other data that you have collected. While you don't want to force the idea on interviewees, there is no harm in asking a simple question about their experience of the concept (e.g., "Have you ever experienced harassment in your workplace?" "Are there any taboo topics in this department?" etc.). Your question may spark a response and more indicators for analysis, or it may not—which is also data!

THEORETICAL SATURATION

Theoretical saturation refers to the constant comparison of conceptual indicators in the data to the point where additional indicators yield no further theoretical specification or elaboration. Glaser (2001) describes theoretical saturation as "intense property development" (p. 191), suggesting that this stage of theory development is "necessary to lift the theory above description and enable its integration through theoretical propositions (hypotheses) as abstract conceptual theory" (Holton, 2007a, p. 281). By theoretically sampling to maximize the diversity in both comparative groups and varieties of data, the analyst will enhance saturation of both the properties and dimensions of concepts. Probing questions, during data collection and analysis, will assist the densification of conceptual properties (Glaser, 1978).

As the theory develops, the theorist learns which categories require the most and the least saturation and which ones can be dropped; thus, the emerging theory generates its own selectivity (Glaser & Strauss, 1967). Core categories should be saturated as completely as possible. Failure to saturate the core and related concepts will leave the theorist with a thin theory of loosely connected concepts and little explanatory power. However, continuing to collect data for concepts that have saturated or for those that are not related in some way to the emerging theory's core category is a waste of researcher time and resources. "The criteria for determining saturation then are a combination of the empirical limits of the data, the integration and density of the theory and the analyst's theoretical sensitivity" (Glaser & Strauss, 1967, p. 62).

Perhaps You Are Wondering . . .

Do I need to saturate my concepts in one location/ comparative group before I theoretically sample for those concepts in another location/comparative group?

It is difficult to know when a concept will be theoretically saturated. It is possible that the concept may saturate in one comparative group and that you may not identify any additional properties or dimensions of that concept in subsequent theoretical sampling of other groups. However, theoretical sampling in a number of comparative groups may well capture new properties or dimensions or possibly even new concepts with relevance to your emerging theory. As the theorist, it is your decision as to when you feel that concepts have been saturated and there are no obvious gaps in the emerging theory that need to be followed up with additional sampling. It is a judgment call based on the explanatory power, or explanatory gaps, of the emerging theory.

THEORETICAL CODING

Once the core category has emerged, having identified those concepts that bear some relationship to the core and having theoretically sampled to saturate the core and related concepts, the analyst is ready to begin the process of theoretical coding as the final shaping of the emergent theory. It is at this point, however, that some theorists fail to achieve the full explanatory power of classic GT by not pursuing its integration through theoretical coding. Instead, they default to simply offering conceptual description rather than pressing on to this final stage of GT development. As Bacharach (1989) reminds us, "while descriptions may be the source material of theories, they are not themselves theoretical statements" (p. 497) and "just as a collection of words does not make a sentence, a collection of constructs and variables does not necessarily make a theory" (p. 496).

The integration of a grounded theory through theoretical coding captures our innate ability for perceiving latent patterns that organize and integrate relevant related concepts to provide a full explanation of the emergent theory's resolving or managing of a main concern. Glaser and Strauss (1971) speak of "the emergence of a natural integration" (p. 190). Theoretical codes conceptualize (i.e., model) how substantive codes may relate to each other as propositions or hypotheses to be integrated into a theory.

Theoretical coding occurs only after all substantive coding is completed and the core category and related concepts have been theoretically saturated: "Theoretical codes give integrative scope, broad pictures and a new perspective" (Glaser, 1978, p. 72) and help the analyst maintain a conceptual level in writing about concepts and their interrelations. They "conceptually punctuate the emerging theory with an organizing pattern."[1] As discussed in Chapter 6, the core category of a grounded theory is always presented (or modeled) as some form of theoretical code—a process, typology, range, or other. It is during the hand sorting of memos that ideas begin to emerge about the relationships between the core category and related concepts. The analyst begins to sense some sort of overall pattern (or model) that organizes the emerging theory through an appropriate theoretical code (or codes) that explains the relationships, thereby giving the emerging theory its overall shape.

Perhaps You Are Wondering . . .

Can I use extant theories in theoretical coding?

It is important here to differentiate between using the substance of extant theories and using how those theories are modeled. Using the substance of an extant theory may lead the analyst to "borrow" concepts from the extant theory and introduce (i.e., potentially force) them onto the emerging grounded theory. On the other hand, being *theoretically sensitive* to how different extant theories are modeled may help the analyst to see how the emerging grounded theory might be integrated and modeled in a similar way. Playing with this model in relation to the emerging grounded theory is fine. It is only when the

(Continued)

(Continued)

analyst forces the emerging theory to fit a specific theoretical model that the full integrative potential of GT may be compromised.

The researcher who does not reach outside extant theory for theoretical coding possibilities runs the risk of producing adequate but rather mundane conceptual theory. Such theory makes a limited contribution to knowledge and, although certainly preferable to purely conjectured theory, it will lack the impact that the creative emergence of a novel or nontraditional theoretical code may offer. No matter how intellectually seductive, fashionable, or discipline-dictated a theoretical code may be, to cross the line from theoretical exploration to forced integration with a preconceived theoretical model undermines the generative nature of grounded theory (Holton, 2007a, p. 283).

While the emergence of a theoretical code that works to integrate one's theory is often a flash of realization—what Glaser (1978) has termed the "Eureka moment"—developing one's theoretical sensitivity to a wide range of theoretical codes enhances the ability to see their emergent fit to a developing theory. Reading widely opens a researcher to serendipitous discovery of new theoretical codes from other disciplines, offering novel frameworks and models for integrating grounded theories. The essential requirement is that the code must emerge from theoretical sorting of memos; it is not preselected and *forced* on the theory (Glaser, 1992).

Glaser (2005a) advocates reading theory in other substantive areas and disciplines as a means of enhancing one's theoretical sensitivity by building a repertoire of theoretical codes. Reading theory in other fields enhances the theorist's pattern recognition abilities, opening the possibility of serendipitous discovery of new theoretical codes with emergent fit. Glaser (1978, 1998, 2005a) offers many options for theoretically coding a grounded theory. The critical criterion is that the appropriate theoretical code(s) must emerge through sorting of memos; they are not assumed or selected in advance (see, e.g., Walsh et al., 2013, who use translation theory [Callon, 1986; Latour, 1987], a sociological theory, to help make sense of their data and propose the translated strategic alignment model in rupture with existing literature on the subject of strategic alignment in the field of information systems).

Glaser (1978) advocates the implicitness of theoretical coding: "One talks substantively and thinks theoretically of the relationship between codes" (p. 72). In writing the theory, however, theoretical codes may be expressed implicitly or explicitly. For example, Sandgren et al. (2007) refer explicitly to the theoretical code of typology in organizing their theory of *doing good care*, whereas Sandgren et al. (2006) never directly refer to a specific theoretical code in their theory of *striving for emotional survival* but implicitly suggest the theoretical code of strategies. Holton (2007b) describes her grounded theory of *fluctuating support networks* as a basic social structural process with its core category of *rehumanizing* as a basic social psychological process.

Perhaps You Are Wondering . . .

Is grounded theory always a basic social process?

The concept of the basic social process is a generic theoretical construct in sociology explaining fundamental patterns in the organization of social behavior as it occurs over time, involving a change over time with discernible breaking points or points of transition or passage from one stage to another (Glaser, 1978). You will read accounts of GT methodology as requiring identification of basic social processes (Bryant & Lasky, 2007; Starks & Trinidad, 2007), but the basic social process is just one theoretical code that may be appropriate to the theoretical integration of a grounded theory. "All BSPs [basic social processes] are core variables, but not all core variables are BSPs" (Glaser, 1978, p. 96). As one example, the seminal work of Glaser and Strauss (1965a, 1968) employed a typology of awareness contexts and a trajectory of the dying process in hospitalized terminal care.

The emergent nature of theoretical coding is achieved through hand sorting of accumulated theoretical (analytic) memos:

> Facilitating the emergence of relevant theoretical codes requires close attention to the ideas memoed, submersion at the conceptual level, a balance of logic and creativity, openness to the unexpected, and confidence in following what emerges regardless of how counter-rational it may seem to extant theoretical perspectives. (Holton, 2007a, p. 284)

As such, theoretical coding reminds us that *the essential principle of earned relevance in GT is not confined to conceptual emergence but is equally important in theoretical integration through the emergence of relevant theoretical codes.*

Perhaps You Are Wondering . . .

Is axial coding the same as theoretical coding?

While theoretical coding is not mentioned per se in Glaser and Strauss (1967), the coding paradigm of conditions, contexts, actions, interactions, and consequences that underlie Strauss and Corbin's (1990, 1998) axial coding approach is implicit in the *Awareness* study (Glaser & Strauss, 1965a), in which Glaser and Strauss explain how, early on, they "systematically worked out the concepts (and types) of death expectations and awareness contexts, and the paradigm for the study of awareness contexts . . . [and how] . . . a concern with death expectations and awareness guided the preliminary data collection; the systematic formulation of these concepts and of the paradigm guid[ing] further data collection and the ensuing analysis" (p. 287). Strauss (with Corbin) would go on to incorporate the use of this coding paradigm—the conditional matrix—as an essential step in their process, referring to it as axial coding.

Glaser (1978) would extend the scope of theoretical coding to include a wide range of potential models for theory integration by elaborating on 18 different coding families (pp. 74–82) and insisted that the appropriate model(s) must emerge from theoretical sorting. Glaser (1992) challenged Strauss and Corbin's (1990) insistence on the use of axial coding as *forcing* a preconceived theoretical code, undermining the emergent potential of GT and reducing it to conceptual description. Later, he would further elaborate and extend the range of theoretical coding possibilities (Glaser, 2005). To sum up, axial coding relies solely on one theoretical code (paradigm) applied to the data for theoretical integration, whereas classic GT remains open to the emergence (through theoretical sorting) of a wide range of potential theoretical codes around which to integrate and model an emerging grounded theory.

This insistence on the emergence of theoretical codes through hand sorting of memos is a hallmark of classic GT not espoused by those who follow other approaches. For example, Charmaz (2014) advocates theoretical codes for clarifying and sharpening analysis but implies that the basic social process is the theoretical code underlying all grounded theories. While the basic social process is certainly a dominant theoretical code in grounded theories, such preconception effectively precludes the integrative potential for other emergent theoretical codes. At the same time, it is worth noting that Charmaz (2014) appears ambivalent regarding the need for a core category, preferring the more ambiguous notion of "focused coding." This is perhaps consistent with her constructivist stance and its notion of multiple social realities. It is not, however, consistent with classic GT.

Glaser (1998) encourages the grounded theorist to develop a repertoire of as many theoretical codes as possible as a means of offering theories that transcend the somewhat predictable offerings of extant theories. Skill in drawing upon such a repertoire also offers some assurance against slipping into what Glaser (2005) terms *pet* or *grabby* theoretical codes. Here the theorist becomes so enthralled with the discovery of an enticing theoretical code—one with imagery that grabs—that he or she begins to see it everywhere! As with substantive coding, theoretical codes must earn their relevance.

Theoretical Sorting

Hand sorting of memos provides theoretical order and integration of ideas and requires the theorist to theoretically discriminate as to where each idea fits in the emerging theory. The goal is to find the emergent fit of all ideas so that everything fits somewhere with parsimony and scope and with no relevant concepts omitted. The physical act of hand sorting memos further facilitates the preconscious processing of matured ideas and guides the organization and integration of the overall theory. Many researchers use sticky notes to help with their theoretical sorting. Piko (2014) describes how she used sticky notes on a large window to help her visualize the emergent integration of her grounded theory. Over a period of weeks she sorted, compared, and resorted her notes, moving them around on the window and making additional notes until she achieved full integration. Some colleagues provided us with photographs of the theoretical sorting of one of their grounded theories (see Figure 7.1).

Figure 7.1 Theoretical Sorting (Sautrey & Mourmant, 2015. Research in progress)

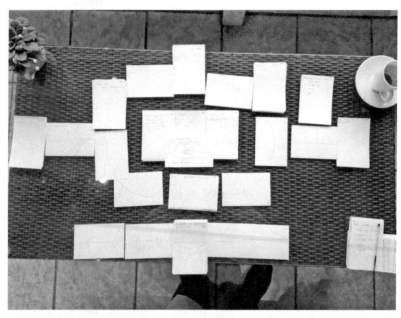

One Student's Experience

To begin, I printed out my memos, sat on the floor, and put them in a pile in front of me.

I placed like with like and grouped together memos with apparent links. As I picked each new memo off the pile, I compared it to the others, asking, "Where does this fit?" and wrote further memos explicating these relationships and theoretical connections. A lot of my memos contained more than one idea relating to different concepts, and so I used scissors to cut them into relevant sections, sometimes into individual paragraphs or even sentences. This increased the amount of paper I had to manage. As I sorted memos, I wrote further memos about the relationships between ideas and integrated these into my sort. By the time my final theory was written, my memo bank had expanded to over 400 memos. Although other researchers have been able to use CAQDAS during this process, I struggled to see how this messy three-dimensional (3D) process could translate onto a two-dimensional (2D) computer screen. As I considered the spread of papers in front of me and shifted the paper about, I was excited by the potential for my ideas to come together in any number of ways. This preliminary sort also enabled me to weed out those immature memos that did not relate significantly to the core category. I retained these in a separate file, meaning that I could go back to retrieve them if their relevance later emerged.

Finally, after 2 months of sorting and trying to find the best theoretical code, I settled on a basic social process (BSP). The BSP is the most common theoretical code in CGT and structures the categories into distinct stages. (For further reading on the BSP, see Glaser & Holton, 2005.) As I tried to write up my theory, however, I became more and more confused. Seeing the lack of integration on paper confirmed my fear that I had been guilty of forcing an inappropriate theoretical code on my data. In my mental fatigue and confusion, I had resorted to settling on a BSP, despite it not having best fit. I knew that I still had a pile of memos that I had not been able to integrate into my chosen structure, but had chosen them because I was fearful that the best theoretical code would never emerge. Buoyed by Glaser's advice that often "wrong tracks lead to right ways," I began sorting again. I explored different theoretical codes by rereading *Theoretical Sensitivity* and *Doing Grounded Theory*. I looked again at the theoretical coding families that I had found too difficult to understand and looked for examples of them in other CGT studies. Interestingly, most of the theories I read were examples

(Continued)

(Continued)

of BSPs, which is perhaps part of the reason behind my subconscious forcing of a BSP onto my data. Glaser has warned against the popularity of the BSP, emphasizing that not all core categories will be a staged process occurring over time. While I had not intended to go looking for a process per se, as a novice researcher, I was perhaps swayed towards the simplicity and 'grab' of a process. Having increased my theoretical sensitivity, I was able to see new possibilities. In particular, Glaser's binary theoretical code resonated with my participants' main concern: being person driven in a service-driven organization. Glaser provided the following definition:

"This coding has to do with compliance to institutional or normal roles—binary retreat; or with non-compliance with role requirements—binary deconstruction. Thus, for example, when a professional meets with a client, to what degree do they interact in their roles—binary retreat; or drop the roles and just be their human selves—binary deconstruction" (Glaser, 2005a, p. 22).

It was exciting to read this definition for the first time, and it sparked an intense period of sorting and a flood of memos as I realized that the binary theoretical code had significant fit and relevance to my data. By prioritizing client realities, practitioners deconstructed service ideals, making service delivery individualized and driven by the person. Conversely, the equilibrium point could be shifted in the opposite direction as practitioners reinstated service ideals over client realities, retreating within their roles and service boundaries. I thus conceptualized *Revisioning* as being dual directional, whereby practitioners made adaptations to their practice in order to go one way or another. (Breckenridge, 2013, pp. 14–15)

Some theorists find that diagramming helps them to visualize potential ways of theoretically modeling their emerging theories. Glaser (2014) quotes one experienced grounded theorist:

I draw figures of the different options of theoretical codes to see how my concepts relate to each other. Some of my drawings may not be so grounded all the time, but it helps me to trigger my creativity so when I go back to my memos and write more memos on memos I see how everything finally fits together. (pp. 16–17)

At the same time, however, Glaser (1998) cautions against using such models as a *short-form* approach to presenting a grounded theory.

He views a diagram as a cop-out, leaving the hard work of elaborating the theory to the reader who may not grasp its rich explanatory power:

> A diagram is but a precursor to a write up of [the theory]. Thus, it is an aide to comprehending the meanings of the written theory. It is not a theory in and of itself . . . The meaning has to be written (p. 169)

As an illustration of this, the diagrams presented in Walsh and colleagues (2013) started to be drawn in 2008. However, it took close to 5 years for the theory to fully emerge and be elaborated in a manner that could be understood by, and useful to, other people. When doing GT, one of the authors of the present book uses diagrams as memos, and these diagrams keep being modified as new data are collected. She finds that they improve her theoretical sensitivity: They help in identifying theoretical codes and the emergence of the theory. This is illustrated in Appendix E.

It is quite possible that in sorting, the theorist may see the possibility of more than one theoretical code that might work to organize the emerging theory. It is the theorist's responsibility to select the code that best fits to integrate the relationship between the core category and related concepts. One theoretical code always dominates, although sub-core relationships may require additional theoretical codes to fully explain the complexity inherent in some grounded theories.

Theoretical Coding

While the core category of a grounded theory is always some type of theoretical code, some theories may require more than one theoretical code for full integration. Holton (2006) illustrates her theory of rehumanizing knowledge as a basic social process with three stages (finding and likening, igniting passions, and mutual engagement) and a number of amplifying causal loops creating the energy that motivates and sustains the rehumanizing process.

Analytic Rules

Glaser (1978) has suggested that failure to hand sort memos results in a thin, linear, and less than fully integrated theory. Sorting also leads to more memo writing as the theorist begins to see and record the relationships among concepts. This helps to further raise the conceptual level of

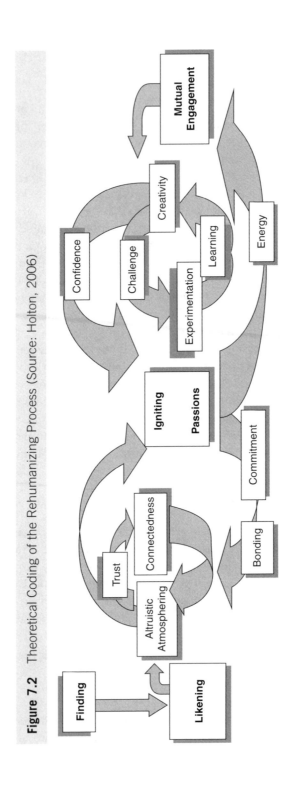

Figure 7.2 Theoretical Coding of the Rehumanizing Process (Source: Holton, 2006)

the theory and reduces the potential for the analyst to slip into description. Glaser (1978) has set out a number of analytic rules regarding the processes of sorting, carrying forward, and integrating a grounded theory. The following is a summary of Glaser's (1978, 2014) analytic rules:

1. Starting to sort—Start anywhere. Sorting will force its own beginning, middle, and end for writing. **The important thing is to start.** Trying conceptually to locate the first memos will force the analyst to start reasoning out the integration. Once started, the analyst soon learns where ideas are likely to integrate best, and sorting becomes generative and fun.

2. Core variable—Sort all other categories and properties **only** as they relate to the core category or BSP. This rule forces focus, selectivity, and delimiting of the analysis. Theoretical coding helps the analyst decide on and figure out the meaning of the relation of a concept to the core variable. **This theoretical code should be written and sorted into the appropriate pile with the substantive code.**

3. Promotion or demotion of core variables—This helps the GT analyst to explain some variation of a problem as it is processed, thus achieving some theoretical coverage. The goal is neither to cover all possible theoretical possibilities nor to explain all variation.

4. Memoing—Once sorting on the core variable begins, the constant comparisons are likely to generate many new ideas, especially on theoretical codes for integrating the theory. Stop sorting and start memoing! Then, sort the memos into the integration.

5. Carry forward—Analyst carries forward to subsequent sorts (pages when writing) the use of each concept from the point of its introduction into the theory. Requires only the use of the concept, not all illustration. The concept is illustrated only when it is first introduced (to develop the imagery of its meaning).

6. Integrative fit—All ideas must fit in somewhere in the outline, or the integration must be changed or modified. This rule is essential—if the analyst ignores this step, he will break out of the theory too soon, and necessary ideas and relations will not be used. This rule is based on the assumption that the social world is integrated and the job of the grounded theorist is to discover it. If he cannot find the integration, he must resort and

reintegrate his concepts to fit better. The analyst moves back and forth between outline and ideas as he sorts, forcing underlying patterns, integrations, and multivariate relations between the concepts. This step is intensely generative, yielding many theoretical coding memos to be resorted into the outline.

7. Sorting levels—Conceptual ordering of sorting is on at least two levels, for example, the core category, then subcore categories and conceptual properties or dimensions. Or, for a monograph or a book, the ordering would be chapters and then sections in each chapter.

8. Idea problems—Sorting forces the analyst to introduce an idea in one place and then establish its carry forward when it is necessary to use it again in other relations. When in doubt about a place to sort an idea, put it in that part of the outline where the first possibility of its use occurs, with a note to scrutinize it and pass it forward to the next possible place.

9. Cutting off rules—Theoretical completeness implies theoretical coverage as far as the study can take the analyst. He must explain with the fewest possible concepts and with the greatest possible scope as much variation as possible in the behavior and problem under study, sufficiently explaining the main concern and its resolution with concepts that fit, work, have relevance, and are saturated.

10. Mechanics of sorting—Cut up memos to facilitate ease of sorting ideas. Keep notes as you are sorting, and sketch out models of potential theoretical codes for theory integration. Stop sorting to memo. Even before intentional sorting begins, keep files for memos arranged for some initial integration. Move quickly when sorting. Avoid overthinking about any one sort as the *sort* will change over time as the appropriate theoretical coding emerges.

11. Theoretical pacing—Have a flexible but regular schedule with periods of uninterrupted sorting through memos to help in balancing the buildup of ideas preconsciously with the writing of memos that capture preconscious processing. At the theoretical coding stage, the sorting and emergence of ideas is at a deeper level as the theorist begins to see the emerging theory as an integrative whole. (Glaser, 1978, pp. 120–127; 2014, pp. 108–122)

Table 7.1 summarizes our discussion of theoretical sampling, theoretical saturation, and theoretical coding as essential techniques for shaping the overall elaboration and integration of a grounded theory.

One very effective way to *test* the integration and overall shape of a grounded theory is to draft a working paper. Start with a very brief explanation of the context and the main concern and how the core category works to process, manage, or resolve that issue or concern. Hand sorting of memos leads to seeing how best to conceptually organize this initial write-up and assists in writing the theory both conceptually and parsimoniously without reverting to detailed description.

Table 7.1   Techniques for Shaping a Grounded Theory

Theoretical sampling	Theory-driven process of data collection based on further developing the emerging theory
	Pursuing different slices of data for theoretical elaboration
	Iterative process of cycling between existing data and collecting new data as required to pursue and develop emerging ideas
Theoretical saturation	*Intense* conceptual property and dimension elaboration
	Constant comparison of conceptual indicators until additional comparisons yield no further theoretical specification or elaboration
	Saturation bounded by empirical limits of the data, integration, and density of the theory and researcher's theoretical sensitivity
Theoretical coding	Emergent latent pattern recognition
	Core category of a grounded theory is always some type of theoretical code (e.g., process, range, continuum, typology, etc.)
	Conceptualizes how substantive concepts may relate to each other as hypotheses
	Overall integration of the emergent theory using processes, frameworks, models, etc.
	Earned relevance (i.e., modeling is emergent through hand sorting of conceptual memos)
	Often more than one theoretical code needed

IN SUMMARY

In this chapter, we have explored the role of theoretical sampling, theoretical saturation, and theoretical coding in shaping an emerging grounded theory. We have discussed the techniques of theoretical sampling and theoretical saturation to build emergent concepts and categories and the importance of hand sorting of memos for emergent integration of the final theory through theoretical coding. We take up the issues regarding writing grounded theory in Chapters 8 and 9.

TEST YOUR KNOWLEDGE

In the following questions one or several answers may be correct.

1. Theoretical sampling
    a. Is the sampling of different existing theories or theoretical framework
    b. Is deciding what data to collect next based on the theory that is emerging from already collected data
    c. Is the sampling of only one type of data
    d. May include any type of data
    e. None of the above

2. Theoretical saturation
    a. Refers to intense development of conceptual properties
    b. Is the comparison of extant theories to an emergent grounded theory
    c. Continues until no new properties or dimensions of concepts emerge from additional data
    d. Is achieved through theoretically sampling diverse comparison groups and data
    e. None of the above

3. Theoretical coding
    a. Is done when the grounded theory has emerged
    b. Is done to help a core category emerge from the data
    c. Is done after theoretical sampling has helped with saturating the core category
    d. None of the above

4. Memo writing
    a. Helps record the relationships among concepts
    b. Helps raise the conceptual level of the theory

    c. Helps avoid falling into simple description

    d. None of the above

5. Theoretical sorting

    a. Is the process of sorting conceptual memos

    b. Is in aid of discovering relationships between the core category and related concepts

    c. Can be done by hand or by computer

    d. Can be a tedious process requiring several attempts at resorting of memos

    e. Draws on the researcher's creativity and theoretical sensitivity

    f. None of the above

6. Analytic rules

    a. Help to raise the conceptual level of a grounded theory

    b. Guide the process of theoretical sorting

    c. Foster integrative fit of the emerging theory

    d. Provide a step-by-step guide to doing classic GT

    e. None of the above

FURTHER READING

Gibson, B., & Hartman, J. (2014). Rediscovering skills for theoretical sampling. In *Rediscovering grounded theory* (Chapter 7). London: Sage.

Glaser, B. G. (1978). Analytic rules. In *Theoretical sensitivity: Advances in the methodology of grounded theory* (pp. 120–127). Mill Valley, CA: Sociology Press.

Glaser, B. G. (1978). Theoretical coding. In *Theoretical sensitivity: Advances in the methodology of grounded theory* (pp. 72–82). Mill Valley, CA: Sociology Press.

Glaser, B. G. (1978). Theoretical sampling. In *Theoretical sensitivity: Advances in the methodology of grounded theory* (Chapter 3). Mill Valley, CA: Sociology Press.

Glaser, B. G. (2005). *The grounded theory perspective III: Theoretical coding.* Mill Valley, CA: Sociology Press.

Glaser, B. G. (2014). Analytic rules. In *Memoing: A vital grounded theory procedure* (pp. 108–122). Mill Valley, CA: Sociology Press.

Glaser, B. G., & Strauss, A. L. (1967). Theoretical sampling. In *The discovery of grounded theory: Strategies for qualitative research* (Chapter 3). New York: Aldine de Gruyter.

ENDNOTE

1. E-mail correspondence with Barney Glaser, March 9, 2007.

8

Writing as an Important Part of Doing Classic GT

After studying this chapter, you will:

- *understand why and how writing is, in itself, an essential part of the classic GT methodological protocol*
- *appreciate and recognize readiness to sort and write moments*
- *understand possible barriers that can block your writing and be aware of some solutions to remove these barriers*

We saw in a previous chapter the iterative nature of data analysis toward the emergence of a grounded theory. Writing in GT is part of this iterative process and begins with the first data collected, as you start writing memos to help the analysis and conceptualization. Memoing was covered in Chapter 6. In this chapter, we are concerned with writing up the components of your emerging theory and how they are integrated together. When doing GT, writing and thinking are embedded and intertwined: "Writing is the practical expression of thinking . . . writing is a fundamental act of enquiry as valuable, if not more so, as generating or collecting, reading and coding data" (Birks & Mills, 2012, p. 126).

Charmaz (2014) describes writing and rewriting GT as part of the discovery process:

You'll gain further insights and create more ideas about your data while you're writing. You'll see clearer connections between categories and draw implications from them. Thus writing and rewriting become crucial phases of the analytic process. Writing demands more than mere reporting. Through writing and rewriting drafts, you can bring out implicit arguments, provide their context, make links with extant literatures, critically examine categories, present your analysis, and provide data that support your analytic arguments. Each successive draft grows more theoretical and comprehensive. (p. 289)

THE PROCESS LEADING TO ●
THE *READINESS TO WRITE* MOMENT

Writing in itself is considered by some researchers as a method of inquiry (Richardson, 2000). This perspective is particularly well suited to a GT approach as writing up is part of classic GT. Writing is not something to do after the research has been completed. "The write-up is a vital part of the method . . . Its timing is sequential, its doing not optional" (Glaser, 2012, p. 12) because it helps conceptualization: "Writing and thinking are inextricably intertwined in the construction of a grounded theory" (Birks & Mills, 2012, p. 130).

After data have been collected and constantly analyzed, concepts have been generated, and memos have been written, the grounded theorist often reaches a state of ideational overload. At this stage, researchers are often facing a huge pile of memos, signaling a **readiness to sort** memos. As discussed in Chapter 7, the physical act of hand sorting memos helps the researcher preconsciously process this overload, thereby guiding the organization and integration of the emerging theory.

Once the core category of your grounded theory has emerged, memo writing accelerates as theoretical sampling progresses to elaborate the core and related concepts and initial efforts are undertaken to theoretically sort memos for emergent patterns (theoretical coding). When theoretical completeness appears to be achieved, memos are again sorted, leading to a "readiness to write" (Glaser, 2012, p. 4) moment that will prompt the researcher to write the first draft of the theory. The **readiness to write** moment is built into classic GT and should not be bypassed; if it is bypassed, it may be definitively lost. It is an essential moment to allow the relationship between the researcher and her data to evolve (Glaser, 1978).

Glaser (2012) describes in great detail memo sorting as a crucial episode in the classic GT research process. To sort memos, researchers should pick up any memo, anywhere in the pile, and place it on a table, on the floor, or anywhere big enough to accommodate a large number of small pieces of paper (Figures 8.1 and 8.2). They then pick up another memo and compare it to the first one; they either place it on, or next to, the first one or place it in a new pile while writing another short memo about how this memo relates to the first one.

This new memo is then placed between the two piles (perhaps suggesting a potential theoretical code). This process continues until all initial memos are sorted into different piles with new memos linking all piles. Then the researcher writes the theory that he sees unfolding from his data on the table. If there are any gaps or clarifications needed, the researcher goes back to the field to theoretically sample. Once sorting is completed, the memos are merged and integrated into a readable text with good flow. Thus, there is no preconceived outline when you write as part of the classic GT process.

The process leading to the *readiness to write* moment is summarized in Figure 8.3.

When sorting memos, the researcher does not put a memo down idly. If it does not fit somewhere, it is put aside in a "left out" pile as nonfitting or nonrelevant; usually this pile is small. If a memo can fit in several places, it should be placed where it fits best to help the write-up of the

Figure 8.1 Theoretical/Memo Sorting on a Table (Source: Walsh, 2014a)

Figure 8.2   Sorting Memos on the Floor (Source: Sautrey & Mourmant, 2015. Research in progress)

emergent theory. Sorting helps generate the theory and writing it up. When sorting memos, Glaser (1998, 2005a) advocates talking and writing substantively but thinking theoretically. The idea here is that the researcher stays close enough to the substantive area to ensure that the emergent theory remains relevant to those in the substantive area and that in organizing and writing up the theory, it does not become so conceptually abstract that it no longer works to explain the main concern and its resolution. On the other hand, the researcher must resist the temptation to fall into copious description that inevitably bogs down the theory, holding it hostage to one specific setting (i.e., specific people, time, and place), and stealing the explanatory power of its broader general implications.

Figure 8.3 The Process Leading to the *Readiness to Write* Moment

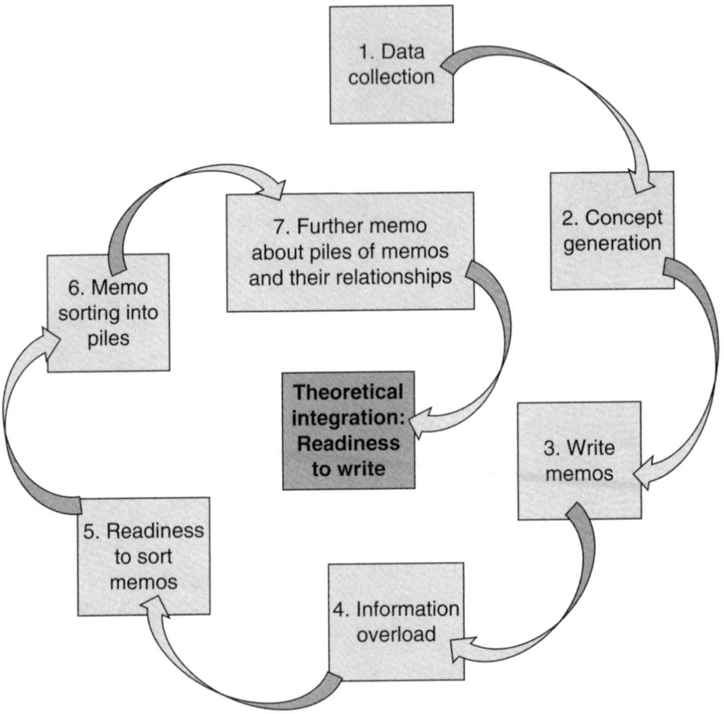

- ## APPROACHING THE LITERATURE IN A GT STUDY

Once the researcher has completed analysis of empirical data, and after the core category has emerged, he can turn to the literature of his relevant field as more data to be constantly compared in elaborating and saturating emergent concepts, developing further their properties and dimensions (for an illustration, see Appendix C). Glaser (1978) describes the literature as a "prominent class of outside comparisons" (p. 51). Of course, in doing so, the researcher must determine whether the literature is empirically grounded. Even "conjectured" theory can yield interesting ideas, but its *groundedness* will need to be empirically confirmed through further theoretical sampling to merit a place in the final write-up of a grounded theory. Another approach to addressing the literature is to compare it with your emergent theory, discovering and considering what aligns, what modifies, and what challenges extant theory. In so doing, the researcher begins to identify how the emergent grounded theory supports, extends, corrects, and contributes to extant knowledge. As we saw in a previous chapter, the literature from other fields of research may also be used to help make sense of collected data, build new theory, and, more generally, write a compelling account of the emerging theory.

WRITING GT WITH MIXED QUANTITATIVE AND QUALITATIVE DATA

Writing as part of the GT process is particularly delicate and essential when you use mixed quantitative and qualitative data. A researcher may use quantitative and qualitative data and analyze them as one set in an exploratory GT stance with the help of those quantitative and/or qualitative techniques that the researcher thinks will best serve the purpose of her research (e.g., Schall, 1983; Walsh, 2014a). In some instances, neither qualitative nor quantitative data/methods are sufficient to fully develop your theory; rather, all are necessary (Figure 8.4). The different quantitative and qualitative data, methods, and techniques are mixed and supplement each other within a single project. For instance, and as highlighted in Walsh (2014c), the researcher may need to qualify quantitative data (e.g., make sense of the results of the factor analysis of quantitative data with the help of collected qualitative data) or quantify qualitative data as a compromise between numerical precision and narrative complexity (Sandelowski et al., 2009).

Figure 8.4   Using Mixed Data to Write a Grounded Theory

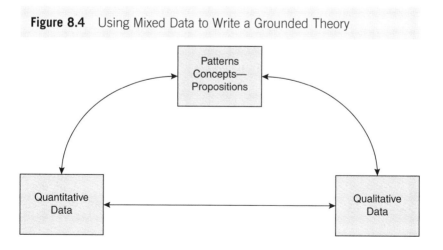

When using mixed data, it is even more essential to write the emerging grounded theory as it unfolds, when data becomes daunting and memo sorting becomes compelling, so as not miss the *readiness to write* moment. Attempting to later capture back elements that were bypassed and not written will be extremely difficult because of the embeddedness of the qualitative and quantitative analyses.

The Consequences of Bypassing the Readiness to Write Moment: Testimony by Isabelle Walsh on How the Publication of Walsh (2014a; see Appendix C) Was Unnecessarily Delayed

The grounded theory proposed in Walsh (2014a) had to be written and rewritten a number of times because the *readiness to write* moment was bypassed. Even though, when sorting the various memos, I felt compelled to write what was emerging from my data, I just did not know how to write what I saw in my data: at the time, there were very few examples of mixed GT studies.

When I first wrote this mixed GT study (and submitted it to a top-tier information systems journal), I first presented all quantitative results, then all qualitative results, then attempted to integrate them all. But this was not how the theory had emerged. I was very lucky to have reviewers who were very patient and very open to grounded theory. They made me go back to my data and account faithfully to what had emerged, when and how. Not all reviewers are as patient and open as these reviewers were. Guided by the reviewers' queries and criticisms, I had to work very hard to recapture the true emergence of the theory.

Eventually, I found that the easiest way to write mixed GT was *not* to try and isolate quantitative and qualitative data/results that were embedded. Instead, I found that it was best to relate my stories as they unfolded, as impossible as it may appear at first. If quantitative and qualitative data/results were embedded, then I wrote "as was." However, I wrote *quantitatively*, that is, with acronyms for variables/categories/concepts and numbers, when I used quantitative data, and I wrote *qualitatively*, with fully developed names for variables/categories/concepts and verbatim, when I used qualitative data. What I wrote was then easy for me, the reviewers, and (I hope) the readers to read, follow, and understand. However, the whole process took me years and some very indulgent and patient reviewers (I have not always been that lucky! Other reviewers might have rejected my work during the first round), whereas, if I had done the writing as the theory emerged and when the *readiness to write* moment was at hand, the whole process would have been easier, less risky, and much faster.

THE FIRST DRAFT ●

Writing as part of the GT process must be done as simply as possible to highlight patterns as they emerge and to help move toward conceptualization and increased abstraction. Once the memos are theoretically sorted, the researcher is usually eager to write up the theory that he *sees* in the data to produce a first rough draft of his conceptual ideas. This first draft, or working paper, is "a 'write up' of piles of ideas [the piles of memos] from theoretical sorting" (Glaser, 1978, p. 128). It is "writing concept to concept relations integrated into a conceptual theory" (Glaser, 2012, p. 111) and certainly not like writing fiction. Perfection in terms of style, grammar, and spelling is not required for this first draft, which is not written to please a supervisor, a committee, an editor, or reviewers. The purpose of this first draft is only to put the theory on paper. In turn, this first draft becomes a memo in itself.

In writing up your GT, it is important to stay on a conceptual level. One very effective way to do this is to write in the present tense; that is, talk about your theory as if it is going on *now*, for it surely is . . . somewhere! Writing in the past tense (as research *findings*) tends to drift into description, producing an *account* of what happened during data collection rather than a conceptual explanation of the discovered latent pattern of social behavior. Employing "illustration dosage" (Glaser, 1998, pp. 198–199) by adding brief data excerpts to illustrate key concepts helps control conceptual density, improving readability as well as enhancing understanding. Too many lengthy quotes, however, can bog down your theory, interrupting the conceptual flow and making it difficult to read.

As part of an academic process, first drafts may eventually be submitted to international conferences in order to present one's ideas within one's research field. Even though Glaser often advises not to voice one's ideas and not to present them for other people's judgment until the theory has fully emerged, it may be useful and important for young scholars in search of legitimacy to offer a working paper for peers' judgment. In our experience, the peer review process mostly helps strengthen results and identify weaknesses as long as the researcher takes the comments as provisional and stays true to what is in the data. When reviews are positive, they provide great encouragement to complete a research project, which might otherwise have been put aside.

Another Type of Memoing

One of the authors of this book regularly submits her first drafts to international conferences. She also encourages her doctoral students to do the same.

For instance, the grounded theory of "IT culture creep" was published in 2010 (Walsh et al., 2010). However, the first draft was published in 2008 at the Americas Conference in Information Systems (Walsh & Kefi, 2008). Comments from peers obtained during the conference helped finalize the theory of IT culture creep and eventually publish it in a top tier research outlet.

Another example is the grounded theory of the "translated strategic alignment model" that was published in a top tier research outlet in 2013 (Walsh et al., 2013). The first draft of this theory was published in 2010 at the Americas Conference in Information Systems (Walsh et al., 2010), before categories were fully saturated.

These publications at international conferences may be considered as a type of memoing and will eventually help the final write-up of your theory.

Proposing first or intermediate drafts of their grounded theories to international conferences for peers' perusal and informed comments will help prepare researchers for what we consider scholars' ultimate purpose: writing toward publishing in a recognized and well-ranked research journal of their field. This issue is addressed at length in the next chapter.

● WRITING BLOCKS

Writing as part of the GT process may be impeded in many ways for many reasons, and in some extreme cases, blocked. In his 2012 monograph about the act of writing grounded theory, Glaser investigates in depth the different elements that may block writing. These writing blocks may be personal. For instance, the researcher may suffer from performance anxiety, lack of experience, poor reading ability that induces a lack of knowledge of existing literature, or an inability to see patterns and conceptualize. Writing may also be blocked by methodological issues. For instance, conflicts between GT and other approaches researchers might wish to use in combination. Finally, writing blocks may be induced by circumstances that are contextual or external to the researcher. For instance, supervisors, committee members, or universities may hinder writing through insisting on some prescribed writing formats. Difficult life circumstances (health, family) may also hinder writing.

Personal Blocks

Some examples of personal blocks are provided in Figure 8.5 and discussed in this section. The fear of writing needs to be acknowledged as legitimate for most inexperienced researchers; it will usually diminish with time and practice. It is mostly linked to performance anxiety, more especially when a researcher lacks confidence, has no writing experience of any sort, or when the format prescribed to the researcher (e.g., by his supervisor) is too constraining.

Novice grounded theorists may be overwhelmed by their data, which could feed not one theory but multiple theories, leading to *perpetual outgrowing* (Glaser, 2012, p. 112). This can be worsened when researchers "fall in love" with their data and search for perfection or when too many redundant descriptive elements are blurring the overall theory. If writing is done as memos are sorted, then perpetual outgrowing can be minimized. It will also probably help alleviate what

Figure 8.5   Overcoming Some Personal Writing Blocks

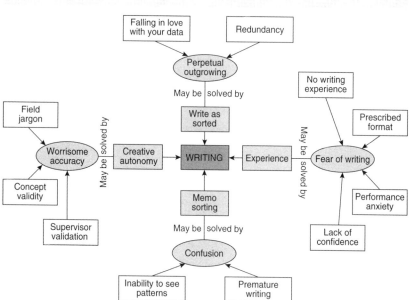

we named "postpartum blues" (!) when one doctoral student, whom one author of this book helped supervise, seemed to fall into depression once her dissertation document had been submitted to her committee. If parting with your theory is done a little at a time, the final break will be less difficult to accept.

What Glaser (2012) names "worrisome accuracy" (p. 119) is another possible writing block induced by superfluous descriptive details, the need to conform to field jargon, or the desire to obtain a supervisor's validation. Fighting for and obtaining creative autonomy will solve this issue. Even though writing is an intrinsic part of classic GT, attempting to write up one's theory before memos are sorted into piles will lead to confusion and may well tempt the researcher into preconceiving the theory. It has to be remembered that writing as part of the GT process is a "write-up of sorted memos" (Glaser, 2012, p. 120) as they provide conceptual meaning and will help fight confusion.

Methodological Blocks

Sometimes, writing may be hindered by some methodological blocks. For example, the researcher may feel compelled to use some methods or techniques that violate GT principles. These methods or techniques have then to be revised and adapted. We have found that any methodological blocks may be addressed by going back to the seminal texts, Glaser and Strauss (1967) and Glaser (1978), and keeping clearly in mind GT's main foundational pillars as highlighted in Chapter 3: *emergence, theoretical sampling,* and *constant comparative analysis.* We have found that if this is done, while remaining in an exploratory stance that is an essential aspect of a GT approach, GT methodological protocol may be applied with any data, collected through a variety of methods, and analyzed with the help of many data analysis techniques. In using quantitative data in particular, we have found that many methods and techniques may be adapted to fit GT's main foundational pillars (see boxed text).

Using Quantitative Techniques in a GT Stance

Factor analysis of quantitative data may be used in an exploratory fashion. Its purpose is "to examine the underlying patterns or relationships for a large number of variables and to determine whether the information can be condensed or summarized in a smaller set of factors or components"

(Hair, Black, Babin, Anderson, & Tatham, 2006, p. 101). This quantitative technique may help with the selective and theoretical coding of quantitative data by sorting the data "into the appropriate pile" (Glaser, 2004, p. 19[1]). When applying this technique with the help of some software, make sure not to inform the software with the number of factors you might expect (based on previous qualitative phases and results); rather, let the slices of quantitative data inform the emerging number of factors.

Cluster analysis is another statistical technique that we have found useful when doing GT with quantitative data. It is a statistical data analytic method viewed mainly as an exploratory technique (Hair & Black, 1998) and whose main purpose is "to group objects based on the characteristics they possess" (Hair, Anderson, Tatham, & Black, 1995, p. 423). High within-cluster homogeneity and between-cluster heterogeneity is the aim. Cluster analysis is very close to the GT comparative method. It searches for nonobvious patterns and relationships between important sets of data. However, the way one uses cluster analysis (or any other multidimensional scaling instrument) will, of course, determine whether theory is allowed to emerge from the data or whether theory is forced upon those data.

Even techniques like structural equation modeling, traditionally considered as a confirmatory technique, may be adapted to fit a GT stance. For instance, when using mixed qualitative and quantitative data, you may choose partial least squares (PLS) path modeling to investigate the quantitative data. This approach is generally viewed more as an exploratory, soft modeling approach than as a confirmatory one (Gefen, Rigdon, & Straub, 2011; Hair, Sarstedt, Ringle, & Mena, 2012; Ringle, Sarstedt, & Straub, 2012; Vinzi, Trinchera, & Amato, 2010). All possible paths between the various constructs under scrutiny may be investigated before deciding which paths are the most probable when considering quantitative and qualitative data together as one set.

External/Contextual Blocks

Context may also hinder writing. This is when the "outside world" imposes unwarranted constraining demands on the researcher. Every researcher will have her own ideal *physical* writing preferences, for example, being completely isolated from anybody else, listening to music while writing, and so on. However, researchers will often have to deal with nonideal contextual situations imposed by family life obligations or the demands of a dissertation supervisor, for example, the requirement to review the literature ex ante, which goes against classic GT's main pillars or meeting impossible deadlines. This will create a block that can be alleviated (as proposed by Lowe, cited by Glaser, 2012) by engaging momentarily in other, purely menial, tasks and then eventually coming back to the problematic contextual issue after having taken time to ponder over it.

The most serious external or contextual writing block may sometimes stem from your PhD supervisor or your dissertation committee who may not be experienced grounded theorists and may try to impose their own pet approaches, which may violate some of GT's foundational pillars. Beyond all precious advice that one may find in various publications (see, e.g., Glaser, 2012), we have found that the best way to get around possible issues with supervisors or committee members is to have your work recognized by your peers, through publication in top tier international conferences and/or peer reviewed journals before you present your finished work to them. Writing for publication is addressed in the next chapter.

IN SUMMARY

Writing in itself is an intrinsic part of GT. If ideational overload is overlooked and the *readiness to write* moment is bypassed, the completion of your work will be delayed. Some personal and contextual blocks to writing may be overcome through memo sorting and simply writing things as they emerge and as you see them through collected data, on the way to building up your creative autonomy and developing your GT writing experience.

TEST YOUR KNOWLEDGE

In the following questions one or several answers may be correct.

1. When doing GT
   a. You have to write memos all the time as you analyze your data and ideas emerge
   b. You have to write your memos properly so that anybody can understand them
   c. You have to wait to be ready to write your theory before you start memoing
   d. None of the above

2. When you are overtaken by information/ideational overload, you should
   a. Stop doing GT
   b. Change your codes
   c. Start memo sorting
   d. None of the above

3. The *readiness to write* moment
   a. Comes after memo sorting
   b. Is when you are ready to write a first draft of some theoretical statement
   c. May be bypassed
   d. None of the above

4. Drafts of your theory
   a. Must include the relationships between concepts that emerged from your data
   b. Involve writing up the memos that you have sorted into piles
   c. Eventually become memos until another, more densified, theory emerges
   d. None of the above

FURTHER READING

Glaser, B. G. (1978). *Theoretical sensitivity: Advances in the methodology of grounded theory* (Chapter 5). Mill Valley, CA: Sociology Press.

Glaser, B. G. (2012). *Stop, write: Writing grounded theory*. Mill Valley, CA: Sociology Press.

Schall, M. (1983). A communication-rules approach to organizational culture. *Administrative Science Quarterly*, 28(4), 557–581.

Walsh, I. (2014). A strategic path to study IT use through users' IT culture and IT needs: A mixed-method grounded theory. *Journal of Strategic Information Systems*, 23, 145–173.

ENDNOTE

1. All articles in FQS are licensed under a Creative Commons Attribution 4.0 International License. Authors hold the copyright and retain publishing rights without restrictions.

9

Writing Classic GT for Publication

After studying this chapter, you will:

- *understand that you can rarely publish a grounded theory as it actually emerged from your data*
- *accept reviewers' opinions and address their concerns even though you might not always agree with them*
- *have some general guidelines to help you get your work read, accepted, and published*

Whether or not you have read the previous chapters, having arrived at this stage of the book probably means that you are convinced that using GT as a research paradigm, a methodology, or an analysis framework is important and significant for your research. However, writing as part of the classic GT process, that is, of "doing" GT, and writing classic grounded theory for an audience, to share and disseminate your ideas, are two rather different processes.

• DOING VERSUS WRITING

Writing—the way we write—matters "theoretically and practically. . . . How should we write our research? *Who* is our audience? . . . What are our goals? . . . What readers will we write for? . . . How should we write so that our writing matters?" (Richardson, 1990, p. 9). These questions highlight many implicit issues, which can be broadly classified as rhetorical, ethical, and methodological.

Rhetorical Issues: The Way We Write

The first issue with writing grounded theory for an audience is the fact that no written words can fully describe the iterative GT process, the incessant iterations between data and conceptualization, or the final conceptual leap that illuminates a grounded theory. If one attempts to describe fully in writing, and in truth, the way their GT research was conducted, it is most probable that few people would read or understand it. When you write a classic grounded theory, it is therefore essential to give sufficient information to guarantee the reader that all classic GT guidelines have been followed, but, at the same time, you must also organize your work in a way that respects the conventions of the intended audience.

There are many different ways to write and account for your research depending on your chosen outlet. When you write your dissertation, you have to first please your thesis supervisor, then your committee members and external examiners. When you write an article to be published in an academic outlet, you have to please the reviewers and the associate and senior editors. When you write a monograph, you mostly please yourself. Finally, when you write a methodological book like this book, your purpose will be fulfilled if your readers find it easier to apply the method(s) you describe after reading your book.

Writing options and writing outlets are numerous. Even though Lyytinen, Baskerville, Iivari, and Te'eni (2007) have pointed to differences in publication culture whereby European scholars have tended in past years to favor book publications, most academics are currently hired, promoted, and tenured on the basis of publications in so-called top-tier journals. As academics, we depend essentially on promotion and tenure committees and on other committees or public bodies that allocate resources to academic units and individual researchers. These various committees will judge your work based mostly on your publications in top tier journals (Takeda, 2011).

Furthermore, if, while doing your PhD, you publish your classic grounded theory in a top-tier journal, or (as revision processes of such journals are very lengthy) you at least avoid the dreaded "desk reject" at the outset and engage your work in the revision process of such a journal, it is unlikely that your thesis supervisor will object or question the use of GT or the way you write your research, whatever way you wish to do so. When you are a young researcher, your peers' positive judgment is a very convincing argument that is difficult to contradict, even by an established professor. Therefore, we will concentrate in this chapter on the type of writing required to publish in those so-called top-tier outlets.

Different journals emphasize different topics, methodologies, or both. To find out about a journal's preferences, you can investigate their mission statement and submission guidelines, which are available on journal websites. To publish in any research journal, your work has to be presented in a way that meets the writing conventions of that journal and the respective editors' and reviewers' expectations. Therefore, you have to find ways to reconcile these conventions with classic GT precepts.

If you choose to publish in a research journal (rather than, for instance, in a monograph or a book), another issue that you face when writing classic grounded theory is that journal articles "have become increasingly narrow in scope and focused on a little bit of knowledge— as if knowledge 'really' were a bin of bits" (Richardson, 1990 p. 16) and were only progressing incrementally. However, if you have successfully applied classic GT, you should have produced a theory that has the potential to be *in rupture* with existing literature, hence difficult to reduce to incremental progress and a single journal article. One way to counteract this drawback is to rationalize, as much as possible, the way you write and fit in, as much as possible, the prescribed formats, with established rhetorical devices that may be found in most social sciences (de Vaujany, Walsh, & Mitev, 2011).

Different Writing Formats

The editor in chief of a top-tier research journal, whom we know well, once confirmed to us that research articles are traditionally more suitable for incremental discoveries. This came up when, new to the game of publishing, one of the authors of this book asked for his advice on publishing a conceptual piece of work that would create some upheavals if published. The editor in chief had read and liked this piece of work. He strongly advised us to publish it as a book because the intellectual leap that it proposed was too broad to fit in a research article and would involve a length of manuscript that would be difficult to adhere to any research journal's writing conventions. As we did not wish to go through the book format, the original article was divided into several articles, to which we added empirical data. The original piece of work thus "gave birth" to a number of journal articles, most of which have now been published.

Finally, and as highlighted by Fetters and Freshwater (2015), when aiming to publish, "effective authors compose their articles for the understanding of the reader, and not their own egos" or seeking "to impress others" (p. 204). These authors propose that we consider every word and sentence we write and ask ourselves the following questions: "Will this make sense for the reader? Will this help the reader understand what I want to convey?" (p. 204).

Ethical Issues: Adjusting Your Work to Fit Established Conventions

Academic papers are encoded with academic conventions (e.g., the main current paradigmatic positions of the research field covered by a given journal) and writing conventions (e.g., length, focus, methodological stance) fitting traditional standards that readers expect will be met (Richardson, 1990). To help you identify these conventions and verify that they are compatible with whom you are and with your work, Richardson (2000) implicitly provided some valuable guidelines even though prescription was certainly not her purpose as she was solely aiming to identify different writing formats in qualitative research. However, using some of her ideas out of context helped us to highlight some interesting propositions that can be applied while writing classic grounded theory geared toward publication in a top-tier outlet.

We would propose for you to choose an article published in a top tier outlet of your own field, an outlet where you would like to publish. Choose an article that is fairly recent (published during the past 3 years) because cyclic changes in editorial boards may change some of the applied writing conventions (de Vaujany et al., 2011). As the chosen article has been published in the chosen outlet, it exemplifies in some ways this outlet's writing conventions and will guide you toward framing your work within these conventions. This article should be one that you admire, one that you believe makes important contributions to the field, and one whose philosophical assumptions are globally *in tune with yours.*

Provided reviewers do not subsequently ask you to forfeit some of your own philosophical assumptions, you then might be able to fit your work within the conventions of the given journal. That being said, and whatever the writing conventions and philosophical assumptions of the editorial board of a journal, our experience is that if your work is considered innovative and important for your field, and if your writing is clear enough to allow the reader to understand your contribution, you will eventually be published in a top-tier journal—perhaps not in the journal that you originally aimed for (you may have to investigate other top-tier journals with broader-minded editors in chief), but you *will* be published.

Learning From Experience

It took me many years to be able to publish my first GT article in a top tier journal. Before I actually succeeded in publishing it, I had to submit it twice. After the initial submission in the first journal, I was asked to review and resubmit while removing the methodological GT approach as well as the core category of my grounded theory! Although there was no doubt that my work was not convincing enough and that other elements of these initial reviews helped me improve it, I did not review and resubmit to the same journal. I felt that, if I did so, I would be lying about my research and that I would somehow forfeit my identity as a researcher. Instead, I improved my work based on some other elements of the initial reviews that I felt highlighted some serious flaws in my work, but I submitted to another journal, which incidentally was higher ranked and globally considered as "better" than the first one. Interestingly, during the reviewing process of this second submission, and after I had addressed all revisions required by the reviewers, the associate editor advised me, for the last round of review, to bring in a coauthor who could guide me to write within the conventions of the journal. This did not jeopardize my philosophical assumptions, nor did it entail disguising my research. It only meant that my writing format was not the right format for the chosen outlet. I brought in an experienced coauthor who helped me understand the associate editor's and the journal's writing expectations, and the article was eventually published.

—Isabelle Walsh

Methodological Issues: Writing to Be Read and Published

Even though doing GT is never a linear process, the writing format of GT is rarely otherwise if one wishes to be read, easily understood, and published in a top-tier journal. As hypothetical-deductive research has left an enduring imprint in most of the so-called top tier outlets, and although sections found in published empirical articles are sometimes named differently and sometimes merged, the basic standard and expected structure of a journal article that relates empirical research is, globally, fairly linear and includes six sections. Each of these sections as outlined in the following box aims to answer particular questions.

The Standard and Expected Structure of a Journal Article and Questions to Be Answered

1. Introduction

- Why should the reader bother to read your article? (What is the issue you are investigating or addressing? Why is it important?)
- What are the major contributions of your work?
- How is your work organized?

2. Literature Review

- What does the literature tell us about the object of your research?
- What is the gap that is being addressed?

3. Methodology

- What are the data, data collection methods, and data analysis techniques used in your research?

4. Results

- What have you found?

5. Discussion

- How do your findings fit in with existing literature?
- What are the limitations and contributions of your work?

6. Conclusion

- How has the research issue, highlighted in the introduction, been addressed?

On one hand, this expected structure, in itself, may raise a number of issues in relation to a classic GT stance. On the other hand, it need not raise any issues if we keep in mind that *doing research* and *writing to publish* are different processes, even though they are linked, and writing research should reflect, at least in some manner and to some extent, the way the research has been conducted.

When you do classic GT, you basically start with a general area of interest and methodological guidelines that you will apply in congruence with your philosophical positioning, but you do not even know which data are going to be collected or how you are going to collect them. You start by listening and observing in the field. It is only after you have identified the main concern and after a core category has emerged to explain this main concern that you turn to the literature. But this does not mean this is the way you should actually structure your story for publication. It also does not mean that you have to *lie* or pretend you did what you did not do. For instance, when you write the introduction, in which traditionally the reader expects to see your research question, the fact that you comply with this does not mean that the focus of the study was decided at the outset of the study through preconceived notions. You can, in the introduction, indicate that you began the study with an area of interest and phrase the research question in an open manner (e.g., What is the experience of knowledge workers regarding work-related informal networks?). Even when placing your literature review after the introduction and before the results, you can clearly indicate that it was done ex post but is presented ex ante in order to help the reader understand your work. This confirms that, as per classic GT precepts, the literature was held in abeyance until the core category of your grounded theory emerged.

Being a scholar means that you read a lot. Doing GT does not mean that you stop doing so. Sometimes, an existing framework developed in a different field of research (or a different domain in your field) and discovered by chance through your readings helps you understand and code your data, not because you tried to apply it and forced your data into this framework but, rather, the opposite; that is, this theoretical framework was not preconceived but rather emerged from other literature (which is also data as such) and helped you make sense of some of your data (see the use of translation theory, a theory from the field of sociology, in Walsh, 2010, or the use of values, needs, and motivation theories, from the psychological field of research, in Walsh et al., 2010).

To illustrate the difference between *doing* and *writing* GT, we give the example of an article published in a top tier journal of the information systems field of research (Walsh et al., 2013), which was first published online in 2013 and won a best paper award in May 2014. Table 9.1 presents a summary of how the research was conducted and how it was presented for publication.

Table 9.1   Conducting a GT Research Project Versus Writing an Article for a Research Journal

The Way the Research Was Conducted			The Way the Journal Article Was Written	
Phases		Description	Sections	Description
1	Open coding Constant comparison	Identification of the main concern	1	Introduction with traditional research question as formulated in Phase 6 of the research (Introduction)
2		Theoretical sensitivity to translation theory	2	Theoretical anchorage (Literature review)
3	Selective coding Constant comparison	Emergence of the core category	3	Research settings, samplings, data collection, coding (Methodology)
4		Literature review	4	Description and conceptualization (Results)
5		Theoretical saturation	5	Proposed theory and discussion with respect to existing literature (Discussion)
6	Theoretical coding	Integration and elaboration of the grounded theory Articulation of traditional research question	6	Summary of what was accomplished and answer to the research question (Conclusion)

The actual chronology of this research, as befitting classic GT, was identification of the main concern during many years of practical experience, consultancy missions, and preliminary research investigations in three firms in 2008 and 2009. This main concern was the failure of information technology (IT) projects in firms. It must be highlighted that *this was not our (the researchers') main concern*, as the consultancy missions conducted in the three firms (and later theoretically sampled for our research) were not concerned with IT projects as such but with change management. The main concern identified was, indeed, *the participants' main concern*.

Later, while preparing a class in 2008 about organizational theories, we (by chance) *discovered* translation theory and actor network theory (ANT; Callon, 1986; Latour, 1987). Theoretical sensitivity to this framework allowed us to move on from open coding to relate various categories, thus highlighting the core category (which had not been highlighted before as such in the literature). The core category, *Aligning stakeholders' needs*, emerged in 2009, after which we started selective coding leading to theoretical coding. The literature review was conducted from 2010 to 2012 by a supervised doctoral student, who co-signed the final published article. All categories in our theory were fully saturated in 2012. The research question was formulated at the end of 2012 while finalizing the writing of the article before submission to a journal. If one looks at the way the article was written and published after three rounds of revision and substantial modifications required by reviewers, it reads as follows:

Introduction: Up front, the introduction includes an argument on the fact that our area of interest (the alignment between information systems and business strategy) is an important issue for both managers and researchers (it is considered as essential in firms to drive toward competitive advantage), the limitations of the existing literature (the concept of strategic alignment has mostly been studied through Henderson and Venkatraman's 1993 strategic alignment model, and this static model relies on assumptions that are no longer valid), and the research question (How do organizations achieve strategic alignment in practice?).

Literature Review: The second part of the article, titled "Theoretical Anchoring and Analytical Framework," describes the model that predominates in the literature and why it is challenged. Then ANT is introduced as well as the important concept of *translation*, which helped us relate, make sense of, and understand our empirical data.

Methodology: This part describes research settings and samplings, data collection and coding, and our coding categories.

Results: The results include a descriptive part (the emerging landscape in the three firms investigated in depth) and our conceptualization of seven dynamic needs alignments to maximize the chances of success of an IT project.

Discussion: The theory that we propose (the translated strategic alignment model [TSAM], which is a processual, non-functionalist model) is discussed in this section together with its contributions and how it addresses previous models' shortcomings, hence the gap filled in the literature, as well as the managerial (practical) implications.

Conclusion: The conclusion summarizes the work accomplished and how the research question was addressed in the article.

We were familiar with the journal where the article was submitted and knew that several members of the editorial board were grounded theorists. Despite this familiarity, we were still expected to deliver a certain standard format that could be easily read and understood by any researcher or practitioner, whether or not they knew about GT. In truth, and as far as we have experimented, no research process that leads to theorizing in rupture with existing literature is linear. However, top-tier journals expect our writing to be so. To complicate issues further, they also expect a compelling story and significant results. An article, beautifully fitting the conventions and standards of a given research field and journal but which does not have a compelling story to tell, nor interesting results, stands little chance of being published in a top-tier journal.

WRITING CLASSIC GT USING MIXED DATA   ●

Another major and delicate issue in writing classic GT is aiming to do so while using both qualitative and quantitative data and techniques. Data, methods, and techniques have become, wrongly (Walsh, 2014c), implicitly embedded in paradigms: quantitative data and techniques in positivist hypothetical-deductive research that uses a mathematical type of writing and corresponding symbols; qualitative data and techniques in interpretive research that uses a more narrative style of writing. However, research is currently moving beyond these extreme caricatures, and a solution has to be found to write mixed design research while retaining sense-making for the reader. Writing a compelling qualitative GT study toward publishing it in a top tier journal is already difficult enough. Doing so for a mixed GT study is an even greater challenge; it may, however, help greatly in the production of formal theories of great value because these theories are often in rupture with existing literature (Walsh, 2014c).

Beyond remaining within the established conventions of top tier outlets and rationalizing the presentation of our work, we found through trial and error that the easiest way to write the results of a "mixed design GT" study is, in the results section of the work, to stick as close as possible to the way the theory unfolded. Walsh (2014a) mixed method grounded theory was written several times trying different writing strategies before it was accepted in a top-tier journal. It was first submitted to what is considered a well-established and "traditional" quantitative positivist journal. To have it be considered for publication by such a journal, the qualitative data slices and the GT stance were "obliterated." It was, of course, rejected, but we were very lucky to have a senior editor who went to the trouble of pointing out weaknesses. Unsurprisingly, the weaknesses were positioned where we had obliterated qualitative data.

The work was then submitted in full to a journal where we had previously published qualitative GT. When we submitted the article, we warned the editor in chief that the design was unusual and required reviewers to be familiar with classic GT and at ease with both qualitative and quantitative data and techniques. Here again, we were very fortunate, as one of the reviewers challenged us to write our results as close as possible to the way our theory had unfolded. When we first submitted it, we had tried to describe the results obtained from the quantitative data collected and the techniques applied, then the qualitative ones, and finally the theory that had unfolded. But this did not work because both qualitative and quantitative data, methods, techniques, and analyses were embedded. Next we tried mixing them since they had truly been embedded in the reality of our research journey, but we lost the reader because our explanations were too complicated. Finally, in the third round of revision, we used a subterfuge: We listed our theoretical propositions and explained how we had reached each of them using mixed data, methods, and techniques. To be easily understood by the reader, we *talked and wrote quanti* (using in the text, numbers, acronyms to designate the variables, and mathematical symbols) when we were describing quantitative data and techniques, and we *talked and wrote quali* (using in the text nothing but words and full extended names for the variables) when we were describing qualitative data and techniques. In other words, we used established *philosophical caricatures* to make our work understood. Then, the fact that we used both qualitative and quantitative data and techniques to develop some propositions did not hinder understanding.

This article (Walsh, 2014a) was the follow-up to a previous qualitative grounded theory that had already been published (Walsh et al., 2010), so with the primary data set collected for this second work, we used as secondary data what had been collected and used in the previous study. But we could not say so as, otherwise, reviewers could have identified us and this would have jeopardized the double blind reviewing process. We resolved this issue by using our previous work as data (obtained from existing literature). For further information on methodological aspects of this article, the reader can refer to Appendix C and an example of the mixed writing described earlier. The introduction of elements extracted from the literature as data is provided in the following boxed text.

Using the Literature as One of the Sources of Data

Proposition 2: Individual IT culture has a positive influence on contextual IT needs.

Walsh et al. (2010) found that the users who were highly IT-acculturated also had high levels of contextual IT needs. When we investigated the path IITC → CONITNEE, we found β = 0.400, significance: p < 0.001. However, this path was investigated with quantitative data obtained within an academic context and a highly-computerized organization. Some elements resulting from our qualitative data set alerted us. For instance, interviewee P4 is a young assistant professor with a couple of previous teaching experiences and who has started a new job in "X" school; she grew up in a computerized home environment with a father who is an IT engineer. She told us: *I certainly could not do my job in 'X' school without IT. This was not the case in my previous institution, although I personally feel I need IT to do my job as a professor [...] for instance, it's the first time I have been asked to use PowerPoint slides to teach. In my old school, nobody ever used PowerPoint.* Thus, this professor did not perceive the same contextual

(Continued)

(Continued)

IT needs when she taught in an old-fashioned, IT-conservative university as when she teaches in a forward-looking, highly-computerized university. This more generally suggests that the same person with a given level of IT acculturation may perceive different contextual IT needs, depending on the organization they work in.

In the wording of the items for the construct of contextual IT needs ... it is quite clear that we specify the organization that we refer to. Therefore, in the present study, the influence of the organization is included in the construct of contextual IT needs and explains why this path was quantitatively supported; it might not be so in a different organization and proposition 2 might not extend to other substantive areas and other contexts. (Walsh, 2014a, p. 155)

● WRITING CONVENTIONS

Writing, like power, is a "sociohistorical construction" (Richardson, 1990, p. 51), and we inscribe values in our writing. Therefore, we cannot improvise if we want our research to be published in the top journals of our research fields. It is a long learning process. "Styles of writing . . . are not fixed or neutral but reflect the historically shifting domination of particular schools or paradigms" (Richardson, 1990, p. 16). For instance, when we started publishing our GT works, we found that GT appeared to be more easily accepted in European journals of our research field even though these journals were also well recognized in North America. This guided our choice of relevant outlets for our work. This was even more the case when we were trying to publish mixed design GT that used mixed qualitative and quantitative data. This might be explained by the fact that Paul Lazarsfeld's works, to which GT is anchored, were, at the time, extremely well accepted in Europe, where they have led to an important school of thought in statistics, led by Benzécri (1973).

The situation is currently[1] evolving, and North American journals are being made more and more aware of what GT may bring to research, and its use has been increasing exponentially during the past two decades (Figure 9.1). Some fields, for instance, medicine and nursing, have widely recognized the added value of GT (Figure 9.2). Other fields, such as the management/business field (Figure 9.2), are still lagging behind, although a significant increase in the number of GT papers published during the past decade can be witnessed even within these fields (Figure 9.3).

Figure 9.1   Number of GT Works Published per Annum (All Research Fields Included)

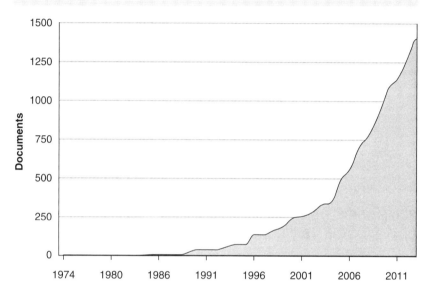

Figure 9.2   GT Works Published by Subject Area

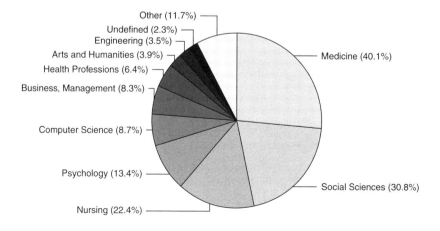

Figure 9.3   GT Works Published in the Business Research Field

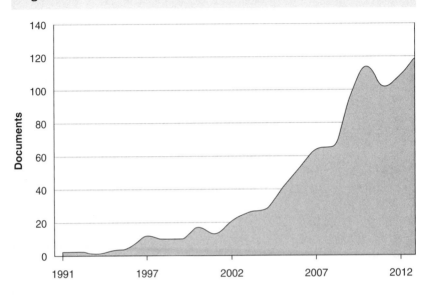

● SOME GUIDELINES FOR PUBLISHING CLASSIC GT IN TOP TIER RESEARCH JOURNALS

If you are an experienced researcher who has already published a number of works, you probably know your research field and its writing conventions fairly well. Then, you might try to publish your GT work in any research outlet and "fight" for it to be recognized even though it might not be congruent with the historical writing conventions of the outlet that you have chosen. The "fight" might be long and arduous. If, however, you are a novice researcher, you might not be prepared to take this chance. Here we provide some guidelines for novice researchers.

Present your ongoing works in conferences and to colleagues within and outside your institution, within and outside the GT research community, and as often as you can, before submitting to a journal. Encourage and accept criticism. This will help you improve your work and maximize your chances of being published.

When you think you are ready to submit to a research outlet, study the top tier journals of your field thoroughly, as well as their writing conventions and the philosophical assumptions of the editorial board. For instance, if you pick a journal that has always published 100% quantitative positivist research, it is completely unlikely that a qualitative interpretive grounded theory will be accepted in this journal. On the contrary, if you pick a journal renowned for its qualitative or mixed methods research, you might have a chance proposing an interpretive qualitative grounded theory or a critical realist mixed design grounded theory, respectively.

Once you have identified the journal(s), select articles that are meaningful and interesting to you and use them as models of the expected writing conventions. This does not mean that you reproduce them but, rather, that you use them as models of the type of writing that is expected and commonly accepted in the chosen outlet(s). Rewrite your work to fit the identified writing conventions as long as this does not cause you to forfeit some of your own basic philosophical assumptions or "disguise" your research beyond what you deem acceptable. If this is the case, choose another outlet.

If you are lucky enough not to receive a "desk reject," your article will be sent to reviewers. Be patient and humble when you read the reviewers' comments. All reviewers cannot be wrong. Reviewers are usually chosen within a population of researchers who have already published in the outlet that you have chosen. These reviewers are usually specifically appointed to review your work because of their competence in your research area and sometimes for their methodological competence. Hence, if they question some aspects of your work, there is a fair chance that the readers of the outlet you have chosen to publish in will as well.

Keep in mind that reviewing is a thankless and unpaid task. Even though we have, on occasions (though extremely rarely), encountered some reviewers who did not understand our work, the other reviewers appointed at the same time usually allowed the associate editor to minimize the impact of the "bad" reviewer and our work was eventually published. Do not be discouraged if and when your work is rejected. This is part of the learning process, and we all learn much more through being rejected than accepted. As long as your work is reviewed, even if it is eventually rejected, you can draw some valuable lessons from this process and keep improving your output.

Not Quite Ready . . .

The paper we gave as an example earlier in this chapter (Walsh et al., 2013), whose results were eventually voted by a scientific board as most important for both the research and practitioner communities, was previously rejected by another top-tier journal. At the time of this first submission and subsequent rejection, it just was not ready for publication and the research *flow* was still obviously difficult to follow. However, through this first rejection, and the detailed reviews that accompanied the rejection, we learned a lot and were able to readjust our writing format to better suit a top-tier outlet.

Be humble and do not hesitate to call in, as a second author, some-one with experience and know-how in a domain where your own competence is lacking. If you choose this person correctly, what you might learn in the process of coauthorship will be extremely valuable and might open some doors that you did not even know existed.

IN SUMMARY

Doing GT and *writing GT* with the goal of publishing in a research jour-nal involve different processes. It is often necessary to organize the way we write our grounded theories to fit, at least approximately, the writ-ing conventions of the outlets in which we choose to publish. All reviewers cannot be wrong, and we should remain *humble.* If one of our works submitted for publication is rejected, and if we want our works to be read and understood, we should take the opportunity to learn from, rather than refuse, the judgment of our peers.

TEST YOUR KNOWLEDGE

In the following questions one or several answers may be correct.

1. In order to publish a grounded theory in a research outlet
    a. You should forfeit your philosophical assumptions
    b. You should unconditionally fit in the research outlet's writing conventions
    c. You do not have to show that you have followed all of GT's foundational guidelines
    d. None of the above

2. Writing GT for an audience
    a. Has to be done through the GT process
    b. Has to faithfully describe the full GT process
    c. Has to be done in iterative cycles
    d. None of the above

3. Writing conventions
    a. Are the same for all research outlets
    b. Are all clearly stated in writing by research outlets
    c. May be identified partially through the publications of each outlet
    d. None of the above

4. Writing for an audience
    a. Is always a linear process
    b. Accounts for findings in a mostly linear fashion
    c. Is usually helped by regular exposure of results to one's peers
    d. None of the above

FURTHER READING

Richardson, L. (Ed.). (1990). *Writing strategies: Reaching diverse audiences* (Vol. 21). Newbury Park, CA: Sage.

Richardson, L. (2000) Writing: A method of inquiry. In N. K. Denzin & Y. S. Lincoln (Eds.), *Handbook of qualitative research* (2nd ed., pp. 923–948), Thousand Oaks, CA: Sage.

ENDNOTE

1. The source of the data used in this section is the Scopus database, launched in 2004 by Elsevier. On its website, it claims to be "the largest abstract and citation database of research literature and select results from the web . . . [covering] 27 million abstracts, 230 million references and 200 million web pages." In this database, we investigated works that include the term *grounded theory* in the title, abstract, or keywords.

10

Evaluating Classic Grounded Theory

After studying this chapter, you will:

- *understand the criteria for evaluating classic grounded theory*
- *recognize the quality of a classic grounded theory by applying these criteria*

Different approaches to research necessitate different criteria for evaluating the quality of the research outcomes. Establishing such criteria is a somewhat contentious aspect of the shifting nature of research paradigms.

THE CONSEQUENCES OF THE PARADIGM WAR

Patton (2002) refers to the traditional dichotomy in research approaches as competing inquiry paradigms: "using quantitative and experimental methods to generate and test hypothetical-deductive generalizations and using qualitative and naturalistic approaches to inductively and holistically understand human experience and constructed meanings in context-specific settings" (p. 69). He acknowledges a range of qualitative research approaches with alternative criteria and concludes that issues of quality and credibility in qualitative research relate to three concerns: rigorous methods, credibility of the researcher, and philosophical belief in the value of qualitative inquiry (p. 584).

Venkatesh, Brown, and Bala (2013) propose an integrative framework for mixed methods inference quality and provide several examples of validity in quantitative and qualitative research. For quantitative research, they propose to check on design validity (i.e., internal and external validity), measurement validity (i.e., reliability and construct validity), and inferential validity (i.e., statistical conclusion validity); for qualitative research, they propose to check on design validity (i.e., descriptive validity, transferability, and credibility), analytical validity (i.e., theoretical validity, dependability, consistency, and plausibility), and inferential validity (i.e., interpretive validity and confirmability). However, their work still appears somewhat biased by the *paradigm war* that we described in Chapter 2; also it cannot be applied "as is" to evaluate classic grounded theories. For instance, external validity, that is, "whether the cause-effect relationship holds over variation in persons, settings" (p. 13), does not hold for a classic grounded theory. External validity will depend on the researcher's philosophical stance and if the investigated theory is a simple substantive theory bounded in time, space, and context; a general substantive theory that extends to a substantive area; or a conceptually formalized theory that extends to many different substantive areas.

As highlighted in Chapter 2 and discussed by Walsh (2014c) and Walsh and colleagues (2015b), we must be careful not to enroll in paradigmatic caricatures. We must not automatically assimilate the use of quantitative data with hypothetical-deductive research or the use of qualitative data with interpretive research. Guba (1990) refers to a paradigm dialogue, noting a plethora of alternative approaches to research that have emerged over the past decades to challenge conventional positivism: "United in what they oppose, they are nevertheless divided, sometimes sharply, on what they espouse" (p. 9). To engage further in this dialogue is beyond the scope of this text, but given the extensive use of qualitative data in GT, novice researchers can find themselves attempting to justify their work in relation to a *menu* of criteria. As for the use of quantitative data, or mixed data, with an exploratory stance, it is still so rare in many fields that researchers, even experienced ones, who adopt this path may also find themselves in need of justification for their work to be understood and validated. Therefore, here, we focus our attention on exploring criteria for evaluating the quality of a classic grounded theory with any type of data, qualitative and/or quantitative, and from any philosophical stance that a researcher may choose (although such a stance should be clearly stated early on in a GT work to enlighten the reader and make the work transparent).

● CRITERIA FOR EVALUATING GROUNDED THEORY

First, let us consider some general criteria for evaluating the quality of theory-building research. Bacharach (1989) contends that "the goal of theory is to diminish the complexity of the empirical world on the basis of explanations and predictions" (p. 513). Eisenhardt (1989) reminds us that strong theory-building research should result in new, even frame-breaking, insights and that a good theory "should display enough evidence for each construct to allow readers to make their own assessment of the fit with theory . . . a strong theory-building study has a good, although not necessarily perfect, fit with the data" (p. 548). While noting that theory is always provisional, Bacharach (1989) cautions,

> To dangle criteria above the head of a theorist like the Sword of Damocles may stifle creativity. . . . However, during the early stages of theory building, there may be a fine line between satisfying the criteria of the internal logic of theory and achieving a creative contribution. A good theorist walks this line carefully. (p. 513)

Whetten (1989) contends that "sensitivity to the competing virtues of parsimony and comprehensiveness is the hallmark of a good theorist" (p. 490).

While appreciating the perspectives of these experienced methodologists, it is important to remember that GT's distinct research paradigm sits outside the "classically opposed orthodoxies" (Patton, 2002, p. 69). Our consideration should, therefore, begin by recalling the nature and purpose of GT: *to systematically generate theory from data as an integrated set of concepts and as hypotheses about the interrelationships among these concepts that focus a main issue or concern in the area under study and explain how that issue or concern is processed or resolved.* Glaser (1998, 2005a) refers to GT as asymptotic and emphasizes its propositional nature; it never fully reaches *truth* but the more data analyzed, the more plausible the generated theory. As an exploratory approach, GT's credibility cannot be judged on the basis of established knowledge. Its relevance comes from data, not extant literature. "The important question is the usefulness of the theory that has been generated" (Baker, Wuest, & Stern, 1992, p. 1359).

O'Connor, Netting, and Thomas (2008) note the intent of grounded theory is emergent understanding, not testable theory, and suggest "the easy advice for those facing an IRB [Institutional Research Board] would be to demonstrate the clearest standards available, those suggested by its original developers" (p. 36). Glaser and Strauss (1971) offered four specific criteria for evaluating grounded theories: "theory that fits the real world, works in predictions and explanations, is relevant to the people concerned, and . . . is readily modifiable" (p. 176). Charmaz (2006, 2014) proposes the criteria of credibility, originality, resonance, and usefulness.

Glaser (1992, pp. 116–117) reiterates the four criteria of fit, workability, relevance, and modifiability and later elaborates, as follows, to define these terms and propose related questions that may be asked to verify the quality of a classic grounded theory:

1. *Fit* is another word for validity. Does the concept adequately express the pattern in the data which it purports to conceptualize? *Fit* is continually sharpened by constant comparisons.

2. *Workability* means do the concepts and the way they are related into hypotheses sufficiently account for how the main concern of participants is resolved?

3. *Relevance* makes the research important, because it deals with the main concerns of the participants involved. To study something that interests no one really or just a few academics or funders is probably to focus on non-relevance or even trivia for the participants. *Relevance,* like good concepts, evokes instant grab.

4. *Modifiability* is very significant. The theory is not being verified as in verification studies, and thus never right or wrong . . . it just gets modified by new data to compare it to . . . New data never provides a disproof, just an analytic challenge. (Glaser, 1998, pp. 18–19)

In exploring these criteria further, we might draw some comparison of *fit* with notions of validity. As Glaser and Strauss (1967) state,

the theory should provide clear enough categories and hypotheses so that crucial ones can be verified in present and future research; they must be clear enough to be readily operationalized in quantitative studies when these are appropriate . . . that the categories must be readily (not forcibly) applicable to and indicated by the data under study. (p. 3)

We might compare GT's criterion of *workability* with external validity and transferability (i.e., the theory is sufficiently abstract to transcend specific empirical incidents for theoretical generalizability). Indeed, replication is built into the research process through theoretical sampling and constant comparisons (Glaser & Strauss, 1965a, p. 290).

GT's criterion of *relevance* speaks to the practical value or utility of the theory (Patton, 2002, p. 588). Its relevance, credibility, and confirmability are, of course, affirmed through its empirical grounding in data and the "conceptual grab" (Glaser, 1978, p. 100) of the theory. Concepts convey credibility when they are both "analytic—sufficiently generalized to designate the properties of concrete entities (not the concrete entities themselves)" and "sensitizing—they yield a 'meaningful' picture—with apt illustrations" so that the reader can "feel that vicariously he has been in the field" (Glaser & Strauss, 1965a, p. 291). We might align criteria of resonance and usefulness (Charmaz, 2006, 2014) here as well. Bacharach (1989) suggests that "a theory is useful when it can both explain and predict" (p. 501). Glaser (1963) suggests that plausibility is sufficient in developing theory; that "to develop, not test, a model, it is sufficient to explore plausible relations between variables, and not necessary to build a strong case on hard fact" (p. 381). Glaser and Strauss (1965a) suggest that any grounded theory can be "applied and adjusted to many situations with sufficient exactitude to guide thinking, understanding and research" (p. 292).

GT's emphasis on the *modifiability* of a good grounded theory is perhaps unique in expressly acknowledging its propositional nature as distinct from the verificational nature of hypothetical-deductive theory building and from the detailed descriptive nature of many qualitative research works. While contending that the primary goal of a theory is "to answer the questions of *how, when,* and *why*" (Bacharach, 1989, p. 498), Bacharach insists that a theory that is not testable "no matter how profound or aesthetically pleasing it may be, it is not a theory" (p. 512). Indeed, while insisting that the goal of GT is not hypothesis testing, Glaser and Strauss (1967) maintain that "evidence and testing never destroys a theory (of any generality), they only modify it. A theory's only replacement is a better theory" (p. 28).

To the criteria of *fit, workability, relevance,* and *modifiability* we would echo Glaser and Strauss (1967) in noting the criteria of "logical consistency, clarity, parsimony, density, scope [and] integration" (p. 3) as indicators of a good grounded theory. Density refers to levels of conceptualization, development of theoretical properties, and overall conceptual integration (Glaser & Strauss, 1971, p. 190). Bacharach

(1989) notes that "the purpose of theoretical statements is twofold: to organize (parsimoniously) and to communicate (clearly)" (p. 496). Indeed, Glaser and Strauss (1967) acknowledge the importance of the "parsimony of variables" (p. 110) through GT's delimiting the emergent theory to a core category and related concepts. Eisenhardt (1989) reiterates this call for parsimony, cautioning that in studies with a "staggering volume of rich data, there is a temptation to build theory which tries to capture everything. The result can be theory which is rich in detail, but lacks the simplicity of overall perspective" (p. 547). Bacharach (1989) defines scope as "the range of the phenomena encompassed by the theory" (p. 509), suggesting that "for adequate scope . . . the constructs must, in turn, sufficiently, although parsimoniously, tap the domain of the phenomenon in question" (pp. 506–507).

IN SUMMARY

In this chapter, we have explored the distinct criteria for evaluating a classic grounded theory that go beyond the accepted criteria for both hypothetical-deductive and qualitative research. Classic GT's criteria of *fit, workability, relevance, modifiability,* and *parsimony* facilitate the generation of theory with *grab,* or what Charmaz (2006, 2014) proposes as originality. Of course, like all efforts at theory generation, the quality of a classic grounded theory will vary according to the theorist's understanding and thoroughness in applying GT principles and techniques, the theorist's ability to stay open to discovery in the data, the incisiveness of analysis, and the clarity and elegance with which the theorist writes up his or her theory.

TEST YOUR KNOWLEDGE

In the following questions one or several answers may be correct.

1. Criteria for evaluating classic grounded theories
   a. Include objectivity, generalizability, and reliability
   b. Are similar to criteria for interpretive research
   c. Emphasize modifiability and parsimony
   d. Include fit, workability, and relevance
   e. None of the above

2. In a good classic GT
   a. The concepts express patterns in the data
   b. Emerging concepts and their relationships account for how the main concern is resolved
   c. The concepts have grab
   d. The theory may be modified by new data
   e. None of the above

3. In a good classic GT
   a. Replication is built into the research process
   b. The theory does not need to have practical value
   c. It is sufficient to explore plausible relations between variables
   d. It is necessary to build a strong case on hard facts
   e. None of the above

FURTHER READING

Glaser, B. G. (1978). *Theoretical sensitivity: Advances in the methodology of grounded theory* (Chapter 1). Mill Valley, CA: Sociology Press.

Glaser, B. G. (2003). *The grounded theory perspective II: Description's remodeling of grounded theory methodology* (Chapter 9). Mill Valley, CA: Sociology Press.

Glaser, B. G., & Strauss, A. L. (1967). *The discovery of grounded theory: Strategies for qualitative research* (Chapter 9). New York: Aldine de Gruyter.

Conclusion

Many authors have, over the years, written methodological books about GT. In so doing, they have often reinterpreted and "remodeled" GT (Glaser, 2003) from their own philosophical perspectives. In this book, our purpose was to revisit classic GT as a full package while remaining as true as possible to its founders' thoughts. We have reminded the reader of the roots of GT (Chapter 1) and the ultimate purpose of GT, that is, discovering theories no matter what the researcher's philosophical assumptions may be (Chapter 2). We have highlighted GT's foundational pillars (Chapter 3), clarified common sources of confusion related to GT (Chapter 4), helped the reader to find and use all available data (Chapter 5), analyze the data (Chapter 6), shape the emerging theory (Chapter 7), and write as both an intrinsic part of doing GT (Chapter 8) and also toward publishing in top tier research outlets (Chapter 9). Finally, we have offered the reader advice on evaluating the quality of grounded theories (Chapter 10).

Throughout this book, we hope to have shown that GT is much more than a qualitative research methodology befitting only an interpretive philosophical stance, even though it may accommodate such a stance. We have aimed to provide practical guidance while staying true to the classic GT practice. However, it must be highlighted that, as our own philosophical stance is critical realist, it is most probable that, unwittingly we may have, at least partially, remodeled GT that is supposed to be philosophically neutral. In the same way, the frameworks proposed by Strauss and Corbin (1990) or Charmaz (2014) are epistemologically and methodologically biased interpretations and applications of GT. We do not call for a reconsideration of the intrinsic worth of these works, which might suit the philosophical assumptions of some researchers. However, grounded theory being a grounded theory itself as often stated by Glaser, it has to be highlighted that these frameworks are at a lesser level of conceptual formalization than that of classic GT (Glaser, 1978; Glaser & Strauss, 1967), a fact that is often misunderstood and which Glaser has been defending for many years.

To give a few illustrative, non-limitative examples, Strauss and Corbin (1990) and Charmaz (2009, 2014) propose frameworks that use mostly qualitative data—the former with a symbolic interactionist philosophical background, the latter with a constructivist philosophical background. Glaser (2008) uses quantitative data with a post-positivist background. Walsh (2014c) uses mixed qualitative and quantitative data with a critical realist background. All these frameworks have been empirically developed through doing and supervising various research projects with emergent substantive GT research designs (GTDs) and have probably and unwittingly remodeled, at least to some extent, classic GT, whereas Holton (2006, 2007b) uses qualitative data and develops a substantive GT design in her works, from a critical realist perspective in line with classic GT, without remodeling it to become a different framework. This highlights the possibility of viewing classic GT as a meta-theory of inductive research design (Walsh, 2014c).

Figure 11.1.   Classic GT as a Meta-Theory of Inductive Research Design (Adapted from Walsh, 2014c)

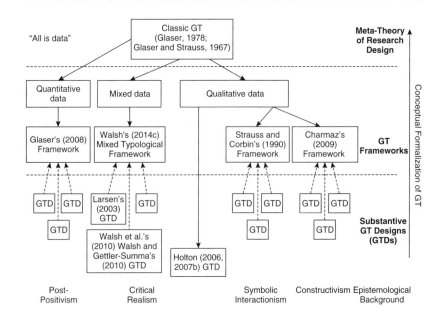

WHAT IS GT, AND WHY THE CONTINUAL REMODELING?   ●

This naturally leads to the question as to what classic GT truly is; a question that has recently been openly asked (see Walsh et al., 2015a, 2015b, and the related special issue of *Organizational Research Methods*). As we saw, many different answers to this question may be proposed. In various fields of research, GT has been described as a *technique* (e.g., Lawrence & Tar, 2013), a *method* (e.g., Amsteus, 2014), a *methodology* (e.g., Manuj & Pohlen, 2012), or a *paradigm* (e.g., Holton, in Walsh et al., 2015b; Levina, in Walsh et al., 2015b; Rodrí-guez-Martin et al., 2013). Based on Glaser (1978), Fernandez (in Walsh et al., 2015b) describes GT "as a basic social process in which researchers engage with their data and participants in creating theory." Bailyn (in Walsh et al., 2015b) sees GT as a "perspective on data and on what one can learn from data." Finally, Walsh (2014c; Walsh et al., 2015b) proposes GT as a meta-theory of exploratory research design.

Is GT a method, a technique, a methodology, a framework, a paradigm, a social process, a perspective, or a meta-theory of research design?

GT is probably all of these at the same time. As such, and depending on the researcher's perspective, it will keep being remodeled. However, if we go back to the four possible different definitions of the word *paradigm* highlighted in the preface of this book, Morgan (2007) showed that all are a "shared belief system that influences the kinds of knowledge researchers seek and how they interpret the evidence they collect" (p. 50). Therefore, it may certainly be stated that, because of its "transcendent" quality (Glaser, 2004), classic GT is a research paradigm befitting the discovery of new theories from any philosophical perspective.

Appendix A

Doing Qualitative Research Does Not Mean You Are Doing Classic GT

● **QUALITATIVE DESCRIPTION DATA COLLECTION AND ANALYSIS[1]**

Note the precise, planned-in-advance sample; the attention to complete data capture through use of a preformulated interview guide, taping, and transcribing; the abundance of codes generated from line-by-line coding of the transcripts; the logical and thematic organization of the resultant codes; and the descriptive (past tense) reporting of findings.

Excerpt From the Study Design

I selected eight individuals from the community for personal interviews. Those selected included four males and four females; six had participated in the focus group at the May reunion while two— one male and one female—had been unable to attend. Interviews were semistructured in that I used a set list of questions but encouraged the interviewees to take the conversation where they wished. Each interview lasted from 60 to 90 minutes and was audiotaped and transcribed. In addition to line-by-line coding the eight interview transcripts, I also completed coding of the focus group transcript. This initial coding was free form and highly intuitive and yielded 155 codes.

After reviewing my coding, some duplication was evident. I reviewed the codes and grouped them to remove duplications, reducing the list to 75 coded concepts. I then identified three overarching categories that I labeled *Aspects of Community, Aspects of Practice*, and *Aspects of Participation*. I explored the correlation of the various codes to the three overarching categories and assigned

43 codes to the *Aspects of Community* category, 38 to the *Aspects of Practice* category, and 24 to the *Aspects of Participation* category.

Beginning with the interviews, I focused my attention to the most frequent codes in each category. I selected those coded to at least 12 of the 18 interviews to represent a reasonable distribution of individual member perceptions within the data. Based on this criterion, I was able to narrow the selection of codes from 75 to 42: 26 correlating to *Aspects of Community*, 10 correlating to *Aspects of Practice*, and 6 correlating to *Aspects of Participation*.

Of the 26 concepts correlating to *Aspects of Community*, I designated five as subcategories—*Community Identity, Bunch of Emotions, Connectedness, Commitment*, and *Power of this Community*. Under these five subcategories I thematically distributed the remaining 21 concepts. Similarly, under the category *Aspects of Practice*, I designated three concepts as subcategories—*Allowed Me to Grow, Sharpening the Saw*, and *Play*—and thematically distributed the remaining seven concepts among these three. Under *Aspects of Participation*, I designated one concept as a subcategory—*Participation in Community*—and assigned the remaining five concepts to this subcategory.

Excerpt From the Study Findings

Members referred to the reassurance they felt in being part of a tight-knit family "able to get together, tell old war stories, create new experiences, make new friends" (A.M., Interview, October 2001) and "a place where egos and agendas don't seem to get in the way of genuine dialogue and caring for one another" (L.G., Interview, October 2001). Images emerged of good times, celebrations, vivid memories, and powerful connections. Shared stories and memories reinforced the closeness. As in a family, members described the sense of belonging as important: "knowing that I can wander into the group 20 years from now and be accepted as one of the gang. I've found a community where I believe I am liked as much for my loony-ness as for my creativity . . . I guess that for me the community, the fun, and the belonging is paramount" (J.M., Interview, October 2001).

Our findings suggest that community identity is forged through shared experiences: "I know that my experience in the community has shaped how I will live the second half of my life. I want to stay connected to others who have that same mid-life grounding point" (M.S., Virtual Interview, October 2001). "It was a slog at times. . . . I was grateful that I have been through some tough times in my military career, because that gave me the ability to see the slog as something that bound us all together. We got through it because of the fun after and during class as well as by having the stamina to suffer the late nights, the lack of sleep in the residencies and the expectations on us to produce" (J.M., Interview, October 2001).

● CLASSIC GT DATA COLLECTION AND ANALYSIS[2]

Note the tentative and emergent approach to sampling, the use of field notes to capture data, the use of constant comparison and theoretical sampling to progress theorizing, the emergence of a core category to explain resolution of the main concern, and the use of theoretical saturation and theoretical coding to fully develop the emergent explanation. Note also that the theory is written conceptually and in the present tense.

Excerpt From the Study Design

I had initially projected my fieldwork to involve approximately 50 participants. In accordance with GT methodology however, sample size could not be definitively established in advance of the fieldwork but rather emerged as the study progressed. In summary, 61 individuals participated in the study: 27 through personal interviews and 34 individuals in focus group sessions. Interviews lasted from 60 to 90 minutes each. The focus groups occurred during two retreats, each lasting three days. These events were not organized specifically for my research efforts but were events to which I was invited by individuals who, because they had already participated in interviews, were aware of my research and felt that I might gain further data for my study.

Field notes were written up directly during and after each interview or focus group session. Consistent with the principles of classic GT development, field notes were collected and analyzed according to the constant comparison method of joint coding and analysis with subsequent data collection directed to theoretical sampling as concepts emerged. In open coding of my data, I first compared incidents to incidents in the data, and I would ask, "What category (concept) does this incident indicate?" "What property of what category does this incident indicate?" and "What is the participant's main concern?" (Glaser, 1998, p. 140). These questions enabled me to transcend the descriptive detail of the data and abstract incidents within my data as indicators of the latent pattern of social behavior that would eventually emerge as a conceptual theory.

Among the substantive codes that emerged were *changing workplace context, coping with change* and *humanizing workplace*. The important thing is that each concept has earned relevance in relation to the theory, its relevance theoretically sampled for and sufficiently validated and its properties and dimensions identified though constant comparison and interchangeable indicators to theoretical saturation. As my analysis progressed, *rehumanizing* emerged as a potential core category. It appeared to account for much of the variation around knowledge worker concerns with the changing knowledge workplace and resultant dehumanization. Accordingly, *rehumanizing* became the focus of further selective data collection and coding efforts.

Subsequent data collection and coding were thereby further delimited to that which was relevant to the emergent conceptual framework (Glaser & Holton, 2004, para. 56–57). Selective data collection and analysis continued until the core and related categories were sufficiently saturated and further coding of new incidents did not yield any new properties. It was time to cease collecting and coding data and to turn to conceptual integration and articulation of the emerging grounded theory.

Excerpt From the Emergent Theory

The instability of many workplace environments results in a loss of autonomy and even identity for many knowledge workers. The concept of rehumanizing explains how knowledge workers resolve their concerns with the dehumanizing impact of a changing knowledge workplace, that is, how they restore the human dimension in their work relationships and working environments. Rehumanizing gives meaning to their work while sustaining energy and commitment. Rehumanizing is characterized by authenticity, depth and meaning, recognition and respect, safety and healing and kindred sharing. The bureaucratic relationships in many knowledge workplaces lack authenticity. They are power-laden transactions. Whether the power can be attributed to position, influence or alliance, the tensional shifts can leave individuals feeling uneasy, anxious, and without a base or grounding. The need to play roles in organizations and to assume corporate identities also leads to inauthentic voices, disconnecting individuals from what they really feel. Identity and purpose in work are eroded as "everyone plays the script." With the increasing intensification and specialization of knowledge, workers feel siloed. The time available for more general interactions is reduced. Removing opportunities for broad interpersonal contact further dehumanizes the work environment and reduces the potential for authentic engagement. Many highly skilled knowledge workers risk vulnerability in moving up in the organization to take on managerial roles that progressively distance them from their areas of specialized expertise. There is a risk of vulnerability, as well, in emotional disclosures in the workplace. Individuals frequently feel they have to restrict emotional displays or run the risk of being seen as weak, a vulnerability that can restrict career progression. Emotions are held in check and authenticity compromised.

ENDNOTES

1. Holton (2001). Unpublished case study.

2. From Holton (2006).

Appendix B

Classic GT Using Qualitative Data

The following is based on Holton (2006)[1] and elaborates her application of classic GT methodology, in particular the process of concept development, to her generation of a grounded theory of *rehumanizing knowledge work through fluctuating support networks* in the knowledge workplace.

THE DATA ●

My data consisted of field notes from personal interviews, casual conversations with knowledge professionals, and observation of various focus group gatherings. Participants were drawn from the public and private sectors and a variety of professional fields under the general rubric of knowledge work. In summary, 61 individuals participated in the study: 27 through personal interviews (13 face-to-face interviews, 12 virtual interviews via e-mail, and 2 telephone interviews) and 34 individuals in focus group sessions. In addition, I encountered opportunities in the field to augment the interview and focus group data with participant observations of informal networks as well as document analysis. Data were analyzed using the full complement of procedures that comprise classic grounded theory methodology. In accordance with classic GT, concepts emerged through the process of constant comparison of interchangeable empirically grounded indicators.

● THE EMERGENT THEORY

My thesis explains the basic social structural process of *fluctuating support networks* through which knowledge professionals self-organize to overcome dehumanized work environments as well as the social structural conditions that precipitate their formation, namely, *the changing knowledge workplace, coping with change, resistance to change, dehumanization,* and *rehumanizing.* Such networks operate outside the formal organization. They are self-emerging, self-organizing, and self-sustaining. Participation is voluntary and intuitive. The core category is *rehumanizing,* a three-stage basic social psychological process through which knowledge professionals engage in *finding and likening, igniting of passions,* and *mutual engagement,* giving meaning to their work while sustaining their energy and commitment. *Rehumanizing* restores *authenticity, depth, and meaning* to their work; it offers them *recognition and respect, safety and healing,* and *kindred sharing* as they cope with the turbulence that inevitably accompanies persistent and unpredictable organizational change. In the process, they are *reenergized,* their *passion for work is reignited,* stimulating *creativity,* the desire to embrace *challenge, experimentation,* and *innovation.*

● STAYING OPEN

Early in my research process, I had to learn the hard way that my research interest was not the main concern of the knowledge professionals that I was interviewing. Like many novice researchers wishing to do GT, I initiated data collection focused on a preconceived professional interest. I developed an interview protocol and diligently taped and transcribed the first five interviews. As I sat transcribing, I was struck not only by how much time the transcribing was taking but also by how dull the interviews were. While my interviewees were completely respectful of my research and dutifully tried to answer each question posed, it was clear to me that they had little genuine interest in my topic. We were all doing our best, but I found myself despairing and anxious as to how any of this was going to produce a theory! My early efforts at open coding of these data, heavily influenced by qualitative data analysis procedures, had yielded 155 substantive codes—data overwhelm!

I went back to further study GT methodology, particularly the work of Barney Glaser (1978, 1998), and realized that my approach was privileging my professional interest and not allowing the main concerns of my participants to surface. So I set aside those first five interviews and started over to collect new data without an interview protocol and without taping. My first two "new" interviews were with managers in a public sector organization. Rather than launching into a long preamble about my research interests, I simply asked them to tell me about their jobs. I listened for what my participants wanted to tell me. I followed up with the question, "What concerns you most in your role?" That's all it took to open the "flood gates." In each case, the interviewees started voicing concerns about organizational change and how the nature of change was impacting their ability to manage the motivation and productivity of their staff. I jotted down key words and phrases during each conversation (e.g., fragmented knowledge pockets, structures eroding, people marginalized, how to free people up, opening people up to possibility).

Immediately after each meeting, I rushed to a nearby coffee shop and started jotting down more detailed field notes using those key words and phrases to remind me of what had emerged in our conversation. What these managers wanted to talk about wasn't what I had set out to research, but I trusted the process. I coded my field notes and memoed. I struggled to let go of my preconceived research interest and simply to trust what was emerging from the data, but as I continued collecting and coding data, this main concern (changing workplace context) emerged over and over.[2]

OPEN CODING ●

With my more *open* field notes, and using the constant comparison process, open coding led to a much reduced list of 57 substantive codes. It is worth noting that this latter list of codes is substantially smaller and more conceptual than that produced in my earlier efforts. This illustrates not only the potential for overwhelming the novice researcher with descriptive data capture but also the very real possibility of losing the true conceptual power of classic GT to transcend the descriptive level (Glaser, 1978, pp. 49–52; 1998, pp. 23–26).

CONSTANT COMPARISON ●

The purpose of constant comparison is to see if the data support and continue to support emerging categories. At the same time, the process further builds and substantiates the emerging categories by defining their properties and dimensions. When comparing incidents to incidents in the data, I would ask, "What category (concept) does this incident indicate?" "What property of what category does this incident indicate?" "What is the participant's main concern?" (Glaser, 1998, p. 140). These questions enabled me to transcend the descriptive detail of the data and abstract the incidents within as indicators of latent patterns of social behavior that would eventually emerge as a conceptual theory.

Each concept is developed through constant comparison of interchangeable (empirical) indicators in the data. The number of indicators per category is not as significant as the requirement to sample sufficiently to achieve theoretical saturation. The important thing is that each concept has earned its relevance in relation to the theory—relevance that is theoretically sampled for and sufficiently validated (theoretically saturated).

Example of the Constant Comparative Method

1. Comparing Incident to Incident

In coding my interviews, I noted several references like these:

... a place where she found "like minds," common passion, and where there was a building of trust ... authentic connection ... Through her subsequent participation, she is "getting to really know others.... Building connections"

" ... way of hearing quiet voices in organizations" ... authentic voices in organizations rather than corporate voices

... corporate relationships are not authentic, they are transactional/power related ... Where do we find the experience of being ourselves in organizations? Where do we learn to be human?

... having a chance to "be heard," to share with others who understand, who they can trust to help and to hold confidences

... the corporate model that most of us work in now squeezes out our humanity. We develop machine relationships—even odd corporate voices ... manner of speaking ... a "dead sound" where our real personality has been excluded, as has emotion and feeling

C. and R. bring that wonderful warmth and spontaneity to the community—nothing can be dull when they're present—lots of depth and experience there—looking forward to getting to know both much better

By comparing incident to incident, I developed the concept of *authenticity*.

2. Comparing Concept to More Incidents

As I continued to code my data, I began comparing new incidents in the data with my concept of *authenticity*. I wrote memos to conceptually elaborate my ideas about the concept. Memos such as the following:

(Memo 1) The instability characteristic of current organizational environments results in a loss of autonomy and even identity for many knowledge workers. Power shifts leave individuals feeling "at sea"—uneasy, anxious, without a base or grounding.

(Memo 2) The prevalence of the "machine" metaphor in organizations has dehumanized work environments. Many workers actually begin to view themselves as "cogs" in a wheel and begin to respond accordingly with automatic, mindless behaviors that further disconnect them from their work. As one interviewee said, "It appears that the corporate model that most of us work in now squeezes out our humanity. We develop machine relationships—even odd corporate voices . . . a manner of speaking a 'dead sound' where our real personality has been excluded as has emotion and feeling." Another interviewee commented, "This machine world is causing us to become ill and depressed . . . We act in this impersonal and unreal way in our whole lives. We even act like this to ourselves and no longer have a real relationship with ourselves. How can we learn and experience being human again? What is the essence of being human? It is surely to hear our real voice."

(Memo 3) The need to play roles in organizations—to assume corporate identities leads to inauthentic voices. This creates disconnect between what individuals really feel and what they feel they must voice. It erodes identity and connection with purpose in work. Individuals put on armor to protect and to project. After a while nothing feels real—people may long for a return to connecting with what they value/what they are passionate about. They long for a place to be real, to feel safe to express their authentic selves, to explore, to play, to risk . . . a place where they can relax, release tensions, open up.

(Memo 4) Fluctuating networks offer a respite from time crunched, transactional, efficiency-driven work environments where there is little tolerance or time for the curiosity, exploration, and fun. What is being sacrificed? Not only the potential for creativity and innovation but the very humanity-centered nature of vocation—the joy in creating and problem solving through collaborative engagement. The Xerox technicians story (Orr, 1990) . . . On their own time, they found a way to integrate the social and technical aspects of their vocation. They raised the solving of work-related problems to an art. Valuable, tacit knowledge was transferred almost effortlessly among the technicians in an open environment where knowledge sharing was the power—building individual reputations ("war stories") while enhancing organizational performance in service to clients. The exercise raised the identity of "master technicians," provided a process for recognizing and sharing expertise, bringing new technicians into a culture of sharing and learning—a culture of mutual benefit—an inclusive meritocracy.

(Continued)

(Continued)

I theoretically sampled for *authenticity* to further elaborate the concept in terms of its properties. For example, openness and honesty, trust, sharing, being heard, safety, power, balance, and so on.

3. *Comparing Concept to Concept*

I began to compare *authenticity* with other concepts that were emerging, writing memos about the relationships to develop hypotheses that linked/ integrated these concepts. Eventually, through hand sorting of memos, *authenticity* would emerge as a property of my core category, *rehumanizing*.

● CONCEPTUAL MEMOING

In classic GT, conceptual elaboration and integration are facilitated through an extensive and systematic process of memoing that parallels the data analysis process. Memos are theoretical notes about the data and the conceptual connections between categories written up during the coding and analysis process as the ideation of the emerging theory's conceptualization. During the course of the constant comparison process, I wrote more than 400 memos capturing the development of my theory.

● CORE CATEGORY EMERGENCE

I started collecting data in 2001. *Rehumanizing* emerged as a potential core category in September 2003. As a concept, it appeared to account for much of the variation around knowledge professionals' concerns with the changing knowledge workplace and resultant dehumanization.

● THEORETICAL SAMPLING

At this point, *rehumanizing* became the focus of theoretical sampling. Subsequent data collection and coding was thereby delimited to that which was relevant to the emergent core and related concepts, facilitating their conceptual elaboration through intense property development.

SELECTIVE CODING AND THEORETICAL SATURATION ●

Selective data collection and analysis continued on 38 substantive codes until the core and related categories were sufficiently saturated and further coding of new incidents did not yield any new properties. The research process had achieved theoretical saturation of the core concept—*rehumanizing*—and its related categories through constant comparison and interchangeability of indicators (Glaser, 2001, pp. 191–193). Further coding and constant comparison yielded no new conceptual ideation. It was time to cease collecting and coding data and turn to conceptual integration and articulation of the emerging grounded theory.

THE CONCEPTUAL ELABORATION OF *IGNITING PASSIONS* ●

To illustrate the process of conceptual development, I offer here a detailed account of the emergence and theoretical saturation of one concept, *Igniting Passions*, the central stage in the basic social psychological process of *rehumanizing*.[3] This same process was applied to each concept that emerged as relevant in relation to the core category of rehumanizing.

Igniting Passions is the catalytic middle stage in the basic social psychological process of *rehumanizing*, facilitating the symbiotic relationship, continuous amplification, and interdependent functioning of *rehumanizing*'s subcore processes of *finding and likening* and *mutual engagement*. The dynamic capacity of *igniting passions* sustains the overall *rehumanizing* process by continuously generating *confidence, energy, commitment,* and *bonding* among network members. A total of 62 specific indicators of the concept of *igniting passions* appear in data collected from 15 interviews and two focus groups conducted between October 2001 and January 2004. A total of 22 memos were written between November 2002 and April 2004 elaborating the concept of *igniting passions*. The memos range in length from several lines to several pages.

As each incident can be an indicator of more than one concept, several of the memos correspond to more than one category or concept. Therefore, to facilitate hand sorting the memos (the final stage in conceptual integration of the theory), the corresponding categories are printed in bold type across the top of the memos. Each memo appears only once in the final theoretical integration of the theory, but its appropriate placement was not known until all concepts had been fully saturated. I was ready to begin hand sorting of the memos for emergent theoretical codes.

The category *passion* appeared in open coding of data collected as early as October 2001. Early memos capture the dimensions of *feedback and recognition* and *learning* as being positively correlated with *igniting passions* for network engagement.

Conceptual Memos

Recognition Needs: Feedback and recognition fuel alignment of individual and organizational passions

Reciprocating Passions: Learning and knowledge sharing ... Being selfish in terms of learning ... Someone commented ... "When we are (selfish), we learn to give to others—greedy to share ..." "vessels" for fulfilling greedy learning/sharing needs—reciprocal fulfillment of passions for earning and sharing. The accidental learning presented is a "smorgasbord" that rekindles the desire to learn—it also restores the learner's control and builds autonomy self-select, sample, take what's desired and needed. Restless spirits sated by continuous learning opportunities—integrated learning and practice

Power in diversity: Diversity of personalities, talents, perspectives, experience— creates a bubbling energy and creative potential. The range of contributions ... is immense—energy, passion, strength, vulnerability, commitment, opening up, connecting, authenticity, tenacity, validation, modeling, confirming, facilitating ... This heady emotional/transformational release. ... This may be applicable to networks and communities like _____ because of the nature of their domain/practice leadership, learning, organizational culture. ... It will be interesting to see whether any of this feeling shows up in their networks.

Additional dimensions of *igniting passions* emerged as data collection and analysis continued with *igniting passions* linked to learning as well as to vocation and to enhancing one's professional skills.

Conceptual Memos

The Passion of Vocation: Networks as keeping personal and professional passions from being eroded, depleted in the hectic, humdrum of daily organizational operations. "*Our job is our work ... our practice is our passion.*" Distinguishing between "practice" and "work"—between "vocation" and "job."

Passionate Learning: "really start to learn when they find a passion for a subject and then make a real connection to another learners and real time practitioners." Individual passion for learning is stimulated and reinforced in community. Further data collection and analysis reveal the dimension of alignment and suggest that networks can assist in enabling individuals to align their personal purpose with their work. As such, passions are ignited through purposeful engagement.

Passion and Purpose: Networks may be a venue/vessel for individuals to be able to bring their passion back into their organizational roles—experiences of participation speak of their reconnecting with previous "dream jobs," core values, interests, and passions—this desire to reconnect passion and purpose may be a motivation for seeking/participating in networks/communities of practice.

Sustaining Passion: Networks as a way to find the people with a passion for organizational work . . . this is a simple principle of self-organization at work—allocating resources to follow the passion. She talks of the organizational challenge of getting past "assigned work" to matching assignments with passions–may not be worth the effort of trying to orchestrate this (i.e. manage the process)—that it may be better to let things take their course and be satisfied with "60%." . . .

Letting the system self-organize . . . organic . . . "if no one has passion, we should not be doing it!" . . . organizations can use networks to monitor "passions" and set strategic directions accordingly . . . The human dimension—passion ignites passion—creates understanding and engagement—networks as a forum to mobilize passion into action . . . bringing diverse talents, skills together—mobilized by shared passion—vision—system sorts itself/self organizes to achieve action—progress the work—enhance the practice.

Engagement: Concept of engagement coming up a great deal lately in a lot of the literature/press on workplace issues. Article in the *Globe and Mail* this week (March 5) by Barbara Moses titled "Embrace the Challenge: Be Engaged" on this issue noting importance of both satisfaction and engagement as key determinants of employee retention in the current environment. Another article in the *Globe and Mail* (same day, by Tara Wohlberg) on spirit in the workplace. One of the great advantages of the "knowledge age" is the seemingly endless potential for combining uniquely personal talents and passions into an unlimited array of new careers/roles. At the same time, we are suffering a "hangover" from the old mental models of the Industrial era which focus on efficiency, productivity, and competition ("push" factors/stressors).

A longer memo begins to integrate emergent conceptual ideas.

Conceptual Memos

Igniting Passions: ".... passion. This is when you are really working with people—not just a "file" that you are responsible for." In work involving "the human dynamic" it is essential to come together face to face—there is a cost benefit to doing so if it engages the passion of organizational members—we speculate about whether perhaps organizations should allocate resources on the basis of matching passions! ...

"Try to develop a passion meter" ... networks as a way to find the people with a passion for organizational work ... this is a simple principle of self-organization at work—allocating resources to follow the passion.

Organizational challenge of getting past "assigned work" to matching assignments with passions—may not be worth the effort of trying to orchestrate this (i.e., manage the process)—that it may be better to let things take their course and be satisfied with "60%" ... *Letting the system self-organize ... organic ...* "if no one has passion, we should not be doing it!" ... organizations can use networks to monitor "passions" and set strategic directions accordingly ... The human dimension—passion ignites passion—creates understanding and engagement—networks as a forum to mobilize passion into action ... bringing diverse talents, skills together—mobilized by shared passion vision—system sorts itself/self organizes to achieve action—progress the work—enhance the practice.

Core Group: These were the individuals who really had a passion ... to go beyond the technical. They were "kindred spirits"—passionate. They are still friends even though most are no longer working in the training departments. ... The task is done, but the community remains. They still have a passion for the work (learning) and are still personally connected. They stay in touch regularly—still goes to them when she "needs boosting." There is one or two whom she uses as "sounding boards" and as sources of information and contacts.

Building Community as Central Value: Like minds, common passions, respect for diversity, trust—authentic connection—reciprocating—building capacity, strength, common good.

Power in Diversity: Diversity of personalities, talents, perspectives, experience—creates a bubbling energy and creative potential. The range of contributions is immense—energy, passion, strength, vulnerability, commitment, opening up, connecting, authenticity, tenacity, validation, modeling, confirming, facilitating ... Practice is "deep," heartfelt, engaging, transformational for individual and the group as a whole. . . . The fractal effect of networks—just imagine the potential to be able to release this within organizations! This heady emotional/transformational release ...This may be applicable to networks like these because of the nature of their domain/practice leadership, learning, org culture ... It will be interesting to see whether any of this feeling shows up in networks in other domains—technology networks, etc.... Need to sample for this ...

The Passion of Vocation: Networks as keeping personal and professional passions from being eroded, depleted in the hectic, humdrum of daily organizational operations. *"Our job is our work ... our practice is our passion." Distinguishing between "practice" and "work"—between "vocation" and "job."*

Passionate Learning: "really start to learn when they find a passion for a subject and then make a real connection to other learners and real time practitioners." Individual passion for learning stimulated and reinforced in community.

Reciprocating Passions: Learning and knowledge sharing ... Being selfish in terms of learning ... Someone commented ..." When we are (selfish), we learn to give to others—greedy to share."

Networks as a "vessel" for fulfilling greedy learning/sharing needs reciprocal fulfillment of passions for learning and sharing. The accidental learning presented in Networks is a "smorgasbord" that rekindles the desire to learn—it also restores the learner's control and builds autonomy self-select, sample, take what's desired and needed. Restless spirits sated by continuous learning opportunities—integrated learning and practice.

Poised to Learn: Individuals must be self-motivated to learn—have an urge, desire to learn—be "greedy" to learn. Someone commented . . ." "When you're ready to learn, a teacher will appear . . ." Networks brings eager, "poised to learn" together with ready teachers.

Passion and Purpose: Networks may be a venue/vessel for individuals to be able to bring their passion back into their organizational roles. Experiences of network participation speak of their reconnecting with previous "dream jobs," core values, interests, and passions—this desire to reconnect passion and purpose may be a motivation for seeking/ participating in networks.

Time Challenge: Struggle to find time to participate—juggling priorities—time vs. needs—geographic distance adds further challenge.

A conceptual memo written January 5, 2004, goes back to earlier data for further analysis.

Conceptual Memo

Passion, Resistance, and Bonding: Rereading field notes from interview with A . . ., noted the many references to passion, in particular, the connection between passion and bonding of network members. Appears that the common passion that brings network members together—part of the likening that creates a network—is also the "glue" that bonds network members. She goes on to describe the "passionate few" as bonding due to the resistance they encounter from the formal system—"the resistance serves as a way to separate out those who really have a passion to keep working" . . . So . . . passion creates likening, resistance creates bonding and reinforces passions. . . . a cyclic process that sustains member engagement in fluctuating networks.

Further data and memoing suggest that passion may be a key variable in work performance with passion being positively correlated to performance and disconnected passion blocking performance.

Conceptual Memo

Disconnected Passion: Individuals who exhibit resistance to change or appear to be risk averse can become labeled in organizations as "non-performers." They may be shunned by others—particularly by managers. This response further isolates the individual and contributes to lower performance—a self-fulfilling prophecy. What may lie at the heart of this superficial assessment of non-performance is a disengagement of the individual from their passion or purpose in work. This disengagement may be a defense or coping mechanism in response to increasing dehumanization from changing workplace context or a botched or poorly executed change effort. Individuals are "having trouble trying to reconnect." They are "disillusioned about the organization and trying to cope with the change" around them. They've become "disconnected from their work." If efforts are made to listen past the disengagement and non-performance, one can often find that there was a time when these individuals "had a real hunger for their work." What they require is a chance to reconnect with their passion, to feel depth and meaning in their work.

They "need to be whole" to have their "eyes light up" again, to feel the energy of a new challenge and new learning. This isn't happening in many organizations because "managers are not listening." The result of their inattention is the veritable blocking of employee capability and desire in their work. The lack of opportunity leaves individuals feeling powerless.

In February 2004, I moved from open coding of data to selective coding for the core category (*rehumanizing*) and related concepts. I went back to data that I had collected earlier in my research. Although these data had been collected using an interview protocol (early in my research and before I fully understood the importance of staying open) I did use it—*all is data*—to selectively code for indicators of *rehumanizing* and related categories—including *Igniting Passions*. My analysis of these earlier data (collected between December 2002 and November 2003) yielded the following conceptual ideation.

Conceptual Memo

Igniting Passions: Maturity of network members enhances purposeful engagement and facilitates their kindred sharing. Maturity may reduce opportunism and transactional interactions. Mature individuals may appreciate the value of authentic connections and kindred sharing more than those with less experience in the work world. Reference to second careers may also be reference to more passionate engagement in the focus of the network—where their hearts are—their passions engaged more so than in their "day jobs" in the formal organization.

Contextual dimensions of network engagement energy, fun, achievement, tension emerged from further data analysis as positively correlated with passion.

Conceptual Memos

Depth and Meaning in Igniting Passions: There's no pretense—no showiness—in network interactions. Members are there for a purpose. There's depth and meaning in their participation—*"problem solving, sorting out ... let's have some discussion on this."* Real purpose and value (meaning) to those engaged and at the same time, it's fun. They enjoy the action, the inevitable debates. It stimulates the environment. It enables members to "eyeball people and get stuff sorted out" so there's real value—progress is made in work.

Igniting Passions: Pressured environment creates an energy that ignites passion. Unpredictability creates energy—fast pace creates excitement and stimulates networking. While there's anxiety created in this environment, it's

(Continued)

(Continued)

an enjoyable anxiety—it's edgy, stimulating. . . . *"What excites me is the pace of it. I like that, I like the energy it gives me and the energy it creates so I like it fast not slow. . . . I think it's very important. It feels like a life! Ahh . . . sometimes it's too much for sure but I'll take any day of too much than too little."*

Challenge emerged as another dimension of igniting passions.

Conceptual Memo

Igniting Passions: Passions are ignited by challenge—the "against all odds" syndrome—finding mutual commitment to a goal that others consider impossible or crazy. Setting themselves apart from the "masses," the ordinary—taking on a challenge and making it work—high achievement orientation—success is sweeter when shared. Believing in the impossible and then making it happen. There's a charge in being challenged and being creative in solving an issue, a problem that ignites passionate engagement within a network—draws members in.

Likening facilitates the challenge and achievement dimensions of igniting passions.

Conceptual Memo

Igniting Passions/Likening/Sustaining: "Newness" is part of likening—the chance to meet others who not only share a sense of energy but who are also open to what others have to offer—the chance to "show and tell" interests, share knowledge and skills—creates an energy and ignites passions—can feel out of control at times but in a good way—skills and abilities are stimulated by joint problem solving and collaborative creativity (see Bennis book on creative collaboration . . .). Moving past challenge to achievement also very important. Novelty likens but achievement sustains.

While igniting passions creates bonds, it can also create insularity.

Conceptual Memo

Igniting Passions/ Sustaining: Passions are not always positive—they can also involve spirited outbursts of anger. This is particularly the case when the core group of a network have developed such a close group identity that it compromises their relationship with others in the external environment—insularity leading to intolerance—impacts upon ability of the network to function within the larger external environment of the formal organization. Interactions become personalized and highly emotional—core becomes segregated—trust erodes and threatens sustainability ... network members may limit/reduce their participation if they feel it jeopardizes their position within the formal organization—cannot risk the consequences.

Challenge and the risk associated with it emerged again as a dimension of igniting passions.

Conceptual Memo

Igniting Passions: Challenge and the chance to achieve ignite passions. The higher the stakes, the greater the passion. That feeling of being on the edge—risking it to overcome and achieve holds a special kind of magic—a pull that can be very empowering. The fear of failure mixed with the high of success.

Passion ignites through an initial spark when individuals connect and liken.

Conceptual Memo

Finding/Igniting Passions: A network forms and fluctuates around an initial spark—this may be a person who takes the lead in identifying and connecting people of "like minds." Once like minds find each other, they quickly self-identify and self-organize. Their mutual passion creates the energy for perpetuating interactions and sustained mutual engagement.

Kindred sharing facilitates igniting passions and sparks creativity, learning, and growth.

Conceptual Memo

Kindred Sharing/Creativity/Igniting Passions/Learning: Kindred sharing involves venting—the chance to "blow off steam"—within a safe and empathetic environment. But kindred sharing moves past venting to strategizing—a proactive and empowering response to dealing with organizational issues—problems and frustrations. It's exploring ways to overcome the hurdle and move forward. It engages collective minds to addressing issues—the collective response not only enables a better response but it also builds momentum and support for moving forward. There's arguing in kindred sharing—those outside the network might see this as negative but it's part of sparking the creativity and problem-solving power of the collective mindset in a network. It's part of the fluctuating nature of the network. Energy builds through fluctuating emotions—passions ignite and creativity is sparked. The outcome is learning and growth.

Igniting passions wards off boredom and stimulates the desire for network participation.

Conceptual Memo

Igniting Passions: Boredom mitigation drives networking—igniting passions accelerates network engagement and participation. Work environments that exude boredom challenge K.W. to seek avenues to sustain energy and ward off dehumanization.

As the concept reaches theoretical saturation, a further memo attempts to integrate the conceptual ideas that have emerged, organizing them into conditions, dimensions, and consequences of igniting passions.

Conceptual Memo

Igniting Passions: ". . . . passion. This is when you are really working with people—not just a 'file' that you are responsible for." In work involving "the human dynamic," it is essential to come together face to face—there is a cost benefit to doing so if it engages the passion of organizational members—we speculate about whether perhaps organizations should allocate resources on the basis of matching passions! ...

"Try to develop a passion meter." Informal networks as a way to find the people with a passion for organizational work ... this is a simple principle of self-organization at work—allocating resources to follow the passion. Organizational challenge of getting past "assigned work" to matching assignments with passions—may not be worth the effort of trying to orchestrate this (i.e., manage the process)—that it may be better to let things take their course and be satisfied with "60%" ... Letting the system self-organize ... organic "if no one has passion, we should not be doing it!" Organizations can use networks to monitor "passions" and set strategic directions accordingly. The human dimension—passion ignites passion—creates understanding and engagement—Informal networks as a forum to mobilize passion into action ... bringing diverse talents, skills together—mobilized by shared passion—vision—system sorts itself/self organizes to achieve action—progress the work—enhance the practice.

Conditions: Energized Environment: Pressured environment creates an energy that ignites passion. Unpredictability creates energy—fast pace creates excitement and stimulates networking. While there's anxiety created in this environment, it's an enjoyable anxiety—it's edgy, stimulating...." "What excites me is the pace of it. I like that, I like the energy it gives me and the energy it creates so I like it fast not slow.... I think it's very important. It feels like a life! Ahh ... sometimes it's too much for sure but I'll take any day of too much than too little." There's no pretense—no showiness—in network interactions. Members are there for a purpose. There's depth and meaning in their participation—"problem solving, sorting out. . . . .let's have some discussion on this...." Real purpose and value (meaning) to those engaged and at the same time, it's fun. They enjoy the action, the inevitable debates. It stimulates the environment. It enables members to "eyeball people and get stuff sorted out" so there's real value—progress is made in work.

Initial Spark: A network forms and fluctuates around an initial spark—this may be a person who takes the lead in identifying and connecting people of "like minds." Once like minds find each other, they quickly self-identify and self-organize. Their mutual passion creates the energy for perpetuating interactions and sustained mutual engagement.

Boredom Mitigation: Boredom mitigation drives networking—igniting passions accelerates network engagement and participation. Work environments that exude boredom challenge K.W. to seek avenues to sustain energy and ward off dehumanization.

(Continued)

(Continued)

Dimensions: Recognition: Passion is positively correlated to recognition. Feedback and recognition fuel alignment of individual and organizational passions.

Personal Alignment: Informal networks may be a venue/vessel for individuals to be able to bring their passion back into their organizational roles. Experiences of network participation speak of their reconnecting with previous "dream jobs," core values, interests, and passions—this desire to reconnect passion and purpose may be a motivation for seeking/ participating in networks. Maturity of network members enhances purposeful engagement and facilitates their kindred sharing. Maturity may reduce opportunism and transactional interactions. Mature individuals may appreciate the value of authentic connections and kindred sharing more than those with less experience in the work world. Reference to second careers may also be reference to more passionate engagement in the focus of the network—where their hearts are—their passions engaged more so than in their "day jobs" in the formal organization.

Purposeful Engagement: Informal networks as keeping personal and professional passions from being eroded, depleted in the hectic, humdrum of daily organizational operations. . . . *"Our job is our work . . . our practice is our passion."* Distinguishing between "practice" and "work"—between "vocation" and "job" . . ." . . . passion. This is when you are really working with people—not just a 'file' that you are responsible for." In work involving "the human dynamic," it is essential to come together face to face—there is a cost benefit to doing so if it engages the passion of organizational members—we speculate about whether perhaps organizations should allocate resources on the basis of matching passions! . . . "Try to develop a passion meter."

Networks as a way to find the people with a passion for organizational work . . . this is a simple principle of self-organization at work—allocating resources to follow the passion. Organizational challenge of getting past "assigned work" to matching assignments with passions—may not be worth the effort of trying to orchestrate this (i.e., manage the process)—that it may be better to let things take their course and be satisfied with "60%" . . . Letting the system self-organize . . . organic—"if no one has passion, we should not be doing it!" Organizations can use networks to monitor "passions" and set strategic directions accordingly. The human dimension— passion ignites passion—creates understanding and engagement—networks as a forum to mobilize passion into action . . . bringing diverse talents, skills together—mobilized by shared passion—vision—system sorts itself/self organizes to achieve action—progress the work—enhance the practice.

Challenge: Passion is positively correlated to challenge. Passions are ignited by challenge—the "against all odds" syndrome—finding mutual commitment to a goal that others consider impossible or crazy. Setting themselves apart from the "masses," the ordinary—taking on a challenge and making it work—high achievement orientation—success is sweeter when shared. Believing in the impossible and then making it happen.

Challenge and the chance to achieve ignite passions. The higher the stakes, the greater the passion. That feeling of being on the edge—risking it to overcome and achieve holds a special kind of magic—a pull that can be very empowering. The fear of failure mixed with the high of success. There's a charge in being challenged and being creative in solving an issue, a problem that ignites passionate engagement within a network—draws members in.

Learning: "really start to learn when they find a passion for a subject and then make a real connection to other learners and real time practitioners." Individual passion for learning is stimulated and reinforced in community. Learning and knowledge sharing. . . . Being selfish in terms of learning . . . Someone commented … "When we are (selfish), we learn to give to others—greedy to share …" Networks as a "vessel" for fulfilling greedy learning/sharing needs—reciprocal fulfillment of passions for learning and sharing. The accidental learning presented in networks is a "smorgasbord" that rekindles the desire to learn—it also restores the learner's control and builds autonomy self-select, sample, take what's desired and needed. Restless spirits sated by continuous learning opportunities—integrated learning and practice. Individuals must be motivated to learn—have an urge, desire to learn—be "greedy" to learn. Someone commented … "When you're ready to learn, a teacher will appear … networks bring the eager, *poised to learn* together with ready teachers."

Consequences: Likening: Passion is positively correlated to likening. "Newness" is part of likening—the chance to meet others who not only share a sense of energy but who are also open to what others have to offer—the chance to "show and tell" interests, share knowledge and skills—creates an energy and ignites passions—can feel out of control at times but in a good way—skills and abilities are stimulated by joint problem solving and collaborative creativity (see Bennis book on creative collaboration …). Moving past challenge to achievement also very important. Novelty likens but achievement sustains.

Rereading field notes from interview with A…., noted the many references to passion, in particular, the connection between passion and bonding of network members. Appears that the common passion that brings network members together—part of the likening that creates a network—is also the "glue" that bonds network members. So … passion creates likening.

(Continued)

(Continued)

Bonding: She goes on to describe the "passionate few" as bonding due to the resistance they encounter from the formal system—"the resistance serves as a way to separate out those who really have a passion to keep working" ... Resistance creates bonding and reinforces passions ... a cyclic process that sustains member engagement in fluctuating networks. Bonding reinforces passions but excessive bonding creates insularity.

Insularity is negatively correlated to network sustainability. Passions are not always positive—they can also involve spirited outbursts of anger. This is particularly the case when the core group of a network have developed such a close group identity that it compromises their relationship with others in the external environment—insularity leading to intolerance—impacts upon ability of the network to function within the larger external environment of the formal organization interactions become personalized and highly emotional—core becomes segregated, trust erodes and threatens sustainability ... network members may limit/reduce their participation if they feel it jeopardizes their position within the formal organization—cannot risk the consequences.

Performance: Passion is positively correlated to performance. Individuals who exhibit resistance to change or appear to be risk averse can become labeled in organizations as "non-performers." They may be shunned by others—particularly by managers. This response further isolates the individual and contributes to lower performance—a self-fulfilling prophecy. What may lie at the heart of this superficial assessment of non-performance is a disengagement of the individual from their passion or purpose in work. This disengagement may be a defense or coping mechanism in response to increasing dehumanization from a changing workplace context or a botched or poorly executed change effort. Individuals are "having trouble trying to reconnect." They are "disillusioned about the organization and trying to cope with the change" around them. They've become "disconnected from their work." If efforts are made to listen past the disengagement and non-performance, one can often find that there was a time when these individuals "had a real hunger for their work." What they require is a chance to reconnect with their passion, to feel depth and meaning in their work. They "need to be whole," to have their "eyes light up" again, to feel the energy of a new challenge and new learning. This isn't happening in many organizations because "managers are not listening." The result of their inattention is the veritable blocking of employee capability and desire in their work. The lack of opportunity leaves individuals feeling powerless.

Creativity: Arguing is part of igniting passions and sparking the creativity and problem-solving power of the collective mindset in a network. It's part of the fluctuating nature of the network. Energy builds through fluctuating emotions—passions ignite and creativity is sparked.

Theoretical sampling of data collected earlier in the study (October and November, 2001) provided additional indicators of several dimensions of *igniting passions* that had emerged previously—fun, challenge, learning, energy, confidence, and bonding.

Conceptual Memo

Igniting Passions: There's a strong desire to continue to network once individual passions have been ignited. Passions are fueled by the desire to continue to experience the energy and synergy that result from mutual engagement—*to work and learn and laugh together.* There's a strong sense of fun, of pushing the envelope. The desire to continue to move the network forward creates its own sense of excitement and fuels a passionate belief in the ability to make a difference.

Conceptual elaboration concludes when the relationships among individually elaborated concepts emerge through the identification and use of relevant theoretical codes to achieve an integrated theoretical framework for the overall theory. The theoretical codes that emerged in this study include basic social process (both psychological and structural processes) and amplifying causal looping. *Igniting passions* earned a pivotal position within the basic social psychological process of *rehumanizing,* the core category of *fluctuating support networks,* itself a basic social structural process.

CONCEPTUAL INTEGRATION AND WRITING UP   ●

Once I had achieved theoretical saturation of my core concept and related categories, I proceeded to review and hand sort memos regarding the core and its properties and dimensions. As I began to sort and look for relationships between the various concepts, theoretical codes began to emerge as an abstract modeling of the latent structural patterns that could integrate and explain the emerging theory. The first indication of emergent theoretical codes was memoed in December 2003.

My study may be viewed as that of a basic social process (BSP)—coping with change (in this case, the substantive area is the knowledge workplace).

(Continued)

(Continued)

As the overarching BSP, coping with change includes both a basic social structural process (BSSP)—fluctuating networks of professional concern[4]— and a basic social psychological process (BSPP)—rehumanizing—which is also the core category, integrating and explaining the BSPP of rehumanizing through the BSSP of fluctuating networks of professional concern. Rehumanizing can be viewed as a structural condition affecting the nature of fluctuating networks of professional concern. These networks have always been there in the workplace as they are inherent to social organization generally, but today's increasingly compressed and dehumanized work environments (changing workplace context) have brought the need for rehumanizing to the fore as a means of addressing the main concern of those involved—coping with change (thereby magnifying the BSPP of rehumanizing as a structural condition of the BSSP of fluctuating networks). As such, the BSSP of fluctuating networks of professional concern has taken on the properties of the BSPP of rehumanizing, including authenticity, depth/meaning, respect, safety, healing . . . As a preliminary suggestion, the stages in the BSPP of rehumanizing may be finding, likening, igniting passions, kindred sharing, experimenting, bonding, and sustaining. Some of these may be combined as research progresses; new ones may be identified . . . the structural process (of fluctuating networks) is of significance because it explains the organization of behavior (as emergent informal organization) to address the main concern of the participants—coping with change within the workplace—through a BSPP (rehumanizing) as antidote to the dehumanizing impact of traditional formal organizational structures. This is starting to feel "right" for me—things are fitting into place and I can now see an overall conceptual framework around which to begin building the theory.

While continuing to consider basic social process as an appropriate theoretical code through which to integrate my emerging theory, I remained open to the emergence of other theoretical codes as I continued to hand sort and integrate memos. A final integration of the theory occurred in March 2004 with the emergence of the theoretical code of amplifying causal looping. The final sorting and integration followed, generating a theoretical outline (conceptual framework) for the full articulation of the theory.

ENDNOTES

1. It is important to remember that this is the work of a novice conducting her first grounded theory study. It is, as such, an exemplar but is by no means offered as a marker of excellence in doing classic GT.

2. As so often happens, there was a connection back to my initial research interest in communities of practice, but my grounded theory explains much more about what is really going on as managers and other knowledge workers voluntarily seek out and engage in work-related communities and networks. My theory explains that the motivation for their participation is not simply learning and practice enhancement. It is much more about their efforts to overcome the dehumanization they experience in their work and their workplace context in the midst of persistent and unpredictable change.

3. My grounded theory is rather complex in that it is a "theory within a theory"—the overall theory of *fluctuating support networks* (a basic social structural process) with its core category of *rehumanizing* (a basic social psychological process) of which *igniting passions* is the central stage in the process (the core category of the *rehumanizing* process).

4. I later renamed this concept *fluctuating support networks* to more effectively reflect their substantive role in providing support to network members.

Appendix C

Doing Classic GT Using Mixed Qualitative and Quantitative Data

This appendix is based on excerpts from Walsh (2014a) and elaborates on her application of classic GT while using mixed qualitative and quantitative data and techniques. The full article "A Strategic Path to Study IT Use Through Users' IT Culture and IT Needs: A Mixed-Method Grounded Theory" may be found in the *Journal of Strategic Information Systems, 23*(2), pp. 146–173. Copyright 2014. (Permission granted by Elsevier, License No. 3674860603800, July 23, 2015). Examples of the mixed qualitative and quantitative data applied in this work may be found in Appendix D.

● 1. A MIXED-METHOD GROUNDED THEORY DESIGN

In this section, we detail the research design that was not set at the beginning of our study; instead, this emerged as our research was conducted, and it was guided by the emerging theory.

1.1 The GT Framework

If one does not take into account any paradigmatic consideration, two main distinct variants of the GT framework may be found in the literature. One of these variants is favored by Glaser and the other by Strauss (Melia, 1996; Urquhart et al., 2009), with main disagreements involving coding issues and the role of extant literature. Our stance is closest to Glaser's but, beyond any difference of opinion between

Glaser and Strauss over the years, and if one goes back to their original (1967) common work, Urquhart et al. (2009) showed that four main characteristics should be found in a GT study: (1) Emergence of both research design and outcome must be rooted in data and not preconceived/imposed on data; (2) constant comparative analysis of the data must take place (i.e., data are constantly compared to previously collected and analyzed data, looking for similarities and differences to help toward conceptualization and theorization); (3) there must be theoretical sampling (i.e., sampling is directed by the emerging theory and continues until the saturation of concepts, categories, properties, and relationships is reached); and (4) the ultimate aim of GT must be theory building, substantive or formal theory (i.e., discovering and constructing, rather than verifying. theory is the end purpose of a GT study).

1.2 A Mixed-Method Approach

In his 2008 work about quantitative GT, Glaser uses Lazarsfeld's work and his techniques of quantitative analysis for discovery. Lazarsfeld "insisted on the combining of qualitative and quantitative analysis" (Glaser, 2008, p. 6), leading to a mixed-method approach. A mixed-method design includes different quantitative and/or qualitative methods, which combine with and supplement each other within a single project. In our work, we did not use qualitative data and methods to draw hypotheses that we verified through quantitative data and methods; this would be what we understand to be a multi-method approach (Morse, 2003, pp. 189–208). In our research, neither qualitative nor quantitative data/methods were sufficient in themselves to theorize; all were necessary. This article combines qualitative and quantitative data and research methods in a mixed-method GT approach.

We used both secondary data (from the existing literature) and primary data (collected for the present study). When we collected primary data (quantitative and/or qualitative), we did so as we needed them to move the emerging theory forward and also to allow for triangulation. Qualitative data were collected when we needed rich description of the emerging relationships between concepts. Quantitative data were collected when we needed to move back from details and obtain a synthetic perspective. All data (qualitative and quantitative) were analyzed as one set.

1.3 Study Context, Sample, and Data Collection

The software that we more specifically investigated is an open source e-learning software platform, Moodle (Modular Object-Oriented Dynamic Learning Environment), which may be used by both professors and students in third-level education and training contexts. We investigated the use of this platform in a European business school, where this software is mostly used as an exchange platform for professors and students. Professors can (if they wish) upload their class materials. Their students have direct and unlimited access to this platform and can download what they need. The platform also allows students to submit assignments, and grading may be done online by the professors. It also provides facilities for instant messaging, and online news, announcements, and timetable details. The use of the platform is not institutionally mandatory, but its use is presented as a great help for both students and professors in fulfilling their tasks; it is, therefore, strongly recommended by administrators for both professors and students. "Well, it's on Moodle, you can find it for yourself" is a recurring answer from some administrative staff when either students or professors ask questions. Most full-time professors use it at least to provide course materials, and students may feel compelled to use it to gain access to these materials, although they could also obtain them from other students if they do not want to use the platform. Some professors might, however, insist that students upload their homework on the platform in order to obtain grades.

Our sampling was guided by the emerging theory. The slices of quantitative data were collected through surveys administered at the end of a school year (June 2012). Therefore, the participants in these surveys had had the opportunity to directly access the investigated exchange platform for a significant amount of time (at least two semesters) and had been offered voluntary training sessions at the beginning of each semester.

The qualitative slices of data were collected through interviews conducted between September 2011 and September 2012 with both students and professors. As we were part of the institution investigated, we also used participant observation. We used Walsh et al.'s (2010) typological work to guide us in our theoretical sampling. We identified users that fit some of the ideal types highlighted by Walsh et al. (2010). More than the seven interviewees we report on were involved; we retained for the present study and report on only those users whose information technology (IT) culture profile we could identify with sufficient precision and who were different in terms of age, nationality, and background to allow for different perspectives. Professors who were interviewed were colleagues that we worked with, sharing classes, chores, or research projects (but not the present one) with them. Students who were interviewed were those with whom we had an above-average number of exchanges as we supervised their master's degree dissertations. Interviewees were treated as case studies rather than as simple interviewees. For the first slice of qualitative data, several extensive interviews were conducted with each interviewee between September 2011 and May 2012; notes were taken and memos written up.

Two surveys (one for professors and one for students)—very similar but with some questions adapted to the different end-users—were put online, and e-mails were sent to faculty and students to invite them to respond in May and June 2012. E-mails were sent to 375 faculty members (85 full-time professors and 290 part-time professors) and 1,076 students, and 84 professors and 198 students answered the surveys (the response rates were 22.4% and 18.4%, respectively). All received answers were used, and no outliers were removed. We verified our results with early and late respondents' data with no significant difference. This indicates that nonresponse bias should not be a problem in the quantitative data collected for the present study (Armstrong & Overton, 1977).

Quantitative data were analyzed with the help of partial least squares (PLS) structural equation modeling (SEM), applied in an exploratory manner. The transcripts of the qualitative data were hand-coded a number of times and sorted out on a table (in parallel with our quantitative investigations. After we had started to explore our quantitative slices of data, together with the qualitative data already collected, we conducted further interviews in July and September 2012 with the seven participants theoretically sampled for the present study, in order to verify our interpretation of the qualitative and quantitative data already collected and to expose this to their perspectives. These last interviews with each interviewee were recorded and relevant elements transcribed. During these interviews, and only then, did we briefly describe to interviewees details of the research that was being conducted. We also introduced them to such terms as *IT acculturation* or *IT culture* and the distinction we drew between the two terms *IT utilization* and *IT use*, which follows Walsh's (2010) definition of these two terms.[1] Had we not done so, and as these terms were part of our own vocabulary, we risked biasing their answers through the way we asked our questions. Also, because some respondents were of different nationalities and spoke different native languages, some of the interviews were conducted in English and others in French. In order to translate adequately important words such as *usage* and *utilization* from one language to the other, the meaning of the terms used had to be fully understood by respondents and our interpretations/translations verified. Therefore, we chose to inform interviewees about the meanings we attributed to these terms in order to avoid misinterpretation on our part of the qualitative data collected. Further notes were made and memos were again written up immediately after these last interviews took place as, in most instances, these final conversations continued after the interviews were recorded. Qualitative data were first open-coded on concepts (e.g., IITC, utilization, global IT needs, contextual IT needs, and situational IT needs) and then theoretically coded in terms of the relationships between these concepts (e.g., individual IT culture → global IT needs, position → contextual IT needs, situational IT needs → utilization). Secondary data (from the literature), primary data (collected for the present study), quantitative data (collected through

Figure C.1   Using All Our Data as One Set[1]

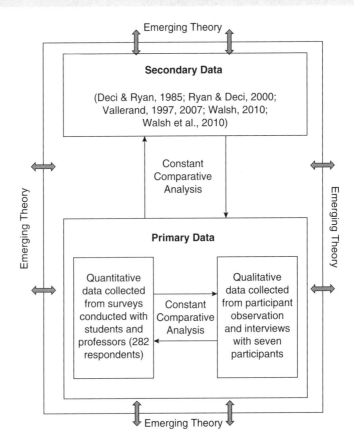

surveys), and qualitative data (collected through interviews and participant observation) were analyzed together, and, in a critical realist stance, we opted for the relationships between concepts that appeared to best fit our whole data set, while considering at the same time broader perspectives reaching beyond our substantive area, in order to start driving toward formal GT.

In order not to confuse the reader, and although many different paths were investigated that are not reported here due to space allocation, we present in the results section only the final models that emerged from and were congruent with our whole data set. As quantitative and qualitative investigations and analyses were done simultaneously, while taking into account all data as one set, and constantly comparing and analyzing all data as they were collected (see Figure C.1), we justify our models with previous works from the literature, quotes from interviews, quantitative reports, or all three of these. Using mixed methods allowed us to avoid the "Texas sharpshooter approach"[2] (Biemann, 2012), a bias that plagues many quantitative studies and that results mostly from their authors' quest for publication (Biemann, 2012).

Throughout the present research, we openly remain in an exploratory stance and iterate between all data. For instance, some relationships were investigated and confirmed through quantitative methods with our substantive quantitative data set, but we neither retained nor reported on them as they did not make sense in our complete data set. Conversely, some other relationships that were not completely confirmed through our quantitative data are discussed, because, based on information obtained through our qualitative data set, they could be important for further research in other substantive areas with different, and less specific, targeted sampling.

1.4 Quantitative Measures

All research variables were quantitatively modeled as reflective using multi-item Likert-type scales (ranging from 1 = "not true at all" to 7 = "completely true"), except for the variables POSITION, IITC, and UTILIZATION.

Reflective measures for the constructs global IT needs (GLOBITNEE), contextual IT needs (CONITNEE), and situational IT needs (SITITNEE) were developed specifically for the present study. To ensure content validity, we used qualitative data from the interviews that were conducted, as well as Walsh et al.'s (2010) qualitative GT work and its detailed online coding appendices. Reflective measures for ease of use (EOU) and usefulness (U) were adapted from Davis (1989). Benbasat and Barki (2007) stressed the "need to make sure usefulness is measured beyond perceptions where possible" (p. 216). The perceptual aspect of usefulness was minimized, as we studied usefulness and ease of use as assessed by users after they had had time to be trained and to test and access the investigated software for a significant period of time.

The control variable POSITION was dummy-coded (Professor = 1 and Student = 2).

For the IITC construct, we used as a starting point the measure proposed by Walsh (2009) and verified by Von Stetten, Wild, and Chrennikow (2011), which we aimed at improving. We modeled IITC as a first-order reflective, second-order formative construct and followed the guidelines provided by Diamantopoulos, Riefler, and Roth (2008). The first-order latent reflective variables we started with were accomplishment needs satisfied through IT usage (ACCNEE), affiliation needs satisfied through IT usage (AFFNEE), primary needs satisfied through IT usage (PRIMNEE), power needs satisfied through IT usage (POWNEE), intrinsic motivation to know IT (INTMOTKNO), extrinsic motivation to use IT through identified regulation (EXTMOTID), and extrinsic motivation to use IT through external regulation (EXTMOTEX). The items of this last construct were worded negatively and had to be reverse-coded to obtain the new variable REV_EXTMOTEX. However, Von Stetten et al. (2011) found that this sub-construct, proposed by Walsh (2009), did not have a significant influence on IITC. We verified and confirmed this point in our preliminary investigations and did not include this sub-construct in the final measurement model of IITC, as we found theoretical reason not to do so: If one considers the self-determination continuum proposed by Gagné and Deci (2005), all sub-constructs of IITC are on the positive end of this continuum except for the questioned variable EXTMOTEX, which rather appears to capture some elements of amotivation (Pelletier et al., 1997). Even recoding and inverting this variable does not solve this theoretical issue, as it has not been proven that amotivation is the reciprocal function of motivation. This is why we chose not to include this sub-construct in the IITC measurement model. Measures of the other dimensions were adapted to improve reliability, and content validity was ensured through the study of various scales in the psychosociological field of research, which we adapted for our purpose.[3]

Concerning the assessment of use, there is a lack of consensus in the literature on how to measure system usage/utilization, and there is a vast array of measures for it, as highlighted by Burton-Jones and Straub (2006). Wu and Du (2012) categorized the existing measures found in the literature as actual usage, reported usage, and measured usage. Actual usage (e.g., the measures used by Devaraj et al., 2008, or Venkatesh et al., 2002) involves objectively collected measures such as computer logs. The other two categories (reported and measured usage) imply subjective self-reported measures. Reported usage (e.g., the measures used by Adams et al., 1992; Keill et al., 1995; Taylor & Todd, 1995) involves measures of duration and frequency that aim at objectivity even though these measures are reported by the users themselves: for instance, the number of hours spent on a system per day. Assessed usage (e.g., the measures used by Davis, 1989; Igbaria & Parasuraman, 1989; Karahanna, Agarwal, & Angst, 2006) involves ordinal measures of intensity and extent, the ordinal scale being the main element of differentiation of this type of assessment. Over the years, other elements of differentiation that involve the user's subjective cognitive abilities were added. As a result of their investigations, Wu and Du (2012) propose the use of rich measures of assessed usage through multiple dimensions that mix different measures. Originally, we had wished to assess IT utilization as defined by Walsh (2010), that is, "the actual, objectively assessed, use of an IT" (p. 152). As actual measures extracted from computerized reports were vetoed by our faculty, we opted for self-reported ordinal measures of utilization. We included in our measure of utilization the number of functionalities used that assessed the extent of utilization (UT_FUNCT) and the frequency of utilization that assessed the intensity of utilization (UT_FREQ). We also wanted to assess the type of utilization, that is, whether users' perception of the platform led them to a self-determined or constrained utilization (variable UT_TYPE). For instance, if users go on the platform "as little as possible" or only when they feel "it is absolutely necessary," their utilization might be considered closer to mandatory than voluntary, and with differing degrees of self-determination. We therefore specifically developed for the present study a three-dimensional formative measure of utilization that included the dimensions UT_TYPE, UT_FREQ, and UT_FUNCT. The construct UTILIZATION was specified as formative, since changes in any of the three indicators would lead to changes in utilization but, conversely, a change in utilization does not imply a change in each of the three indicators.

All measures were pretested with 25 students in a postgraduate class and with a selected sample of 20 faculty members, in order to obtain comments and feedback before the pilot test was finally conducted. After the pretest, the wording of some items was readjusted, and one item was deleted from three of the reflective scales (EXTMOTID,

GLOBITNEE, and CONITNEE) in order to improve reliability; these three scales were, thus, reduced from three to two items each. As these scales were for reflective constructs and we aimed at a parsimonious instrument, this was deemed acceptable.

The measurement models, as well as the relationships between all variables, were analyzed using a PLS approach, and bootstrapping as a resampling technique (500 random samples), to generate t-statistics (Chin, 1998). We used the SMARTPLS software (Ringle, Wende, & Will, 2005). PLS analysis was preferred because it does not require data with a normal distribution (Fornell & Cha, 1994), and it supports both reflective and formative constructs (Gefen, Rigdon, & Straub, 2000). It was also preferred because our research objectives were exploratory (Gefen et al., 2011; Hair et al., 2012; Ringle et al., 2012). PLS analysis is particularly suitable in situations of high complexity, with low theoretical information (Jöreskog & Wold, 1982): We had an important number of variables and little theoretical backup on the relationships we wanted to investigate. Another advantage of the PLS approach is its ability to work with a small sample size (Ringle et al., 2012; Urbach & Ahlemann, 2010).

● 2. THE EMERGING RESEARCH MODELS

As advised by Glaser (1978, 2008), we let our data "speak" and guide the emerging theory. The propositions highlighted could not have been developed if all data had not been interpreted as one set, and if both qualitative and quantitative methods and analyses had not been applied in combination.

Our stance is critical realist (Bhaskar, 1979, 1989, 1998, 2002). Although a debate about critical realist precepts is beyond the scope of this book, before we present our models and propositions, it is essential to clarify what causality is for a critical realist. The notion of causality as a "generative mechanism" is a core and defining feature of critical realism (Bhaskar, 2002). Generative mechanisms are best understood as "tendencies," as their activation is highly context-dependent (Bhaskar, 2002). In contrast with the Humean vision of causality ("A causes B"), commonly accepted in information systems (IS) traditional quantitative positivist circles, a generative mechanism can be reformulated as "A generates B in context C" (Cartwright, 2003; Smith, 2010). For a critical realist, causality is thus a process of how causal powers are actualized in some particular context: a process in which the generative mechanisms of that context (C) shape (modulate, dampen, etc.)

the particular outcomes. For instance, building on Tsang and Kwan (1999)'s example, a car will drive adequately if it has four wheels and an engine but only if somebody also turns on the ignition and a nail does not puncture one of its tires. Therefore, the arrows in the diagrams proposed in this section do not illustrate causality as traditionally understood; they illustrate the activation of causal powers as revealed in the substantive area (the use of the Moodle platform by students and professors) and the context (a European business school) that were investigated. The paths that are reported in the models are those that best fitted our set of data (qualitative and quantitative) within the substantive area and the context that were being investigated. Where possible, however, we used a reflexive approach and extended our results in order for them to be applied in further research in other substantive areas and contexts. When we understood the collected data as sufficient to demonstrate that a proposition would apply whatever the substantive area and context investigated, we added the word *mostly* in the wording of the corresponding proposition. *Mostly*, however, is used only as a heuristic device and should not be taken at face value. It means that, based on the data we collected, the proposition appears to extend to other substantive areas and other contexts beyond those researched for the present study; this would, of course, need to be verified in further research. When *mostly* is not used in the wording of a proposition, it indicates that the corresponding proposition may hold true only within our substantive area and investigated context.

As our main concern was to investigate the path between users' individual IT culture and their utilization of the e-learning platform, and how the various constructs related to their perceived IT needs (global, contextual and situational) fit in this path, we first describe in this section the new path to IT use that we propose through these new concepts. We then embed one of our newly defined variables in the TAM nomological framework to position our work with respect to past literature.

Qualitative and quantitative analyses were embedded, and our results emerged through constant iterations between quantitative and qualitative data as they were collected and through the analysis of all our data as one set. Therefore, for each model, we present our results in a logical sequence that relates our findings as closely as possible to how we arrived at them.

For each proposition, we detail elements from the literature (if available) and/or qualitative clues that led us to it. To avoid unnecessary length, we cite only when needed some verbatim that we consider as most illustrative for our arguments. We also report on the quantitative results that were obtained as we explored the various quantitative paths between the newly defined variables. We report on these through (1) the standardized coefficients β of the investigated paths, which indicate the strength of the relationships between each pair of variables, and have values between 0 and 1; (2) the significance of these paths, obtained through the bootstrapping procedure and expressed by the probability p that the hypothesis underlying this path might not be verified; and (3) the R^2 values for each variable, which inform us how much of its variance is explained by its antecedent(s).

With the help of our whole data set, we found that individual IT culture *mostly* positively influences the global IT needs perceived by users (Proposition 1). In our substantive area and investigated context, individual IT culture also happened to positively influence the contextual IT needs perceived by professors and students (Proposition 2). Both global IT needs and contextual IT needs were found to *mostly* influence the situational IT needs perceived by users for a given IT proposed in their work context and supposed, by deciding instances, to be of some help in fulfilling some of the users' tasks (Propositions 3 and 4). These perceived situational IT needs in turn *mostly* significantly explain the use of this IT (Proposition 5). The position held by an individual within an organization will *mostly* influence his or her contextual and situational IT needs (Propositions 6a and 6b); in our substantive area and investigated context, it also moderated the effect of the perceived situational IT needs on the actual utilization of the investigated IT (Proposition 6c).

ENDNOTES

1. "We define IT-utilization as the actual, objectively assessed, use of an IT, and IT-usage as a socially constructed . . . phenomenon." (Walsh, 2010, p. 8)

2. "The fabled 'Texas sharpshooter' fires a shotgun at a barn and then paints the target around the most significant cluster of bullet holes in the wall. Accordingly, the Texas sharpshooter fallacy describes a false conclusion that occurs whenever *ex post* explanations are presented to interpret a random cluster in some data" (Biemann, 2012, p. 2).

3. The investigated scales were the determination scale (Sheldon, Ryan, & Reis, 1996), basic psychological needs satisfaction scales (currently being researched by a team of researchers, including Deci and Ryan), global motivation scale (Guay, Mageau, & Vallerand, 2003), and the fundamental needs satisfaction scale in the context of sports (Gillet, Rosnet, & Vallerand, 2008).

Appendix D

Some Examples of Theoretical Coding Using Mixed Qualitative and Quantitative Data

Although referring to Walsh (2014a), which is an empirical article, this appendix is extracted and adapted from Walsh (2014c), which is a methodological article. The examples provided refer to the same research project as Appendix C and provides some examples of theoretical coding using mixed qualitative and quantitative data in an embedded mixed GT design. This appendix also illustrates how, once the core category of a grounded theory has emerged, the literature may be used as secondary data.

		Constant comparative analysis of all data as one set		
Theoretical codes	Generalizability	Secondary data (from previous phases and from the literature)	Primary qualitative data	Primary quantitative data
Proposition 1: Individual information technology (IT) culture has a positive influence on the individual's global IT needs.	Substantively formalized	We found, during previous phases of our research, three main attitudinal user groups (proactive, passive, and refusal). These groups include different user profiles, with differing degrees of IT acculturation. We also found that the most IT-acculturated users are proactive. They are perceived by managers as having a facilitating influence during the implementation of new IT in organizations. They are also those users with high levels of global IT needs, whereas passive users have lower levels of global IT needs and refusal users have none.	"For me, there is a clear link between an individual's level of IT acculturation and the need they perceive for IT in their life." (CEO of an IT firm)	IITC → GLOBITNEE: $\beta = 0.598$, $p < 0.001$, R^2 for GLOBITNEE = 35.8%
Proposition 2: Individual IT culture has a positive influence on contextual IT needs.	Bounded by context	We found during previous phases of our research that the users who were highly IT-acculturated also had high levels of contextual IT needs.	"I certainly could not do my job in X school without IT. This was not the case in my previous institution, although I personally feel I need IT to do my job as a professor . . . For instance, it's the first time I have been asked to use PowerPoint slides to teach. In my old school, nobody ever used PowerPoint." (Young assistant professor with a couple of previous teaching experiences and who has started a new job in X school; she grew up in a computerized home environment with a father who is an IT engineer)	IITC → CONITNEE: $\beta = 0.400$, $p < 0.001$

Proposition 3: Global IT needs influence situational IT needs, positively or negatively.	Substantively formalized	Vallerand (1997, 2001) showed that motivation at the situational level results from the effects of both global motivation and "social factors at the appropriate level of generality." (Vallerand, 1997, p. 275)	"I have fairly important IT needs; for example, I have several computers, and I always need to be connected through the Web. When I travel abroad, I remain connected even if it costs me a lot of money. . . . You evaluate the platform and how it helps you fulfill needs linked with your responsibilities. I found that Moodle helped only with uploading the files that I wanted the students to have, and I found other functionalities inadequate, so I use the platform only minimally." (Young informations systems [IS] assistant professor)	POSITION → SITITNEE: $\beta = -0.138$, $p < 0.001$
Proposition 4: Contextual IT needs have a positive influence on situational IT needs.	Bounded by context	N/A	"The link between the need for IT that I perceived as related to the school where I did my Executive Master of Business Administration degree, and the need for the specific tool that was proposed to help us in our tasks as students is significant. . . . It was made clear to us, from the beginning of the course that we were supposed to be IT-proficient." (Mature EMBA student)	CONITNEE → SITITNEE: $\beta = 0.280$, $p < 0.001$

(Continued)

(Continued)

| Theoretical codes | Constant comparative analysis of all data as one set | | | |
	Generalizability	Secondary data (from previous phases and from the literature)	Primary qualitative data	Primary quantitative data
Proposition 5: Situational IT needs, related to some specific system or software, have a positive influence on the use of this specific system or software.	Substantively formalized	If users perceive needs for some specific IT in order to fulfill given tasks, they will be driven to fulfill these needs (Maslow, 1954) and hence use this specific IT.	N/A	SITITNEE → UTILIZATION: $\beta = 0.676$, $p > 0.001$
Proposition 6a: The position held by an individual within a given organization affects the individual's contextual IT needs.	Substantively formalized	Post et al. (1999) show that organization size and users' academic education influence the level of users' contextual IT needs.	"I have done several summer jobs during my studies—from stable work with horses, through factory work, to helping candidates in local elections; obviously, I did not have the same needs for IT in all these jobs. It is probably in my current teaching position that I need IT the most." (Young assistant professor)	POSITION → CONITNEE: $\beta = 0.277$, $p > 0.001$, R^2 for CONITNEE explained by IITC and POSITION = 27.7%

Proposition					
Proposition 6b: The position held by an individual within an organization affects his or her situational IT needs.	Substantively formalized	N/A		N/A	POSITION → SITITNEE: β = 0.454, $p < 0.001$, R^2 for SITITNEE explained by CONITNEE, GLOBITNEE, and POSITION = 35.8%
Proposition 6c: Position has a moderating influence between situational IT needs and utilization.	Bounded by context	N/A	"I teach in several schools and I am not very much into IT. If I were to get used to all the different IT tools in the different schools where I teach, it would take me hours that I don't have. Unless I am 'officially' obliged to utilize a platform, I will not do it even if I need it . . . even if it would make my exchange with the students somehow easier." (Professor who shares his time between consulting and teaching in business schools, and who feels, as he says so himself, "constrained to utilize IT.")	N/A	Quantitative analyses with and without the moderating effect

Appendix E

Examples of Diagrams as Precursors of a Theory

As we saw in Chapter 7, a diagram is not a theory. However, it may help the researcher's theoretical sensitivity, thus nurturing the emergence of a theory, especially if the theory is complex and multiple theoretical codes are emerging from the data.

Two of the following diagrams are extracted from Walsh, Renaud, and Kalika (2013); two are unpublished and were intermediary memos.

Memo 1: Unpublished

Memo 2:   Extracted from Walsh, Renaud, and Kalika, 2013

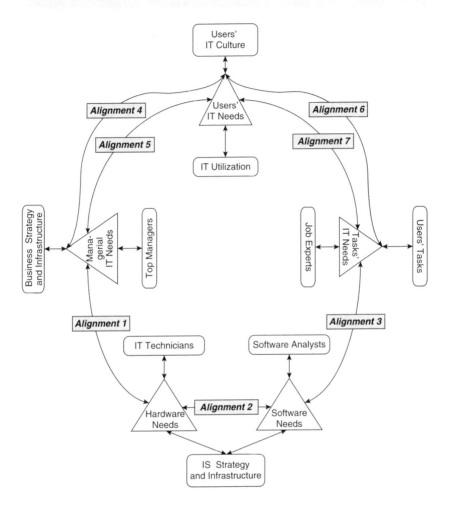

Memo 3:   Unpublished

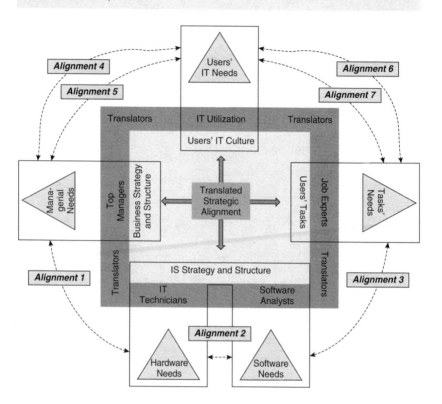

Memo 4:   Extracted from Walsh, Renaud, and Kalika, 2013

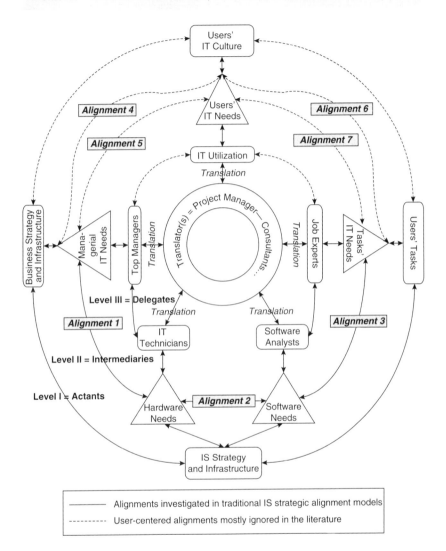

Glossary

Basic Social Process: A generic theoretical construct explaining fundamental patterns in the organization of social behavior as it occurs over time, involving a change over time with discernible breaking points or points of transition or passage from one stage to another. Basic social processes may be psychological (e.g., rehumanizing, becoming, etc.) or structural (network, bureaucracy, routine) or may emerge as a combination of the two (e.g., rehumanizing knowledge work through fluctuating support networks).

Category: The abstraction of individual concepts as a latent pattern.

Classic grounded theory: The systematic generation of theory from data as an integrated set of concepts and as hypotheses about the interrelationships among these concepts that focus on a main issue or concern in the area under study and explain how that issue or concern is processed or resolved.

Code: The label attached to an incident during the substantive coding stage of analysis. Codes are often descriptive, particularly in the initial stages of data analysis.

Concept: The resultant higher level abstraction of a conceptual idea as emerging through the cumulative comparison of codes.

Constant comparison: A foundational pillar of classic GT in which data are analyzed as they are collected and constantly compared with previously collected data for interchangeable indicators of emerging concepts. Comparison first of indicators to indicators, then indicators to emerging concepts and finally concepts to concepts for emerging theoretical integration. Constant comparison is conducted in tandem with theoretical sampling as a means of guiding the direction of further data sampling.

Core category: The category (i.e., theoretical model) that appears to explain how the main concern in the area under study is processed, managed, or resolved by its accounting for much of the variation in the way the main concern is addressed.

Data: The empirical basis for theory building. In GT, "all is data" meaning that data are information that can be counted or expressed numerically (quantitative) or in the form of words (qualitative).

Dimension: A measurable component of a concept or category. Dimensions are not interchangeable; they are complementary to define a concept or category.

Emergence: A result of GT's open and exploratory stance in relation to approaching the research field. A foundational pillar of classic GT, emergence requires the researcher to remain open to discovering a main concern motivating the interest or action within the area under study.

Explication de texte: A technique in French literary analysis describing the close reading of text, line by line, to ascertain precisely what the author is saying without reinterpreting or implying meaning. In GT, *explication de texte* aids in generating concepts that closely fit what is going on in the substantive area by simply naming the concept as an abstraction.

Field notes: Notes recorded by the researcher while in the research setting that serve as *in the moment* reminders of incidents that may indicate potential concepts.

Formal grounded theory: A grounded theory developed at a higher level of empirical generalization and/or conceptual abstraction by extending the general implications of the core category of a substantive grounded theory through subsequent theoretical sampling across a wide range of settings and/or disciplines.

Framework: The general set of guidelines proposed for a specific approach to research, for example, action research, case-study research, classic grounded theory.

Incidents: Indicators of phenomena or experiences as observed or articulated in data.

Interchangeability of indicators: Empirical incidents in data that are interchangeable in indicating a concept (i.e., indicating the same concept) but that may also bring out different properties or values of the conceptual idea to enhance theory elaboration.

Main concern: The issue that emerges across the coded data as the prime motivator, interest, or problem in the research setting.

Memoing: The core ideational processing of theoretical ideas as they emerge through coding and constant comparative analysis, memoing is a continual process that helps to raise the data to a conceptual level and develop the properties of each category.

Methodology: The specific combination of research methods and techniques used in a research project.

Methods: The ways in which data are collected, for example, interviews, observation, filming, or surveys.

Open coding: The initial coding stage in classic GT in which the analyst codes each incident in the data for as many concepts as possibly relevant. Open coding proceeds (in tandem with memoing) until the analyst perceives a pattern emerging that may indicate a potential core category.

Paradigm: A worldview, epistemological stance, or system of shared beliefs held by a community of research practice.

Preconceptions: Assumptions embedded within a researcher's worldview or professional discipline that are taken for granted and assumed to be of relevance.

Preconscious processing: Creative insights and theoretical realizations that occur seemingly serendipitously outside the analyst's conscious efforts to analyze the data.

Property: A latent characteristic of a concept or category (e.g., authenticity, trust, healing) that cannot be directly and objectively assessed.

Readiness to sort: The moment of ideational overload following data analysis when the analyst feels a need to hand sort memos for theoretical realization.

Readiness to write: The moment when theoretical completeness appears to be achieved and memos are sorted, prompting the analyst to write the first draft of the theory.

Secondary data: Data that have been collected for some other purpose.

Selective coding: Subsequent to the emergence of the core category, further data collection and analysis is delimited to achieving theoretical saturation of the core category and related concepts.

Substantive coding: The process of conceptualizing the empirical data in which the theory is grounded. Incidents in the empirical data are coded for indicators of concepts from which a grounded theory is then generated. Substantive coding consists of both the initial open coding of data as well as the selective coding of data once the core category has emerged.

Substantive grounded theory: A grounded theory developed within a specific setting and context and generalizable to a limited number of similar settings or groups.

Techniques: The instruments used to help analyze and make sense of the collected data, for example, text analysis, elaboration analysis, cluster analysis, and structural equation modeling.

Theoretical coding: The final stage in classic GT theory generation, theoretical coding conceptualizes and models how the substantive codes may relate to each other as hypotheses to be integrated into the final theory. Theoretical coding is not selected and imposed on the theory but emerges through earned relevance as the *best fitting* theoretical integrator of the core category and related concepts.

Theoretical sampling: A foundational pillar of classic GT, the process through which empirical data are selected and collected while guided by the emerging theory as opposed to some predefined sample or unit.

Theoretical saturation: When in coding and analyzing data, no new properties emerge but rather more indicators of the same properties continually emerge.

Theoretical sorting: The hand sorting of memos to provide emergent theoretical order and integration of ideas as the theorist seeks to theoretically discriminate as to where each idea fits in the emerging theory.

References

Adams, D., Nelson, R., & Todd, P. (1992). Perceived usefulness, ease of use, and usage of information technology: A replication. *MIS Quarterly, 16*(2), 227–247.

Alvesson, M., & Sandberg, J. (2014). Habitat and habitus: Boxed-in versus box-breaking research. *Organization Studies, 35*(7), 967–987.

Amsteus, M. N. (2014). The validity of divergent grounded theory method. *International Journal of Qualitative Methods, 13*, 71–87.

Armstrong, J. S., & Overton, T. S. (1977). Estimating nonresponse bias in mail surveys. *Journal of Marketing Research, 14*(3), 396–402.

Bacharach, S. B. (1989). Organizational theories: Some criteria for evaluation. *Academy of Management Review, 14*(4), 496–513.

Backman, K., & Kyngas, H. A. (1999). Challenges of the grounded theory approach to a novice researcher. *Nursing and Health Sciences, 1*, 147–153.

Baker, C., Wuest, J., & Stern, P. (1992). Method slurring: The grounded theory/phenomenology example. *Journal of Advanced Nursing, 17*, 1355–1360.

Baskerville, R., & Pries-Heje, J. (1999). Grounded action research: A method for understanding IT in practice. *Accounting, Management and Information Technologies, 9*, 1–23.

Benbasat, I., & Barki, H. (2007). Quo vadis, TAM? *Journal of the Association for Information Systems, 8*(4), 211–218.

Benzécri, J.-P. (1973). La place de l'a priori. In *Encyclopédia universalis* (Vol. 17, Organum, pp. 11–24). Edinburgh, UK: Encyclopaedia Britannica.

Bhaskar, R. (1979). *The possibility of naturalism*. New York: Harvester Press.

Bhaskar, R. (1989). *Reclaiming reality*. London: Verso.

Bhaskar, R. (1998). Philosophy and scientific realism. In M. Archer, R. Bhaskar, A. Collier, T. Lawson, & A. Norrie (Eds.), *Critical realism: Essential readings* (pp. 16–47). London: Routledge.

Bhaskar, R. A. (2002). *Reflections on meta-reality: A philosophy for the present*. New Delhi: Sage.

Biemann, T. (2012, August). *What if we are Texas sharpshooters? A new look at publication bias*. Paper presented at the Academy of Management Conference, Boston.

Bigus, O. E., Hadden, S. C., & Glaser, B. G. (1994). The study of basic social processes. In B. G. Glaser (Ed.), *More grounded theory methodology: A reader* (pp. 38–64). Mill Valley, CA: Sociology Press.

Birks, D. F., Fernandez, W., Levina, N., & Nasirin, S. (2013). Grounded theory method in information systems research: Its nature, diversity and opportunities. *European Journal of Information Systems, 22*(1), 1–8.

Birks, M., & Mills, J. (2012). *Grounded theory: A practical guide* (2nd ed.). Thousand Oaks, CA: Sage.

Blumer, H. (1956). Sociological analysis and the "variable." *American Sociological Review, 21*(6), 683–690.

Breckenridge, J. (2009). Demystifying theoretical sampling in grounded theory research. *Grounded Theory Review, 8*(2), 113–126.

Breckenridge, J. (2013). Doing classic grounded theory: The data analysis process. In *Sage Research Methods Cases* [Online database]. Retrieved from http://srmo.sagepub.com/view/methods-case-studies-2014/n269.xml

Bringer, J. D., Johnston, L. H., & Brackenridge, C. H. (2004). Maximizing transparency in a doctoral thesis: The complexities of writing about the use of QSR*NVIVO within a grounded theory study. *Qualitative Research, 4*(2), 247–265.

Bryant, A., & Charmaz, C. (Eds.). (2007). *The SAGE handbook of grounded theory.* London: Sage.

Bryant, J., & Lasky, B. (2007). A researcher's tale: Dealing with epistemological divergence. *Qualitative Research in Organizations and Management: An International Journal, 2*(3), 179–193.

Bryman, A. (1998). Quantitative and qualitative research strategies in knowing the social world. In T. May & M. Williams (Eds.), *Knowing the social world* (pp. 138–157). Buckingham, UK: Open University Press.

Burton-Jones, A., & Straub, D. (2006). Reconceptualizing system usage: An approach and empirical test. *Information Systems Research, 17*(3), 228–246.

Callon, M. (1986). Some elements of a sociology of translation: Domestication of the scallops and the fishermen of St. Brieuc Bay. In J. Law (Ed.), *Power, action and belief: A new sociology of knowledge* (pp. 196–223). London: Routledge & Kegan Paul.

Cartwright, N. (2003). *Causation: One word, many things.* London: Centre for Philosophy of Natural and Social Science.

Charmaz, K. (1990). "Discovering" chronic illness: Using grounded theory. *Social Science & Medicine, 30*(11), 1161–1172.

Charmaz, K. (2006). *Constructing grounded theory: A practical guide through qualitative analysis.* London: Sage.

Charmaz, K. (2009). Shifting the grounds: Constructivist grounded theory methods. In J. M. Morse et al. (Eds.), *Developing grounded theory: The second generation* (pp. 127–154). Walnut Creek, CA: Left Coast Press.

Charmaz, K. (2014). *Constructing grounded theory* (2nd ed.). London: Sage.

Chin, W. W. (1998). The partial least squares approach to structural equation modeling. *Modern methods for business research, 295*(2), 295–336.

Clarke, A. (Ed.). (2005). *Situational analysis: Grounded theory after the postmodern turn.* Thousand Oaks, CA: Sage.

Clarke, A. E., & Friese, C. (2007). Grounded theorizing using situational analysis. *The SAGE handbook of grounded theory* (pp. 363–397). London: Sage.

The conceptualization of data [Blog post]. (2010, May 1). *From the Mirror.* Retrieved from http://thespeculum.blogspot.ca/2010_05_01_archive.html

Corbin, J. M. (1991). Anselm Strauss: An intellectual biography. In D. R. Maines (Ed.), *Social organization and social process: Essays in honor of Anselm Strauss* (pp. 17–42). New York: Aldine de Gruyter.

Creswell, J. W. (2007). *Qualitative inquiry and research design: Choosing among five approaches.* London: Sage.

Creswell, J. W. (2013). *Qualitative inquiry and research design: Choosing among five approaches* (3rd ed.). London: Sage.

Creswell, J. W. (2014). *Research design: Qualitative, quantitative, and mixed methods approaches* (4th ed.). Thousand Oaks, CA: Sage.

Davis, F. D. (1989). Perceived usefulness, perceived ease of use, and user acceptance of information technology. *MIS Quarterly, 13*(3), 318–339.

de Bono, E. (1968). *New think: The use of lateral thinking in the generation of new ideas.* New York: Avon Books.

de Vaujany, F.-X., Walsh, I., & Mitev, N. (2011). An historically grounded critical analysis of research articles in IS. *European Journal of Information Systems, 20*(4), 395–417.

Devaraj, S., Easley, R. F., & Crant, J. M. (2008). How does personality matter? Relating the five-factor model to technology acceptance and use. *Information System Research, 19*(1), 93–105.

Dey, I. (1993). *Qualitative data analysis: A user-friendly guide.* New York: Routledge.

Dey, I. (1999). *Grounding grounded theory: Guidelines for qualitative inquiry.* San Diego, CA: Academic Press.

Diamantopoulos, A., Riefler, P., & Roth, K. P. (2008). Advancing formative measurement models. *Journal of Business Research, 61*(12), 1203–1218.

Draucker, C. B., Martsolf, D. S., Ross, R., & Rusk, T. B. (2007). Theoretical sampling and category development in grounded theory. *Qualitative Health Research, 17*(8), 1137–1148.

Eisenhardt, K. M. (1989). Building theories from case study research. *Academy of Management Review, 14*(4), 532–550.

Evermann, J., & Tate, M. (2011). Fitting covariance models for theory generation. *Journal of the Association for Information Systems, 12*(9), 632–661.

Fetters, M., & Freshwater, D. (2015). Publishing a methodological mixed methods research article. *Journal of Mixed Methods Research, 9*(3), 203–213.

Fine, G. A., & Deegan, J. G. (1996). Three principles of serendipity: Insight, chance, and discovery in qualitative research. *International Journal of Qualitative Studies in Education, 9*(4), 434–447.

Fornell, C., & Cha, J. (1994). *Advanced methods of marketing research.* Cambridge, MA: Blackwell Business.

Gagné, M., & Deci, E. (2005). Self-determination theory and work motivation. *Journal of Organizational Behavior, 26*(4), 331–362.

Gefen, D., Rigdon, E. E., Straub, D. W. (2011). Editors' comment: An update and extension to SEM guidelines for administrative and social science research. *MIS Quarterly, 35*(2), iii–xiv.

Gibson, B., & Hartman, J. (2014). *Rediscovering grounded theory*. London: Sage.

Gillet, N., Rosnet, E., & Vallerand, R. J. (2008). Développement d'une échelle de satisfaction des besoins fondamentaux en context sportif. *Revue Canadienne des Sciences du Comportement, 40*(4), 230–237.

Giske, T., & Gjengedal, E. (2007). "Preparative waiting" and coping theory with patients going through gastric diagnosis. *Journal of Advanced Nursing, 57*(1), 87–94.

Glaser, B. (2004). Remodeling grounded theory. *Forum Qualitative Research, 5*(2), Art. 4.

Glaser, B. G. (1961). *Some functions of recognition in a research organization* (Unpublished doctoral dissertation). Columbia University, New York.

Glaser, B. G. (1963). Attraction, autonomy, and reciprocity in the scientist-supervisor relationship. *Administrative Science Quarterly, 8*(3), 379–398.

Glaser, B. G. (1964a). Comparative failure in science. *Science, 143*(3610), 1012–1014.

Glaser, B. G. (1964b). *Organizational scientists: Their professional careers*. New York: Bobbs Merrill.

Glaser, B. G. (1965). The constant comparative method of qualitative analysis. *Social Problems, 12*, 436–445.

Glaser, B. G. (1966). [Review of the book *Professional employees: A study of scientists and engineers*, by Kenneth Prandy]. *American Journal of Sociology, 72*(3), 331–332.

Glaser, B. G. (1978). *Theoretical sensitivity: Advances in the methodology of grounded theory*. Mill Valley, CA: Sociology Press.

Glaser, B. G. (1991). In honor of Anselm Strauss: Collaboration. In D. R. Maines (Ed.), *Social organization and social process: Essays in honor of Anselm Strauss* (pp. 11–16). New York: Aldine de Gruyter.

Glaser, B. G. (1992). *Basics of grounded theory analysis: Emergence vs. forcing*. Mill Valley, CA: Sociology Press.

Glaser, B. G. (1995). A look at grounded theory: 1984-1994. In B. G. Glaser (Ed.), *Grounded theory 1984-1995* (Vol. 1, pp. 3–17). Mill Valley, CA: Sociology Press.

Glaser, B. G. (1998). *Doing grounded theory: Issues and discussions*. Mill Valley, CA: Sociology Press.

Glaser, B. G. (2001). *The grounded theory perspective: Conceptualization contrasted with description*. Mill Valley, CA: Sociology Press.

Glaser, B. G. (2002). Conceptualization: On theory and theorizing using grounded theory. *International Journal of Qualitative Methods, 1*(2), 23–38.

Glaser, B. G. (2003). *The grounded theory perspective II: Description's remodeling of grounded theory methodology*. Mill Valley, CA: Sociology Press.

Glaser, B. G. (2005a). *The grounded theory perspective III: Theoretical coding*. Mill Valley, CA: Sociology Press.

Glaser, B. G. (2005b, August 23). *The roots of grounded theory.* Keynote address to the 3rd International Qualitative Research Convention, Johor Bahru, Malaysia.

Glaser, B. G. (2007). *Doing formal grounded theory.* Mill Valley, CA: Sociology Press.

Glaser, B. G. (2008). *Doing quantitative grounded theory.* Mill Valley, CA: Sociology Press.

Glaser, B. G. (2009). *Jargonizing: Using the grounded theory vocabulary.* Mill Valley, CA: Sociology Press.

Glaser, B. G. (2010). The future of grounded theory. *Grounded Theory Review, 9*(2), 1–14.

Glaser, B. G. (2011). *Getting out of the data: Grounded theory conceptualization.* Mill Valley, CA: Sociology Press.

Glaser, B. G. (2012). *Stop, write: Writing grounded theory.* Mill Valley, CA: Sociology Press.

Glaser, B. G. (2013). *No preconceptions: The grounded theory dictum.* Mill Valley, CA: Sociology Press.

Glaser, B. G. (2014). *Memoing: A vital grounded theory procedure.* Mill Valley, CA: Sociology Press.

Glaser, B. G., & Holton, J. (2004). Remodeling grounded theory. *Forum Qualitative Sozialforschung/Forum: Qualitative Social Research, 5*(2), Art. 4. Retrieved from http://www.qualitative-research.net/fqstexte/2-04/2-04 glaser-e.htm

Glaser, B. G., & Holton, J. (2005). Basic social processes. *Grounded Theory Review, 4*(3), 1–21.

Glaser, B. G., & Strauss, A. L. (1965a). *Awareness of dying.* Chicago: Aldine.

Glaser, B. G., & Strauss, A. L. (1965b). Discovery of substantive theory: A basic strategy underlying qualitative research. *American Behavioral Scientist, 8*(6), 5–12.

Glaser, B. G., & Strauss, A. L. (1967). *The discovery of grounded theory: Strategies for qualitative research.* New York: Aldine de Gruyter.

Glaser, B. G., & Strauss, A. L. (1968). *Time for dying.* Mill Valley, CA: Sociology Press.

Glaser, B. G., & Strauss, A. L. (1971). *Status passage: A formal theory.* Mill Valley, CA: Sociology Press.

Goulding, C. (1999). Consumer research, interpretive paradigms and methodological ambiguities. *European Journal of Marketing, 33*(9/10), 859–873.

Goulding, C. (2002). *Grounded theory: A practical guide for management, business and market researchers.* London: Sage.

Gregor, S. (2006). The nature of theory in information systems. *MIS Quarterly, 30*(3), 611–642.

Guay, F., Mageau, G., & Vallerand, R. (2003). On the hierarchical structure of self-determined motivation: A test of top-down, bottom-up, reciprocal, and horizontal effects. *Personality and Social Psychology, 29*(8), 991–1004.

Guba, E. G. (Ed.). (1990). *The paradigm dialog.* Newbury Park, CA: Sage.

Guthrie, W. (2000). *Keeping clients in line: A grounded theory explaining how veterinary surgeons control their clients* (Unpublished doctoral dissertation). University of Strathclyde, Glasgow, UK.

Gynnild, A. (2006). Growing open: The transition from QDA to grounded theory. *Grounded Theory Review, 6*(1), 61–78.

Hair, J., Anderson, R., Tatham, R., & Black, W. (1995). *Multivariate data analysis with readings* (4th ed.). New York: Macmillan.

Hair, J., & Black, W. (1998). Cluster analysis. In J. H. Hair, R. E. Anderson, R. L. Tatham, & W. C. Black (Eds.), *Multivariate data analysis* (5th ed., pp. 469–518). New York: Prentice Hall.

Hair, J., Black, W., Babin, B., Anderson, R., & Tatham, R. (2006). *Multivariate data analysis* (6th ed.). London: Pearson Education International.

Hair, J. F., Sarstedt, M., Ringle, C. M., Mena, J. A. (2012). An assessment of the use of partial least squares structural equation modeling in marketing research. *Journal of the Academy of Marketing Science, 40*(3), 414–433.

Hall, R. (2012). Mixed methods: In search of a paradigm. In T. Lê & Q. Lê (Eds.), *Conducting research in a changing and challenging world* (pp. 71–78). Hauppauge, NY: Nova Science.

Hämäläinen, M. (2014). *Renaissance entrepreneurship: A grounded theory of entrepreneurial recycling* (Doctoral dissertation). Aalto University, Helsinki, Finland.

Hernandez, C. A. (2010). Getting grounded: Using Glaserian grounded theory to conduct nursing research. *Canadian Journal of Nursing Research, 42*(1), 151–163.

Higgins, A., Barker, P., & Begley, C. M. (2008). "Veiling sexualities": A grounded theory of mental health nurses responses to issues of sexuality. *Journal of Advanced Nursing, 62*(3), 307–317.

Holton, J. A. (2006). *Rehumanising knowledge work through fluctuating support networks: A grounded theory study* (Unpublished doctoral thesis). University of Northampton, Northampton, UK.

Holton, J. A. (2007a). The coding process and its challenges. In A. Bryant & C. Charmaz (Eds.), *The SAGE handbook of grounded theory* (pp. 265–289). London: Sage.

Holton, J. A. (2007b). Rehumanising knowledge work through fluctuating support networks: A grounded theory study. *Grounded Theory Review, 6*(2), 23–46.

Holton, J. A. (2008). Grounded theory as a general research methodology. *Grounded Theory Review, 7*(2), 67–93.

Holton, J. A. (2011). The autonomous creativity of Barney G. Glaser: Early influences in the emergence of classic grounded theory methodology. In A. Gynnild & V. Martin (Eds.), *Grounded theory: The philosophy, method and work of Barney Glaser* (pp. 201–223). Boca Raton, FL: BrownWalker Press.

Holton, J. A., & Grandy, G. (2015). *Voiced inner dialogue as relational reflection-on-action: The case of middle managers in healthcare.* Manuscript submitted for publication.

Igbaria, M., & Parasuraman, S. (1989). A path analytic study of individual characteristics, computer anxiety and attitudes toward microcomputers. *Journal of Management, 15*(3), 373–388.

Johnson, R., & Onwuegbuzie, A. J. (2004). Mixed methods research: A research paradigm whose time has come. *Educational Researcher, 33*(14), 14–26.

Jones, R., & Kriflik, G. (2006). Subordinate expectations of leadership within a cleaned-up bureaucracy: A grounded theory study. *Journal of Organizational Change Management, 19*(2), 154–172.

Jöreskog, K., & Wold, H. (1982). The ML and PLS technique for modeling with latent variables: Historical and comparative aspects. In K. G. Jöreskog & H. Wold (Eds.), *Systems under indirect observation* (Part I, 1263–1270). Amsterdam: North-Holland.

Jørgensen, L. B., Dahl, R., Pedersen, P. U., & Lomborg, K. (2013). Four types of coping with COPD-induced breathlessness in daily living: A grounded theory study. *Journal of Research in Nursing, 18*(6), 520–541.

Junglas, I., Niehaves, B., Spiekermann, S., Stahl, B. C., Weitzel, T., Winter, R., & Baskerville, R. (2011). The inflation of academic intellectual capital: The case for design science research in Europe. *European Journal of Information Systems, 20*(1), 1–6.

Karahanna, E., Agarwal, R., & Angst, C. (2006). Reconceptualizing compatibility beliefs in technology acceptance research. *MIS Quarterly, 30*(4), 781–804.

Kearney, M. H. (2007). From the submime to the meticulous: The continuing evolution of grounded formal theory. In A. Bryant & C. Charmaz (Eds.), *The SAGE handbook of grounded theory* (pp. 127–150). London: Sage.

Keill, M., Beranek, P., & Konsynski, B. (1995). Usefulness and ease of use: Field study evidence regarding task considerations. *Decision Support Systems 13*(1), 75–91.

Kelle, U. (2005). "Emergence" vs. "forcing" of empirical data? A crucial problem of "grounded theory" reconsidered. *Forum Qualitative Sozialforschung/ Forum: Qualitative Social Research, 6*(2), Art. 27. Retrieved from http:// nbn-resolving.de/urn:nbn:de:0114-fqs0502275

Kelle, U. (2007). The development of categories: Different approaches in grounded theory. In *The SAGE handbook of grounded theory* (pp. 191–213). London: Sage.

Klag, M., & Langley, A. (2013). Approaching the conceptual leap in qualitative research. *International Journal of Management Reviews, 15*(2), 149–166.

Langley, A. (1999). Strategies for theorizing from process data. *Academy of Management Review, 24*(4), 691–710.

Latour, B. (1987). *Science in action*. Cambridge, MA: Harvard University Press.

Lawrence, J., & Tar, U. (2013). The use of grounded theory technique as a practical tool for qualitative data collection and analysis. *Electronic Journal of Business Research Methods, 11*(1), 29–40.

Lazarsfeld, P. F., & Henry, N. W. (1968). *Latent structure analysis*. Boston: Houghton Mifflin.

Lazarsfeld, P. F., & Thielens, W., Jr. (1958). *The academic mind: Social scientists in a time of crisis.* Glencoe, IL: Free Press.

Lee, A. S., & Baskerville, R. L. (2003). Generalizing generalizability in information systems research. *Information Systems Research, 14*(3), 221–243.

Lee, A. S., & Hubona, G. S. (2009). A scientific basis for rigor in information systems research. *MIS Quarterly, 33*(2), 237–262.

Leonardi, P. M., & Bailey, D. E. (2008). Transformational technologies and the creation of new work practices: Making implicit knowledge explicit in task-based offshoring. *MIS Quarterly, 32*(2), 411–436.

Lincoln, Y. S., & Guba, E. G. (Eds.). (2000). *Naturalistic inquiry* (2nd ed.) London: Sage.

Locke, K. (2001). *Grounded theory in management research.* London: Sage.

Locke, K. (2007). Rational control and irrational free-play: Dual-thinking modes as necessary tension in grounded theorizing. In A. Bryant & C. Charmaz (Eds.), *The SAGE handbook of grounded theory* (pp. 565–579). London: Sage.

Lyytinen, K. (2009). Data matters in IS theory building. *Journal of the Association for Information Systems, 10*(10), 715–720.

Lyytinen, K., Baskerville, R., Iivari, J., & Te'eni, D. (2007). Why the old world cannot publish? Overcoming challenges in publishing high-impact IS research. *European Journal of Information Systems,* 317–326.

Manuj, I., & Pohlen, T. L. (2012). A reviewer's guide to the grounded theory methodology in logistics and supply chain management research. *International Journal of Physical Distribution & Logistics Management, 42*(8/9), 784–803.

Maslow, A. H. (1954). *Motivation and personality.* New York: Harper.

McCallin, A. (2006). Grappling with the literature in a grounded theory study. *Grounded Theory Review, 5*(2/3), 11–27.

Melia, K. (1996). Rediscovering Glaser. *Qualitative Health Research 6,* 368–373.

Merton, R. K. (1967). *On theoretical sociology.* New York: Free Press.

Merton, R. K. (1968). *Social theory and social structure.* New York: Free Press.

Mingers, J. (2001). Combining IS research methods: Towards a pluralist methodology. *Information Systems Research, 12*(3), 240–259.

Mingers, J. (2004). Realizing information systems: Critical realism as an underpinning philosophy for information systems. *Information and Organization, 14*(2), 87–103.

Monette, D., Sullivan, T., & Delong, C. (2011). *Applied social research: A tool for the human services.* Belmont, CA: Brooks/Cole.

Morgan, D. (2007). Paradigms lost and pragmatism regained: Methodological implications of combining qualitative and quantitative methods. *Journal of Mixed Methods Research, 1*(1), 48–76.

Morse, J. M. (2003). Principles of mixed methods and multimethod research design. In Tashakkori and Teddlie (Eds.), *SAGE Handbook of mixed methods in social & behavioural research.* Thousand Oaks, CA: SAGE.

Morse, J. M., & Mitcham, C. (2008). Exploring qualitatively-derived concepts: Inductive–deductive pitfalls. *International Journal of Qualitative Methods, 1*(4), 28–35.

Nathaniel, A. (2008). Eliciting spill: A methodological note. *Grounded Theory Review*, 7(1), 61–65.

O'Connor, M. K., Netting, F. E., & Thomas, M. L. (2008). Grounded theory: Managing the challenge for those facing Institutional Review Board oversight. *Qualitative Inquiry*, 14(1), 28–45.

Orr, J. E. (1990). Sharing knowledge, celebrating identity: Community memory in a service culture. In D. Middleton & D. Edwards (Eds.), *Collective remembering* (pp. 169–189). London: Sage.

Partington, D. (2000). Building grounded theories of management action. *British Journal of Management*, 11(2), 91–102.

Partington, D. (2002). Grounded theory. In D. Partington (Ed.), *Essential skills for management research* (pp. 136–157). London: Sage.

Patton, M. Q. (2002). *Qualitative research and evaluation methods* (3rd ed.). Thousand Oaks, CA: Sage.

Pelletier, L., Tuson, K., & Haddad, N. (1997). Client motivation for therapy scale: A measure of intrinsic motivation, extrinsic motivation and amotivation for therapy. *Journal of Personality Assessment, 68*(2), 414–435.

Pergert, P. (2008). *Façading in transcultural caring relationships: Healthcare staff and foreign-born parents in childhood cancer care* (Doctoral thesis). Karolinska Institutet, Stockholm. Retrieved from http://openarchive.ki.se/xmlui/handle/10616/37795

Piko, L. M. (2014). Discovering Glaser: My experience of doing grounded theory. *Grounded Theory Review*, 13(2). Retrieved from http://groundedtheoryreview.com/2014/12/19/discovering-glaser-my-experience-of-doing-grounded-theory/

Post, G., Kagan, A., & Keim, R. (1999). A structural equation evaluation of CASE tools attributes. *Journal of Management Information Systems, 15*(4), 215–234.

Richardson, L. (Ed.). (1990). *Writing strategies: Reaching diverse audiences.* Newbury Park, CA: Sage.

Richardson, L. (2000). Writing: A method of inquiry. In N. K. Denzin & Y. S. Lincoln (Eds.), *Handbook of qualitative research* (2nd ed., pp. 923–948). Thousand Oaks, CA: Sage.

Ringle, C. M., Wende, S., & Will, S. (2005). SmartPLS 2.0 (M3) Beta [Software]. Retrieved from http://www.smartpls.de

Ringle, M., Sarstedt, M., & Straub, D. (2012). A critical look at the use of PLS-SEM in *MIS Quarterly. MIS Quarterly, 36*(1), iii–xiv.

Roderick, C. (2009). Learning classic grounded theory: An account of the journey and advice for new researchers. *Grounded Theory Review, 8*(2), 49–63.

Rodríguez-Martín, B., Martínez-Andres, M., Cervera-Monteagudo, B., Notario-Pacheco, B., & Martínez-Vizcaíno, V. (2013). Perception of quality of care among residents of public nursing-homes in Spain: A grounded theory study. *BMC Geriatrics, 13*(1), 65.

Runkel, P. J., & Runkel, M. (1984). *A guide to usage for writers and students in the social sciences.* Totowa, NJ: Rowman & Allanheld.

Sandelowski, M. (2000). Combining qualitative and quantitative sampling, data collection, and analysis techniques in mixed-method studies. *Research in Nursing & Health, 23*(3), 246–255.

Sandelowski, M., Voils, C., & Knafl, G. (2009). On quantitizing. *Journal of Mixed Methods Research, 3*(3), 208–222.

Sandgren, A. (2010). *Deciphering unwritten rules: Patients, relatives and nurses in palliative cancer care* (Doctoral thesis). Linnaeus University, Kalmar, Sweden. Retrieved from http://www.diva-portal.org/smash/record.jsf?p id=diva2%3A310790&dswid=8891

Sandgren, A., Thulesius, H., Fridlund, B., & Petersson, K. (2006). Striving for emotional survival. *Qualitative Health Research, 16*(1), 79–96.

Sandgren, A., Thulesius, H., Petersson, K., & Fridlund, B. (2007). "Doing good care"—A study of palliative home nursing care. *International Journal of Qualitative Studies on Health and Well-Being, 2*(4), 227–235.

Sautrey, J., & Mourmant, G. (2015, June 12). *The practical modern artist.* Paper presented at Journée AIM, IT and Culture, Technologies de l'Information et de la Communication et Culture: enjeux et perspectives dans le domaine de l'art, Lyon, France.

Schall, M. (1983). A communication-rules approach to organizational culture. *Administrative Science Quarterly, 28*(4), 557–581.

Schön D. (1983). *The reflective practitioner: How professionals think in action.* London: Temple Smith.

Scott, H. (2009). Data analysis: Getting conceptual. *Grounded Theory Review, 8*(2), 89–111.

Shah, S. K., & Corley, K. G. (2006). Building better theory by bridging the quantitative-qualitative divide. *Journal of Management Studies, 43*(8), 1821–1835.

Sheldon, K., Ryan, R., & Reis, H. (1996). What makes for a good day? Competence and autonomy in the day and in the person. *Personality and Social Psychology Bulletin, 22*, 1270–1279.

Simmons, O. E. (2010). Is that a real theory or did you just make it up? Teaching classic grounded theory. *Grounded Theory Review, 9*(2), 15–38.

Smith, M. L. (2010). Testable theory development for small-N studies: Critical realism and middle-range theory. *International Journal of Information Technology and Systems Approach, 3*(1), 41–56.

Starks, H., & Trinidad, S. B. (2007). Choose your method: A comparison of phenomenology, discourse analysis, and grounded theory. *Qualitative Health Research, 17*(10), 1372–1380.

Stjernsward, S., & Ostman, M. (2008). Whose life am I living? Relatives living in the shadow of depression. *International Journal of Social Psychiatry, 54*(4), 358–369.

Strauss, A. L. (1987). *Qualitative analysis for social scientists.* Cambridge, UK: Cambridge University Press.

Strauss, A. L., & Corbin, J. M. (1990). *Basics of qualitative research: Grounded theory procedures and techniques.* Newbury Park, CA: Sage.

Strauss, A. L., & Corbin, J. M. (1998). *Basics of qualitative research: Techniques and procedures for developing grounded theory* (2nd ed.). Thousand Oaks, CA: Sage.

Suddaby, R. (2006). What grounded theory is not. *Academy of Management Journal, 49*(4), 633–642.

Takeda, H. (2011). *Examining scholarly influence: A study in Hirsch metrics and social network analysis* (Unpublished doctoral dissertation). Georgia State University, Atlanta. Retrieved from http://scholarworks.gsu.edu/cis_diss/44/

Taylor, S., & Todd, P. (1995). Assessing IT usage: The role of prior experience. *MIS Quarterly, 19*(4), 561–570.

Tsang, E., & Kwan, K. (1999). Replication and theory development in organizational science: A critical realist perspective. *Academy of Management Review, 24*(4), 759–780.

Tukey, J. W. (1980). We need both exploratory and confirmatory. *American Statistician, 34*(1), 23–25.

Urbach, N., & Ahlemann, F. (2010). Structural equation modeling in information systems research using partial least squares. *Journal of Information Technology, 11*(2), 5–40.

Urquart, C., Lehmann, H., & Myers, M. (2010). Putting the theory back into grounded theory: Guidelines for grounded theory studies in information systems. *Information Systems Journal, 20*(4), 357–381.

Vallerand, R. (1997). Towards a hierarchical model of intrinsic and extrinsic motivation. *Advances in Experimental Social Psychology, 29*, 271–360.

Vallerand, R. (2001). Deci and Ryan's self-determination theory: A view from the hierarchical model of intrinsic and extrinsic motivation. *Psychological Inquiry, 11*(4), 312–318.

Vallerand R. (Ed.) (2007). *Les fondements de la psychologie sociale*. Montreal, QC: Gaëtan Morin.

Venkatesh, V., Brown, S. A., & Bala, H. (2013). Bridging the qualitative-quantitative divide: Guidelines for conducting mixed methods in information systems, *MIS Quarterly, 37*(1), 21–54.

Venkatesh, V., Speier, C., & Morris, M. (2002). User acceptance enablers in individual decision making about technology: Toward an integrated model. *Decision Science 33*(2), 297–316.

Vinzi, V. E., Trinchera, L., & Amato, S. (2010). PLS path modeling: From foundations to recent developments and open issues for model assessment and improvement. In V. E. Vinzi, W. W. Chin, J. Henseler, & H. Wang (Eds.), *Handbook of partial least squares* (pp. 47–82). Berlin, Germany: Springer.

Von Stetten, A., Wild, U., & Chrennikow, W. (2011). Adopting social network sites: The role of individual IT culture and privacy concerns. In *Proceedings of the Seventeenth Americas Conference on Information Systems (AMCIS)*, Detroit, MI.

Walsh, I. (2009). Development of an instrument to assess individual IT-culture. In *Proceedings of the Fifteenth Americas Conference on Information Systems (AMCIS)*, San Francisco, CA.

Walsh, I. (2010). Investigating the cultural dimension of IT-usage: IT-acculturation, an essential construct in IS research. In *Proceedings of the 31st International Conference on Information Systems (ICIS)*, St. Louis, MO.

Walsh, I. (2014a). A strategic path to study IT use through users' IT culture and IT needs: A mixed-method grounded theory. *Journal of Strategic Information Systems, 23*(2), 145–173.

Walsh, I. (2014b). Using grounded theory to avoid research misconduct in management science. *Grounded Theory Review, 13*(1), 51–57.

Walsh, I. (2014c). Using quantitative data in mixed-design grounded theory studies: An enhanced path to formal grounded theory in information systems. *European Journal of Information Systems.* Advance online publication. doi:10/1057/ejis.2014.23

Walsh, I. (2015). *Découvrir de nouvelles théories.* Paris: Éditions Management & Société.

Walsh, I., & Gettler-Summa, M. (2010). Users' groups interpreted through the lens of the users' needs and motivation. In *Actes du Congrès de l'Association Information & Management (AIM),* La Rochelle, France.

Walsh, I., Holton, J. A., Bailyn, L., Fernandez, W., Levina, N., & Glaser, B. (2015a). Moving the management field forward. *Organizational Research Methods.* Advance online publication. doi:10.1177/1094428115589189

Walsh, I., Holton, J. A., Bailyn, L., Fernandez, W., Levina, N., & Glaser, B. (2015b). What grounded theory is. *Organizational Research Methods.* Advance online publication. doi:10.1177/1094428114565028

Walsh, I., & Kefi, H. (2008). The role of IT culture in IT management: Searching for individual archetypal IT cultural profiles (Paper no. 185). *Proceedings of the Fourteenth Americas Conference on Information Systems (AMCIS),* Toronto, ON, Canada.

Walsh, I., Kefi, H., & Baskerville, R. (2010). Managing culture creep: Toward a strategic model of user IT culture. *Journal of Strategic Information Systems, 19*(4), 257–280.

Walsh, I., Renaud, A., & Kalika, M. (2013). The translated strategic alignment model: A practice-based perspective. *Systèmes d'Information & Management, 18*(2), 37–68.

Weick, K. E. (1995). What theory is not, theorizing is. *Administrative Science Quarterly, 40,* 385–390.

Whetten, D. A. (1989). What constitutes a theoretical contribution? *Academy of Management Review, 14*(4), 490–495.

Wood, J. E. (2009). *Advancing agendas: A grounded theory of engagement with interagency meetings* (Unpublished doctoral thesis). University College London, UK.

Wu, J., & Du, H. (2012). Toward a better understanding of behavioral intention and system usage constructs. *European Journal of Information Systems.* Advance online publication. doi:10.1057/ejis.2012.15

Xie, S. L. (2009). Striking a balance between program requirements and GT principles: Writing a compromised GT proposal. *Grounded Theory Review, 8*(2), 35–47.

Zachariadis, M., Scott, S., & Barrett, M. (2013). Methodological implications of critical realism for mixed-methods research. *MIS Quarterly, 37*(3), 855–879.

Zetterberg, H. L. (1954). *On theory and verification in sociology.* Stockholm: Almquist & Wiksell.

Zetterberg, H. L. (1961). *To publish books by scholars for scholars.* New York: Bedminster Press.

Zetterberg, H. L. (1962). *Social theory and social practice.* Edison, NJ: Bedminster Press.

Zetterberg, H. L. (1965). *On theory and verification in sociology* (3rd ed.). Totowa, NJ: Bedminster Press.

Index